T0303352

literature, religion, and postsecular studies
lori branch, series editor

secular scriptures

modern theological poetics
in the wake of dante

william franke

The Ohio State University Press • Columbus

Library of Congress Cataloging-in-Publication Data
Franke, William, author.
  Secular scriptures : modern theological poetics in the wake of Dante / William Franke.
    pages cm — (Literature, religion, and postsecular studies)
  Includes bibliographical references and index.
  ISBN 978-0-8142-1292-9 (cloth : alk. paper)
  1. Religion and poetry. 2. Religion and literature. 3. Dante Alighieri, 1265–1321—Reli-
    gion. I. Title. II. Series: Literature, religion, and postsecular studies.
  PN1077.F68 2015
  809.1'9382—dc23

Cover design by Lisa Force
Text design by Juliet Williams
Type set in Adobe Sabon
Printed by Thomson-Shore, Inc.

9 8 7 6 5 4 3 2 1

In the holy of holies, where religion and poetry are married, stands
Dante as high priest and consecrates all modern art to its calling.

—F. W. J. Schelling, "Über Dante in philosophischer Beziehung"

"In *Secular Scriptures*, William Franke rejects the received wisdom that sacred and secular are essentially opposed to one another. He does this by asking us to think about where these alleged oppositions in fact converge—in a venerable Western literary tradition. Surveying a broad spectrum of works written 'in the wake of Dante,' he argues that 'self reflexivity,' subjective human experience and reflection, has become for modern poets the locus of revelation, a form of scripture. Building on his extensive previous explorations of ineffability, 'on what cannot be said,' he uncovers the richness—both literary and philosophical—of inventive language that speaks in order to reveal 'the spiritual mysteries of the letter,' to gain access to what ultimately lies beyond the reach of words."

—Peter Hawkins, Yale Divinity School

"I read *Secular Scriptures* almost without putting the work down. Readers in fields from *fin-de-siècle* decadence to 'post-post-modernism' in poetry, especially those with interest in religion and literature studies, will be delighted by the way Dante is recast here to preface twentieth- and twenty-first-century developments. Franke's way of thinking backwards from recent postsecular theory is beguiling and transformative; the movement forward in the final chapter, via Dante's emerging again at the end as at the beginning, is really rather beautiful."

—Romana Huk, University of Notre Dame

"William Franke has written, in a luminous prose, an enthralling book about a pivotal issue in literary studies: the esthetics of visionary literature. The questions Franke raises—philosophy of language, the nature of mystical insights, their modes of representation, and the revelations of poetic knowledge—find in Dante, in the Romantic poets of Europe, and in the radical philosophical speculations of the twentieth century a fascinating articulation through which the reader can experience the depths of the high culture of the West."

—Giuseppe Mazzotta, Yale University

contents

Most of these essays have been published previously in some form, although sometimes in drastically abbreviated versions, and in most cases they have been substantially rewritten. They have, moreover, been fine-tuned in order to connect with and pick up on one another, but each nonetheless remains a discrete and self-sufficient reflection in its own right. There has been no attempt to make them uniform in approach or in research methods. They have been selected and integrated on the basis of their bearing on the topic and on the overarching ideas that organize the volume. Each in its own different way bears witness to the evolving, common predicament of theological poetics in the modern age. Nevertheless, it is only by appearing together as a book that the full coherence and extended intellectual roots of their distinctive approach to criticism as speculative philosophy and theology becomes visible for the first time.

Translations from other languages into English, unless otherwise indicated, are my own. I generally give the original text as well in parentheses or in notes. This practice begins from the epigraph to the book, which is taken from Friedrich Wilhelm Joseph von Schelling, *Sämmtliche Werke,* ed. Karl Friedrich August Schelling, Part I, vol. 5 (Stuttgart/Augsburg: Cotta, 1859), where it reads:

Im Allerheiligsten, Wo Religion und Poesie verbündet, steht Dante als Hohepriester und weiht die ganze moderne Kunst für ihre Bestimmung ein. (152)

Schelling's 1803 essay "Über Dante in philosophischer Beziehung" appeared originally in the *Kritisches Journal der Philosophie*, edited jointly by Hegel and Schelling, and is now available in an edition by Stefan Dietsche (Leipzig: Reclam, 1981), 412–17.

Special thanks are due to Lori Branch for her encouragement of this project from the beginning and for her contributions to shaping its final realization.

I am grateful as well to the publishers for permission to adapt material from the following publications:

"Dante and the Secularization of Religion through Literature." *Religion and Literature* 45/1 (2013): 1–31.

"'Enditynges of Worldly Vanitees': Truth and Poetry in Chaucer as Compared with Dante." *The Chaucer Review* 34, no. 1 (1999): 87–106. This article is used by permission of The Pennsylvania State University Press. Copyright © 1999.

"Prophecy Eclipsed: *Hamlet* as a Tragedy of Knowledge." In *Core Texts in Conversation*. Eds. Jane Kelley Rodeheffer, David Sokolowski, and J. Scott Lee. Lanham-New York-Oxford: University Press of America, 2000. 149–54.

"Blind Prophecy: Milton's Figurative Mode in *Paradise Lost.*" In *Through a Glass Darkly: Essays in the Religious Imagination*. Ed. John Hawley. New York: Fordham University Press, 1996. 87–103.

"The Logic of Infinity: European Romanticism and the Question of Giacomo Leopardi." *Comparatio: Revue Internationale de Littérature Comparée* 1 (1990): 69–82.

"The Linguistic Turning of the Symbol: Baudelaire and His French Symbolist Heirs." In *Baudelaire and the Poetics of Modernity*. Ed. Patricia Ward. Nashville: Vanderbilt University Press, 2000. 28–40.

"'The Missing All': Emily Dickinson's Apophatic Poetics." *Christianity and Literature* 58/1 (2008): 61–80.

"The Dialectical Logic of Yeats's Byzantium Poems." *Yeats-Eliot Review* 15, no. 3 (Summer 1998): 23–32.

"The Religious Vocation of Secular Literature: Dante and Postmodern Thought." In *Letteratura italiana e religione: Atti del convengo inter-*

nationale (Italian Studies–University of Toronto 11–13 ottobre 2012). Ed. Salvatore Bancheri and Francesco Guardini (Florence: Franco Cesati, Editore, forthcoming).

I. The Argument

The essays in this volume demonstrate ways in which secularization is intrinsic to theological revelation, particularly in Christian tradition, and they highlight the role that literature plays in the realization of such revelation in the incarnate form of the word. God's coming into the world is the "secular" movement par excellence: the divine becoming humanly incarnate defines the revolutionary, world-historical event of the Christian religion. Secularism, however, also (and more typically) means the exclusion of God from the world. Our modern society stands almost completely under the sway of scientific and technological revolutions that can seem to undermine theological explanations in terms of ostensibly other-worldly powers and to supplant them by this-worldly accounts in terms of material or empirical causes.

Secularism, not surprisingly, is often proclaimed as enacting the death of God, or at least as entailing God's irrelevance—and thereby as setting the stage for the demise of religion. The encroachment of the secular, consequently, is an ineluctable challenge for theologically sensitive poets throughout the modern period of writing in the national vernacular languages of Europe, starting especially from Dante and Chaucer even well in advance of the scientific age and in telling anticipation of it. The essays in this volume, accordingly, construct a trajectory through modern poetic literature in its struggle with the sense of loss of the very possibility of theological revelation. Can literature replace religion? Can it do so triumphantly or only mournfully? Is this literary transmogrification of revelation the death of religion or its rebirth in a vital new form?

The claim to revelation in literature is very ancient. Its explicit formulation in literary criticism can be traced from the Neoplatonic thought of Porphyry, specifically from his third-century AD allegorical reading of Homer's "cave of the nymphs" in *De antro nympharum* as a symbolic revelation of the Platonic teaching of metempsychosis or the reincarnation of souls. Such Neoplatonic allegorical interpretation of epic literature as religious revelation reaches Dante (1265–1321) particularly through the late-antique and medieval commentary tradition on the *Aeneid* in the works of Macrobius (fl. early fifth century), Fulgentius (c. 462–c. 567), and Bernard Sylvestris (1085–1178). But Dante begins to filter this claim through his own incipiently modern, intensely self-conscious subjectivity: he also subjects it to searching theoretical reflection, opening new vistas and a new era for the theory and practice of theological revelation in literature.

The revelatory claim of literature is transformed drastically by modern approaches to poetry through the radically divergent epistemological assumptions on which their poetics are based. The essays assembled here suggest some of the richness of this transformation and outline the stakes of seeking to discern religious revelation or spiritual enlightenment in poetry, particularly in and through poetic language. In modernity (from the Italian Renaissance through German and English Romanticism to French Symbolism and some of the more spiritualizing forms of Modernism), such language comes to be viewed not just as instrumental or incidental but as intrinsic to the production of at least quasi-religious revelation as a unique personal experience. Modernity develops as a secular era in which epistemological questions of how it is possible for a human subject to know anything at all about the divine, let alone express it in a finite work in language, become acute and issue in recurrent crises of skepticism. Still, in the midst of this uncertainty, beyond all doubt, the dimension of subjective experience and reflection becomes, in crucial ways, itself the locus of revelation in a new, secular sense.

In premodern times, a number of poetic forms, including oracle and prophecy, as well as lyric and epic inspired by the Muses, were widely accepted as authentic types of divine revelation. Of course, the truth of poetry was also sometimes attacked or denied, most (in)famously by Plato. Nonetheless, philosophical truth and even divine revelation in poetry were passionately pursued by Porphyry and his successors in the immense and varied heritage of Platonist poetics and aesthetics down through the ages. Such sacred truth as is revealed and ritually realized in the poem belonged still to the ideal vision and prophetic project of Dante, and he transmitted it to the modern poets in his wake. He, more than anyone before him, brings to conscious theoretical reflection the intrinsically sacralizing—but also profoundly secularizing—propensities of the language of poetry. This dual vocation of poetry inheres in its sensuously material—but also speculatively metaphorical—mode of expression. Poetic language is palpably present and concrete, yet at the same time is infinitely elusive and suggestive of what can never be defined or delimited, of what foils all maneuvers to confine and circumscribe it and thereby transcends our concepts and understanding. The ambiguous tension between the sacred and the secular plays itself out in the divergent and contrasting approaches to conveying religious revelation in and through literature that are attempted by theological poets in the modern vernaculars, as well as in the efforts of confessedly secular spirits to make poetry function as revelation in a supposedly nontheological, purely phenomenological sense.

In modern poets, divine revelation is transformed and reconfigured by being entrusted to the medium of self-conscious poetic art and invention by individual human talents. Literature thereby becomes a means that is liable to deflect and impede—but at the same time, indirectly, to positively contribute to—the event of the divine Word. Indeed, a theological Word can be poetically revealed only thanks to the human words in which it becomes sacramentally incarnate.

The capacities of words, and preeminently their aptitude for self-reflection, are explored along a variety of axes by modern poets. This verbal and psychological reflexiveness begins already with the troubadours, with William IX of Poitiers (Guilhem de Peiteu) and Arnaut Daniel in remarkably audacious and self-conscious ways. It is catapulted forward to a kind of apotheosis by Dante, particularly in his *Paradiso*, with its unprecedented exploitation of poetic structures of self-reflectiveness for a kind of secularized theological revelation. These structures operate as incantation and as incarnation of the self-reflexivity of a Trinitarian divinity.

In this sense, Dante is the progenitor of modern poets, as Romantic critics, including Friedrich Wilhelm Josef von Schelling and both Friedrich and August Wilhelm Schlegel, clairvoyantly perceived and declared in retrospective prophecies of their own. The German idealists added a speculatively transcendental reflection, following the lead of Kant, and in dependence on the Christian theology of the Trinity, to the philosophical grounding of the self-reflective dimension of subjectivity that had opened up so momentously in Dante. However, already in the late Middle Ages, Chaucer reverses Dante's inspiration from above and finds parody of the social comedy of human life to be a means of revealing worldly insight that complements and counterpoints—when it does not outright contradict—the unattainable height of supposedly divine Truth. The poignancy of human reality laid bare by poetic imitation in the *Canterbury Tales* is so intense as to create a relation—even if it is but a negative relation—to the ultimate truth of Scripture, which can only be fideistically believed, since it cannot be rationally demonstrated and known.

Evincing the further onset of a Renaissance sensibility, *Hamlet* more darkly and deliberately dramatizes the tragedy of loss of the prophetic truth characteristic of the earlier age of revelation. Emblematically, the medieval world is embodied in Hamlet's father, the dead king, now become a ghost. The incipient religious skepticism ushered in by the dawning scientific age insinuates itself as undermining the ancient, particularly the biblical, bases of revelation but also as reaching out desperately toward something new. In the end, *Hamlet* envisages a new, more groping kind of faith in "providence." The novel possibilities that emerge here for theological revelation in poetry as a paradoxical sort of visionary blindness are developed most powerfully by Milton later in the seventeenth century, contemporaneously with the ascendency of a nascent modern science. In Milton, the inadequacy of human words for objective description or depiction of the divine opens a negative register of subjective, emotional expression, especially through self-negating, iconoclastic imagery.

In Milton's train, certain spiritually and prophetically inclined Romantics like Blake revive the ideal of the theological inspiration of poetry and devise new techniques of symbolism, claiming once again to pry open the heavens. However, "heaven" is now constituted in a dimension immanent to human consciousness extended to infinity. Of course, this expanse may also be a desert devoid of all theological meaning, and it *is* that for a thoroughgoing secularist like Giacomo Leopardi. Nevertheless, the idea of poetic language as a privileged channel of revelation continues to work itself out in modern times, signally in German and English Romantic thought, as well as in French Symbolist poetry and the corresponding poetics that it spawns.

Symbolism develops in late- or post-Romantic poetry (like Baudelaire's) and in modernist literature into definitively secular and yet still revelatory types of knowing expressed in original styles of poetic scripture. There is still the claim, for example, in Rimbaud, to exceed more mundane means of knowing through a superior type of *seeing* or "voyance" (*Lettres du Voyant*) that consists in an altered consciousness achieved by the "alchemy" of the poetic word and its component elements, namely, sounds and letters.

Taking the claim to revelation in a somewhat different direction, working rather against the ambitions of the symbol to make language itself the locus of revelation, Emily Dickinson mobilizes the self-subverting capabilities of language that enable her wordlessly to connect with a higher—or, in any event, a stranger—ineffable realm and its religious realities. Yet language still serves, at least negatively, as the fulcrum for prying into this other dimension, this dark or shadowy side of consciousness and existence. Moreover, the notion of language as a symbol that mirrors some higher, ordinarily inaccessible reality is still in play in the poetics of high modernism: such a conception of language is displayed eminently in the poems of William Butler Yeats. Even more recently, postmodern philosophy, through its deconstructive redefinition or shattering of truth, with far-reaching reverberations throughout the arts, opens new paths and possibilities for poetic expression and manifestation of secularized religious revelation: it does so particularly by peering beyond word and symbol and concept altogether into the unsayable, unrepresentable, and unthinkable realm of the apophatic.

The nature of poetic and religious knowledge metamorphoses radically along this historical trajectory. It becomes decisively grounded in the secular world and in human faculties of imagination, as well as in language, with its inherently self-reflective structure and dynamics, particularly its self-critical capacity of negation. Despite this, the poetic word retains and reformulates its claim to a religiously revelatory power or function—and sometimes even to extending and re-actualizing Holy Scripture. Just as religious revelation is subjected to myriad forms of secularization in the modern world, with its newly discovered, humanly manipulated media and technologies, so the secular world is, in manifold ways, subject to sacralization, to becoming itself a sign or a resource in unprecedented new forms of revelation that are ambiguously poetic and religious in that they extend—and even tend to surpass—human mastery. In some of the more extreme instances, the limits of finite space and time are suspended through planetary telecommunications making possible omnipresence and synchronicity—a sort of Kingdom Come on earth. The seemingly "angelic" powers arising from hyper-reality and virtual worlds can inspire new, quasi-sacred forms of art and expression.

In our own postmodern times, so rife with religious revivals, often in highly secularized guises, the phenomenology of truth, and even the claim to divine revelation, are once again in ebullition and are under examination from many new angles. We are rediscovering that poetry and theology can offer models of knowing and unknowing that are as pertinent as empirical research and scientific method are to the ascertainment of truth and the creation of sense or meaning—and that they can sometimes be even more persuasive. This book reexamines, through its own original speculative outlook, and in the throes of this upheaval, some of the most compelling exemplars of religious-poetic revelation in the historical archives of modern Western literature.

II. Scope and Orientation

The essays, taken as an ensemble, revolve around and are bookended by Dante. Their perspective on literature as secularized religious revelation is leveraged from his vantage point between the medieval and the modern worlds. Dante represents the pivot on which these worlds divide and yet also come together, the breaking point at which literature and religion become clearly differentiated and nevertheless are shown to be absolutely inseparable. Understanding literature as achieving a form of secularized religious revelation is a critical project that can be pursued from many different angles of approach, but this volume does so from a Dantist's perspective, and it is turned in two directions: toward the roots of secularized religious vision in antiquity and the Middle Ages, on one side, and toward its fruits in modern poetry and poetics, on the other. The book thereby brings to focus a movement of secularizing Scripture that emerges arguably as the central axis and dynamic of Western literary creation and cultural tradition.

Crucial to this volume is a realization that the continuation of religious and specifically of Scriptural revelation is to be found not so much in any discrete transfer of defined themes or specific contents as in the gnoseological form and revelatory ambition of literature in some of its most audacious moments of flourishing in modern times. The poetic epistemologies of modern writers are means of seeking revelation of a higher order of existence or consciousness beyond the immediate evidence of the empirical world. In the modern period, the mundane world became the indisputable baseline of reality for science and for the culture and civilization founded upon it. But the poets all along subtly critiqued such a view of reality. Their vision transmits an alternative optics hailing, in however radically revised forms, ultimately from ancient traditions of religious revelation in scripture and myth.

In its own transmission of such vision, this collection of essays is more than just their sum. Assembled together, the essays map out an intelligible itinerary through modern poetic literature by focusing selectively on crucial historical junctures and pivotal figures. The affirmation of literature as a form of revelation of some higher or deeper—or more mysterious and intimate—reality transfers certain offices and prerogatives from sometimes fossilized institutions and perfunctory rites of religion to the interior forge of the literary imagination at work immersed in the spiritual mysteries of the letter. Each individual poet's struggle is considered in its own context—in fact, the essays were originally written independently of one another—and yet they cannot help reflecting on each other as grappling with transforms of the same or similar issues in the specific cultural milieu and historical circumstances of each writer.

It must be stressed, furthermore, that the speculatively critical lenses cut, fashioned, and deployed throughout the essays are integral to the kind of insight that emerges from the poetry examined as reflective of each different age of culture. The essays are themselves exercises in speculative philosophical reflection carried out concretely through literary interpretation. They performatively disclose, in each case, an epistemological structure of self-reflection operating at the source of each respective form of theological (or antitheological) revelation in poetic literature. They do so in a way that demands to be understood as communicating philosophically with—and, in a sense, as translating—traditions of religious revelation. Like the poetic literature they interpret, the essays proposed here "secularize" theological revelation by making it understandable in terms of imagination and language as inherently inventive, revelatory processes. As creatively critical endeavors, moreover, the essays participate in the process of religious revelation in literature that they reflect upon and expound. They are, to this extent, themselves immersed in the refiner's fire of poetic creation and interpretation that they aim to elucidate—yet cannot explain so much as refract and transmit.

Bibliographical Note

Carrying forward something of the critical perspective broached by
Schelling (as highlighted in the epigraph to this book) and his contemporaries, notably Friedrich Schlegel, Bernadette Malinowski, in *"Das Heilige
sei mein Wort": Paradigmen prophetischer Dichtung von Klopstock bis
Whitman* (Würzburg: Königshausen und Neumann, 2002), offers manifold illuminating suggestions regarding the crisis of legitimacy of prophetic poetry in modern times that is evoked in this introduction right
from the concluding sentences (and questions) of its opening paragraph.
Her work acknowledges the guidance of Werner Frick, who himself
offers some extremely probing observations on the reprise of the ancient
and medieval traditions of visionary poetics by modern poets in *"Poeta
vates: Versionen eines mythischen Modells in der Lyrik der Moderne,"
Formaler Mythos. Beiträge zu einer Theorie der ästhetischen Formen*, ed.
Matias Martinez (Munich: Schöningh, 1996), 124–62. Also contributing
to this critical perspective, which represents the most sophisticated preceding effort I find to examine the transfer of prophetic-poetic topoi into
modernity, specifically with a view to their adaptation to a secular age, is
Gerhard Neumann, "'L'inspiration qui se retire'. Musenanruf, Erinnern
und Vergessen in der Poetologie der Moderne," *Memoria—Vergessen und
Erinnern (= Poetik und Hermeneutik XV)*, ed. Anselm Haverkamp and
Renate Lachmann (Munich: Fink, 1993), 433–55. These researchers suggest how the loss of credibility of claims to theological revelation in their
originally cultic contexts has opened up a space for the secularized poetic
reshaping and reactualizing of such claims in new and different terms. For
more detailed dialogue with these and with other scholars on this general
topic I must defer to my forthcoming article "Poetry as Prophecy, or Literary Form and Theological Revelation" in the *Oxford Research Encyclopedia of Religion*, ed. John Barton (New York: Oxford University Press,
2015).

dante and the secularization of religion through literature

I. Dante: Pioneer and Prophet of Christian Secularism

Dante stands in certain outstanding respects as the premier secularizing thinker and writer of the modern age. The concrete world of history and human individuality emerges from his work with unprecedented force and clarity. It emerges, moreover, as the revelation of an ultimate, eschatological reality of the other world translated into a symbolic language of the phenomena of this world realistically perceived and represented. This translation of religious revelation and poetic vision from otherworldly into worldly terms is what I am calling "secularization," and it defines in essence the nature of the momentous cultural transition effected by Dante's poem.

In its origins, the term "secularization" referred to the transfer of church property to state or private ownership. It designated the dispossession of monasteries and convents by decree of revolutionary or anti-Catholic governments in Reformation and Enlightenment Europe. "Secularization" also signified the return of "religious" (monks and nuns) into "the world."[1] But the term has gradually taken on broader mean-

---

1. Giorgio Agamben reflects on the history of the term in *Il regno e la gloria. Per*

ing by referring to ideas and patterns of thought that are appropriated from their originally religious matrices to be redeployed in this-worldly, ostensibly nonreligious frames of reference. The typically modern belief in progress, for example, retains the utopian orientation of salvation history that looks forward to fulfillment in a better life for all but without reference specifically to the biblical Kingdom of God as the teleological goal of history.

We are still struggling to understand the implications of the epochal transition commonly called *secularization* and in particular to understand its impact on the viability of theological revelation and religious belief for us today. This is why returning to Dante and learning to read his poem for the philosophical and theological challenge and provocation it affords can be of service in illuminating the secular predicament of modern culture, particularly its covert historical derivation from Christian revelation. This perspective, furthermore, brings to light some unsuspected possibilities that have opened up for religious sensibility and creative expression of it in the modern world.

The derivation of secularity from biblical revelation is widely acknowledged, often through reference to Carl Schmitt's dictum in the opening sentence of his "Politische Theologie": "All significant concepts [Alle prägnanten Begriffe] of the modern theory of the state are secularized theological concepts."[2] Likewise enormously influential is Karl Löwith's argument in *Weltgeschichte und Heilsgeschehen* (*World History and Salvation History*) that German Idealism and the Enlightenment (*Aufklärung*) were secularizations of Christian eschatology and theology of history.[3]

At least since the 1960s, there has been a growing conviction, in any case among theologians, that secularization compellingly expresses the

---

una genealogia teologica dell'economia e del governo. Homo sacer II.2 (Vicenza: Neri Pozza, 2007), 15–18, trans. Lorenzo Chiesa (with Matteo Mandarini) as *The Kingdom and the Glory: For a Theological Genealogy of Economy and Government* (Stanford: Stanford University Press, 2011).

2. Carl Schmitt, *Politische Theologie. Vier Kapitel zur Lehre von der Souveränität* (Berlin: Duncker & Humblott, 1922), chapter 3, trans. George Schwab as *Political Theology: Four Chapters on the Concept of Sovereignty* (Cambridge: MIT Press, 1985).

3. Karl Löwith, *Weltgeschichte und Heilsgeschehen: Die theologischen Voraussetzungen der Geschichtsphilosophie* (Stuttgart: Kohlhammer, 1953), published originally in English as *Meaning in History: The Theological Implications of the Philosophy of History* (Chicago: University of Chicago Press, 1949). The thesis has been vigorously contested, notably by Hans Blumenberg, *Die Legitimität der Neuzeit* (Frankfurt am Main: Suhrkamp, 1966), *Säkularisierung und Selbstbehauptung* (Frankfurt am Main: Suhrkamp, 1974), trans. Robert M. Wallace as *Legitimacy of the Modern Age* (Cambridge: MIT Press, 1985).

true meaning of Christian revelation. This point of view has sometimes been advocated in a "God is dead" spirit, or at least as supposedly entailing the demise of theism and of theology as traditionally conceived and practiced.[4] Throughout his extensive oeuvre, Thomas J. J. Altizer lucidly and passionately represents the secular import of Christianity in this death-of-God tradition, and particularly in *History as Apocalypse* (1985), chapter 6, he recognizes the key place of Dante in his history of Christian secularism. He also underscores that secularization has fostered rediscovery of "authentic Christianity" and has opened the way to appreciating how fundamental Christian theological revelation has been to the making of the modern world.

The Christian genealogy of secularism has been a focus of reflection again recently in the wake of Charles Taylor's *A Secular Age*.[5] Taylor's work has fired intensive discussion of the broad topic of secularization that has placed irretrievably into question any simple opposition between the religious and the secular, as if the latter were simply the death of the former.[6] As Wolfhart Pannenberg writes, "Others have seen the central idea of modern times, that of freedom, as being Christian in origin, and have therefore regarded the modern 'history of freedom' as a process of the realization of Christianity itself in the world."[7] Such is the vision, for example, of Jürgen Moltmann, who in *God for a Secular Society* magisterially demonstrates the theological origins and impetus of secularization.[8] In a very different, but not unrelated, vein, Gabriel Vahanian has likewise argued persistently that the secular is not opposed to the sacred but is generated specifically out of Jewish and Christian theological

4. Important landmarks of this movement include Gabriel Vahanian, *The Death of God: The Culture of Our Post-Christian Era* (1961), Paul van Buren, *The Secular Meaning of the Gospel* (1963), Harvey Cox, *The Secular City* (1966), John Robinson, *Honest to God* (1972), and William Hamilton, *Radical Theology and the Death of God* (1966), coauthored with Thomas J. J. Altizer.

5. Taylor, *A Secular Age* (Cambridge: Harvard Belknap, 2007).

6. For diversified responses to Taylor's theses, see *Varieties of Secularism in a Secular Age*, eds. Michael Warner, Jonathan VanAntwerpen, and Craig Calhoun (Cambridge: Harvard University Press, 2010), and *Rethinking Secularism*, eds. Craig Calhoun, Mark Juergensmeyer, and Jonathan VanAntwerpen (Oxford: Oxford University Press, 2011).

7. Wolfhart Pannenberg, *Christianity in a Secularized World* (New York: Crossroad, 1989), vii. Originally *Christentum in einer säkularisierten Welt* (Freiberg im Breisgau: Herder Verlag, 1988).

8. Jürgen Moltmann, *Gott im Projekt der modernen Welt: Beiträge zur öffentlichen Relevanz der Theologie* (Gütersloh: Gütersloher Verlagshaus, 1997), trans. Christopher Kaiser as *God for a Secular Society: The Public Relevance of Theology* (Minneapolis: Fortress Press 1999).

outlooks.[9] Also highly influential in articulating the complex inter-relations of Christian and secular cultures have been the sociological approaches of David Martin, *On Secularization*, Talal Asad, *Formations of the Secular*, and José Casanova, *Public Religions in the Modern World*, the last of whom usefully distinguishes between secularization as (1) differentiation of secular from religious institutions and culture, (2) decline of religion, and (3) relegation of religion to the private sphere.[10]

Often and throughout its tradition, Christian theology has under-lined the fact that all talk about God is also inevitably talk about human beings and the world. Only a naive reification of God into a wholly separate object—in effect, an idol—obscures this realization. In contrast, the renunciation of characterizing God is more adequate and expressive than any given characterization of him could possibly be. Silence is more necessary to signifying God than anything that can be said about him. Yet another leading voice in twentieth-century theology, Edward Schillebeeckx, has focused attention on the link between secularism and the crisis of speech about God—and even the necessity for silence about God: "We are today conscious, not only theoretically but also practically, of the fact that we have no concepts of God and that every concept that is really put forward as a concept of God is in fact godless, because it denies God's transcendence."[11] Secularism entails a surpassing of previously attained conceptions about God and a necessary silence as new vocabularies and forms of thought are forged. Our modes of expression and representation for the divine become inevitably outmoded as human life develops along secular lines and realizes its own specific possibilities. But precisely as the inconceivable par excellence, "God" can continue to be relevant to secular culture in its quest to surpass all its own limits and even all fixed, finite forms of life and thought. When secularism in its drive to question everything questions even itself and its own concept, the limits of the conceptual per se come into view. But precisely these limits and their imaginable "beyond" very often turn out to be most effectively interpreted by religious images for ultimate realities.

---

9. Gabriel Vahanian, "Theology and the Secular," in *Secular Theology: American Radical Theological Thought*, ed. Clayton Crockett (New York: Routledge, 2002).

10. David Martin, *On Secularization: Towards a Revised General Theory* (Hants, UK: Aldershot, 2006), Talal Asad, *Formations of the Secular: Christianity, Islam, Modernity* (Stanford: Stanford University Press, 2003), and José Casanova, *Public Religions in the Modern World* (Chicago: University of Chicago Press, 1994), 211.

11. Edward Schillebeeckx, "Silence and Speaking about God in a Secularized World," in *The Spirit and Power of Christian Secularity*, ed. Albert Schlitzer (London: University of Notre Dame Press, 1967), 172.

Dante, before he undertook to write his imaginative masterpiece, the *Divine Comedy*, laid out his far-reaching cultural project in a treatise for laymen and women: *Il Convivio* (*The Banquet*). He proposed to take the philosophical and theological knowledge of his day, which was accessible only to the learned, who were versed in Latin, and serve it up in the vernacular language, thereby offering a general banquet, *un generale convivio*, to all those too immersed in worldly obligations to be able to dedicate themselves wholly to the pursuit of learning. For this purpose, he set out to select or to forge a new, secular language. He described it metaphorically as the new light and rising sun of the "illustrious vernacular" (*vulgare illustre*)—in the terms he used for paying homage to this language in his treatise on the vulgar tongue, *De vulgari eloquentia*. Into this language, he sought to translate and thereby to divulgate the "bread of angels" (*pan de li angeli*) that had previously been reserved for those—chiefly clerics—schooled in Latin. He announces this new light or language as replacing the old: "This will be new light, a new sun, which will rise where the old one sets and will give light to those who are in darkness and in shadow because of the worn out sun that does not shine for them" ("Questo sarà luce nuova, sole nuovo, lo quale surgerà là dove l'usato tramonterà, e darà lume a coloro che sono in tenebre e in oscuritade per lo usato sole che a loro non luce," *Convivio* I.xiii).[12]

In effect, Dante invokes this new light as a new gospel by echoing Zacharias's prophecy of salvation at the birth of John the Baptist—"the dayspring from on high hath visited us, to give light to them that sit in darkness and in the shadow of death," Luke 1:78–79)—which is integrated into the Roman Catholic liturgy as the *Benedictus*. Dante's words also echo another liturgical text, the *Nunc Dimittis* or Song of Simeon, the devout Jew who recognized the new light, "a light to lighten the Gentiles, and the glory of thy people Israel," once his eyes had seen salvation in the form of the Christ child presented in the Temple in Jerusalem (Luke 2:29–32). Even Dante's gloating that he will satiate thousands and yet have his own baskets overflowing with bread ("Questo sarà quello pane orzato del quale si satolleranno migliaia, e a me ne soverchieranno le sporte piene," *Convivio* I.xiii) is of evangelical resonance, echoing the miraculous multiplication of loaves and fishes in Luke 9:11–17, and it

12. I quote and translate Dante's works from the following editions: *Convivio*, ed. C. Vasoli, *Opere minori*, vol. 5, tome I, pt. II (Milan: Ricciardi, 1988); *La Divina Commedia secondo l'antica vulgata*, ed. G. Petrocchi, 4 vols. (Milan: Mondadori, 1966–67); and *De vulgari eloquentia. Epistole*, ed. Pier Vincenzo Mengaldo et al., *Opere minori*, vol. 5, tome II (Milan: Ricciardi, 1973).

implicitly compares Dante's project to announcing a new Gospel, or at least to announcing in a novel way God's promise of a new life.

The old sun presumably is the Latin language, which the "new sun" of the vernacular is now overtaking and replacing. However, another, or a further, possibility—though one that needed to remain veiled—is that Dante is proclaiming the supersession of the dark sayings of biblical prophecy by the new, natural light shed on the world by Aristotelian philosophy, which he celebrates from the beginning of the *Convivio* for its rational perspicuousness. The work opens with a quotation—"all men desire by nature to know"—expressly taken from Aristotle's *Metaphysics*. Consonant with Scholastic theology and its synthesis of philosophy and revelation, Dante fuses all knowledge into a Christian Neoplatonic amalgam and concerns himself with translating this sacred heritage into terms intelligible to the new, worldly classes of bourgeois professionals— prominently merchants and bankers—that were rising in the bourgeoning cities of incipient fourteenth-century, proto-Renaissance Italy.

At the same time, Dante, before all others, shows the extent to which the pursuit of a secular understanding of the world can also be a testimony of faith. As argued along divergent lines by the previously cited theologians and religious thinkers, to understand our world as "secularized" is to see it, precisely, as the result of religious vision. And this is clearer in Dante's vision perhaps than at any other point in Western cultural tradition. By zeroing in on Dante near the origins of modern secularization, we stand to deepen our understanding of how it has been called forth by Christian revelation: we can watch this movement building, in certain decisive respects, in one of its earliest and most original architects.

Of course, Dante's secularism is by no means unique or unprecedented. Already in the twelfth and thirteenth centuries, Averroes's (Ibn Rushd's) Arabic interpretation of Aristotle in his *Commentaries,* Moses Maimonides's *Guide to the Perplexed* (*Moreh Nevukhim*), and Thomas Aquinas's *Summa Theologiae* were all, in different ways, monumental works of secularizing religious thought and reflection. All of these thinkers, like Dante, receive vital impulses from Aristotle, leading to the rediscovery and reclaiming of the sensory and sublunary world by human reason. Dante, however, affords an extraordinary opportunity for highlighting the way in which this movement is driven by literary mechanisms: such mechanisms are, in fact, the ineluctable means of a secularizing movement in any written tradition. It is the very nature and structure of language and representation—given their own intrinsic energies and propensities to concretize and objectify—that account for how this momentous process of the secularization of religious revelation has unfolded and continues to unfold in modern history down to our own time.

The secularizing thrust and inspiration of Dante's poetic-religious vision has been grasped in a literary-historical perspective by critics, signally by Erich Auerbach, whose *Dante: Poet of the Secular World* outlined a far-reaching program that is still far from having exhausted its insights or spent its influence. Critical emphasis on Dante's discovery of a this-worldly, secular humanity can, of course, be traced back much further: at least to Francesco De Sanctis in the nineteenth century. Of similarly far-reaching influence is the testimony of the great historian of the Italian Renaissance, Jacob Burckhardt, who in *The Civilization of the Italian Renaissance* wrote with regard to the birth of modernity: "Here, again, as in all essential points, the first witness to be called is Dante."[13]

Such celebration of a modern, secular, Renaissance Dante has remained one of the most prevalent agendas for interpretation of the poet ever since. Admittedly, more recent scholarship has suggested that one needs to carefully distinguish between the *Convivio*'s programmatically secular Aristotelian philosophy and the *Commedia*'s reinvestment in the Scriptural model of revelation.[14] However, by transubstantiating the contents of Scripture into poetry through the alchemy of his artistic imagination, Dante in effect secularizes religious revelation. Not rational philosophy, but the unsoundable working of poetry as theology translated into poetic form, becomes the subtler secularizing medium of Dante's most mature writing.[15]

On the basis of the works cited and of other monumental works, the programmatic secularism of this quintessentially Christian poet has been widely recognized.[16] However, Dante's secularist emphasis has often been

---

13. Jacob Burckhardt, *The Civilization of the Italian Renaissance*, trans. S. G. C. Middlemore, 2 vols. (New York: Harper Torchbooks, 1958), I.151. Originally *Die Cultur der Renaissance in Italien: Ein Versuch* (Basel: Schweighauser, 1860).

14. See, for example, Paola Nasti, *Favole d'amore e 'saver profondo': La tradizione salamonica in Dante* (Ravenna: Longo, 2007). John A. Scott, "The Unfinished *Convivio* as a Pathway to the *Commedia*," *Dante Studies* 113 (1995): 31–56, provides a nuanced account of the gaps and the continuities that mark this transition.

15. Essays in *Dante's 'Commedia': Theology as Poetry*, eds. Vittorio Montemaggi and Matthew Treherne (Notre Dame: University of Notre Dame Press, 2010) and in Piero Boitani et al., *Dante poeta cristiano* (Florence: Società Dante Alighieri, 2001), offer a variety of readings along such lines. Kindred in spirit is also François Livi, *Dante e la teologia. L'immaginazione poetica nella 'Divina Commedia' come interpretazione del dogma* (Rome: Casa Editrice Leonardo da Vinci, 2008).

16. Previous powerful, classic statements of Dante's secularizing thrust that foregrounded especially its political character include Ernst H. Kantorowicz's chapter, "Man-

understood as qualifying or compromising, and in any case as in tension with, the religious ethos of his poem. This tension is typical especially of the more esoteric readings. The poet has even been portrayed as secretly anti-Christian and as hostile to medieval religiosity in his militant embrace of a modern secular humanism.[17] Yet it has also become increasingly clear how deeply secularizing philosophy penetrates even Dante's medieval culture.[18] What Dante's role as secularizer should help us to appreciate is rather that secularization does not disprove or deny the relevance of religion, particularly Christianity, to modern secular culture and its revolutions, but just the opposite. It rather shows the rootedness of the modern world precisely in a theological vision. In fact, in certain crucial respects, secularization emerges undeniably as the logically necessary development and fulfillment of Christian revelation.[19] This can be seen with perspicacity in Dante at a point of departure for the new realization of the Christian theological revelation of human life in terms of the secular world that it alone has made possible.

The very sense of Christianity, as a far-reaching secularization of religion, is revealed by Dante in a way that puts him in line eventually with Hegel, the modern thinker who, in his own self-understanding, completes the interpretation of Christianity as a revelation of divinity in humanity and as realized concretely in history.[20] There are, of course, aspects of Christian revelation that remain indispensable for Dante's religious as well as for his poetic faith that tend to be obscured in Hegel's thought—sig-

---

centered Kingship: Dante," in *The King's Two Bodies: A Study in Mediaeval Political Theology* (Princeton: Princeton University Press, 1997 [originally 1957]), and Charles T. Davis, *Dante and the Idea of Rome* (Oxford: Clarendon, 1957).

17. For example, by Alexis Ladame, *Dante, Prophète d'un monde uni* (Paris: Grancher, 1996), and Gregory B. Stone, *Dante's Pluralism and the Islamic Philosophy of Religion* (New York: Palgrave Macmillan, 2006).

18. Ruedi Imbach, *Dante, la philosophie et les laïcs* (Fribourg: Éditions Universitaires Fribourg Suisse, 1996).

19. Such a thesis is developed philosophically by Marcel Gauchet, *Le désenchantement du monde: Une histoire politique de la religion* (Paris: Gallimard, 1985), and is taken up diversely by philosophers including Alain Badiou, Giorgio Agamben, and Slavoj Žižek, emblematically in their works on St. Paul, which are treated together by Dominik Finkelde, *Politische Eschatologie nach Paulus: Badiou-Agamben-Zizek-Santner* (Vienna: Verlag Turia + Kant, 2007).

20. Merold Westphal, *Hegel, Freedom, and Modernity* (New York: State University of New York Press, 1992), demonstrates Hegel's brilliant defense of a rational, Christian revelation of God in the world against a secular, atheist Enlightenment, on one side, and against a mystical Christian pietism, on the other. Guy P. Raffa, *Divine Dialectic: Dante's Incarnational Poetry* (Toronto: University of Toronto Press, 2000), underlines some significant affinities of Dante's intellectual project with Hegel's.

nally the affirmation of God's utter transcendence of history and humanity. Yet Hegel's emphasis on how the transcendent becomes immanent is nevertheless central to the whole Christian vision as it pivots on the Incarnation. Not by accident, Hegel's thinking, with its dialectical mediation of transcendence by immanence, and of divinity by history, was crucial also to Auerbach's framework for reading Dante and thereby helped to inaugurate a new era for Dante criticism based on a secularizing paradigm.

II. Transcendence in Immanence: Freedom and Incarnation

Many of the *Commedia*'s most obvious claims to originality stem directly from Dante's daring discovery and ardent embrace of a radically secular worldview. His realism envisages the world on its own terms rather than as *merely* symbolic of some other order or supernatural reality. His self-presentation as protagonist is likewise a revelation of a completely new autonomy for the individual human being. Yet the transcendent order still is immanently present in the historical world and in the human individual: it is what gives them value, indeed absolute value. Arguably, the valorization of the individual as an absolute and not just as functional in an impersonal, hierarchical system is first made possible historically in the Christian era. Such valorization presupposes, first, the doctrine of a transcendent God, absolute in himself and the source of all value. He alone is the model for the absolute value of each individual in a democratic society. The transcendence of mere functionality on the part of each singular individual, whose infinite worth exceeds every contextual framing and every kind of use value, becomes recognizable only subsequent to and as a reflection of this monotheistic idea of absolute divine transcendence and freedom. The divine transcendence as such becomes worldly in some novel ways in the Incarnation of Christ. Thereafter, it extends itself to other mortal individuals living their lives within the world as further prolongations of Christ's embodiment in the Church.

Emblematically, in the Incarnation, God came into the world, the infinite into the finite, and this incarnation of divinity continues in every singular human individual who is remade in the image of Christ and becomes part of his mystical body. From this point on, the potential for an immanent, worldly realization of divinity is unlimited. Individuals are not wholly of the world, even while existing within it, since their singularity exceeds any context to which they belong and any system that attempts to account for them.²¹ Realizing precisely this form of transcendence is perhaps the most significant, destiny-laden direction in the development of modern Western culture and history. It has generally been championed in all manner of secular discourses under the banner of the "freedom" of the individual. As an inalienable human value, freedom has generated quasi-religious cults and reverence across the whole spectrum of secular ideologies in their approaches to human life.

A secular worldview is characterized by its preserving a sphere of autonomy for human reason and nature, a worldly or secular realm that maintains an integrity of its own and that therefore can be understood in human and natural terms alone. Such a world is "cut off" (*secatus*) from any other world or superior, divine reality. There were powerful secularizing tendencies in the theology and culture of the twelfth and thirteenth centuries. Some of them were connected, for example, with the discovery of ways of using machines (*ars mechanica*) to construct a more humanly congenial world.²² The rediscovery of Aristotle, particularly of his works on natural philosophy, was key to rethinking the human condition in natural terms, and Scholastic theologians, especially from Albert the Great on, developed secularizing views on a range of topics from natural to political philosophy. All of this registers clearly and leaves an incisive impress upon Dante. There is a passage in the *Convivio* where Dante imagines a perfect conjunction of natural virtues in all of the causes, from the celestial to the parental, contributing to a human birth as producing a perfect human being (like Christ), in effect an incarnate God. He is carried away with enthusiasm for what he conceives of as a quasi-natural incarnation of divinity: "it would be almost another incarnate God" ("quasi sarebbe un altro Iddio incarnato," IV.xxi, 10). This new-found human self-confidence and sense of boundless human dignity induces Dante to praise human nobility, with respect to its being full of virtues and fruitfulness, above even that of the angels ("ardisco a dire che la nobilitade umana, quanto è da la parte di molti suoi frutti, quella dell'angelo soverchia," *Convivio* IV.xix, 6).

Dante maintains that man has, in addition to a divine destination, a natural *telos*—a happiness that he is naturally and necessarily interested in attaining in this life, besides seeking salvation and beatitude in the

---

21. Atheist philosopher Slavoj Žižek, in *The Fragile Absolute—or, Why is the Christian Legacy Worth Fighting For?* (London: Verso, 2000), recognizes the immediate relation of the individual to the absolute as belonging properly to the Christian heritage.

22. See, for example, M. D. Chenu, *La théologie au douzième siècle* (Paris: J. Vrin, 1957).

next. The two are distinct and even imply separate systems of government for secular (or terrestrial) and spiritual (ultimately celestial) life, respectively. Hence Dante's assertion of the supreme power of the Emperor in the secular sphere that is not to be interfered with by the Pope's spiritual authority. Dante develops this theory of two distinct goals for mankind as both an earthly creature and an immortal soul—and of two corresponding orders of ethical activity—in explicit theoretical treatments in his tractate on empire (*De monarchia*), which he specifically designates as *temporalis monarchia,* the only form of government suited for leading human beings to complete fulfillment in this life. And the same conceptions are powerfully advocated in his visionary poem as fundamental ideological coordinates. Even just in terms of the poem's plot, Dante the pilgrim must be restored to original natural righteousness in the Garden of Eden at the summit of Mount Purgatory before he can go on in quest of supernatural blessedness in Paradise. When he reaches the Earthly Paradise, regaining the Garden of Eden at the top of Mount Purgatory, Dante has achieved the temporal goal of humanity. The formula from the investiture of the Emperor, echoed in Virgil's words—"I crown and mitre you" ("te corono e mitrio," *Purgatorio* XXVII.142)—confers full secular autonomy upon Dante, who is thenceforth restored to original justice in his own will and is no longer under Virgil's tutelage or under any other earthly authority.

Like Thomas Aquinas, Dante is a pioneering thinker of the secular world. Despite the classically medieval terms of his outlook, he pushes them in a direction opening upon the modern world. This is evident in one way in his political theory, with its uncompromising insistence on the autonomy of the Emperor as the highest authority in the temporal sphere. Such unified, absolute authority is necessary, in Dante's view, in order to ensure and promote the freedom of each individual for full realization of their rational capacity or "potential intellect" (*De monarchia* I.iii, 6–10): "Therefore it is clear enough that the proper work of the human species as a whole is to constantly actualize its total intellectual potential" ("Satis igitur declaratum est quod proprium opus humani generis totaliter accepti est actuare semper totam potentiam intellectus possibilis," *De monarchia* I.iv, 1). Moreover, the secular inspiration of Dante's vision is just as radical and more original—even if less obvious—with regard to his poetic epistemology or gnoseology. In his striving for understanding and knowledge without bounds, he does still found all knowledge on the vision of God.[23] Yet he gives a particular twist to this theological

---

23. Such is the thrust, for example, of Giuseppe Mazzotta's theologically accentuated

foundationalism. The highest and truest knowledge in the Middle Ages is not humanly discovered or constructed so much as divinely given or revealed, and it is not the instrument of an autonomous individual so much as a way of dwelling in an objective order of mind, a means of participation in a Truth that transcends it. Accordingly, the founding truth of Dante's vision radically exceeds his grasp: he emphasizes that it leaves reason gaping open to what it cannot conceive and suspends poetic language gasping in allusion to what it cannot say.[24] The motif of the ineffable accompanies every approach to the divine vision upon which Dante's poetry converges in his culminating work, the *Paradiso*. Dante delves into the human modalities of experiencing divine transcendence precisely in and through the failure of his poetic powers of expression.[25]

The political passion and the intensive representation of the earth that are such salient characteristics of Dante's *Paradiso* have often seemed to be oddly incongruous in what is otherwise conceived of as a mystical itinerary to the direct vision of God. But the logic of secularization as theological revelation in an emergent, new, and modern key enables us to see these constant emphases of the *Paradiso* as defining precisely the meaning of Dante's vision. It is paradoxically because of their utterly (and unutterably) transcendent nature that theological verities can find only worldly, human, and poetic expression. There is no proper or purely spiritual language for them. Dante, veritable father of modernity, discovers that the essence of religious and even of mystical revelation is necessarily expressed in secular terms. Any more direct or adequate statement of theological truth proves to be impossible, for all our language is worldly and, referred to God, can be but metaphor.[26]

---

readings in *Dante's Vision and the Circle of Knowledge* (Princeton: Princeton University Press, 1993).

24. Already the *Convivio* repeatedly stresses these unsurpassable limits (for example, at III xv, 6), notwithstanding its sometimes inebriated celebration of human reason as a more-than-human operation ("più che umana operazione," III.xiv, 11).

25. My *Dante and the Sense of Transgression: 'The Transgression of the Sign'* (London: Continuum [Bloomsbury Academic], 2013) offers further elaboration of this perspective.

26. Aquinas rigorously demonstrates in *Summa theologiae* I.q. 13 that all our language for God is only analogical. Current forms of this issue are debated in John Caputo and Michael J. Scanlon, eds., *Transcendence and Beyond: A Postmodern Inquiry* (Bloomington: Indiana University Press, 2007). More broadly, modern writers engaging in poetic transcriptions of transcendence into worldly immanence are considered in Regina Schwartz, ed., *Transcendence: Philosophy, Literature, and Theology Approach the Beyond* (New York: Routledge, 2004).

In this apprehension, Dante is actually in line with an ancient tradition of negative theology that we can trace through most epochs of Western culture, a tradition in which rational reflection and faith find that they finally support each other:[27] our language can rationally comprehend only the finite world, but its gaps and impasses and silences can be—or cannot help being—inhabited by the ineffable and infinite that exceed the dimension of the finite universe. This is the dimension which is so richly imagined in the other worlds of the Christian religion and of other faiths. In apophatic discourse, finitude breaks open into an undelimited abyss and thereby dialectically evokes the infinite. This discourse is most crucial to Dante's poetry as it strives to reach its highest peak in the *Paradiso*. And it is not only rational but also affective or volitional human reality and consciousness that are discovered as revelatory of an unknowable divinity in the mystical currents of Dante's own time, especially those blossoming in feminine spiritual movements such as the beguines, or in the mysticism of Meister Eckhart (1260–1328), Dante's nearly exact contemporary.[28]

The full range of human and worldly existence shows itself to be revelatory of the divine in this mystical perspective, yet it defies expression, except in a metaphorical language that, more deeply considered, is not even metaphorical but rather apophatic discourse geared to saying nothing, to annulling signification, or to signifying what exceeds all possibility of expression.[29] Alongside Christian sources, Kabbalah and Sufi writings display similar secularizing tendencies that come to an extraordinary flowering of apophatic discourse at the end of the thirteenth and early fourteenth century in figures such as Moses of Léon (1240–1305),

27. The early stages of this history are related by Raoul Mortley, *From Word to Silence, I: The Rise and Fall of Logos*; and vol. II: *The Way of Negation, Christian and Greek* (Bonn: Hanstein, 1986). Contexts close to and including Dante can be found in *On What Cannot Be Said: Apophatic Discourses in Philosophy, Religion, Literature, and the Arts*, edited with theoretical critical essays by William Franke (Notre Dame: University of Notre Dame Press, 2007.), vol. 1: Classical Formulations.

28. *Meister Eckhart and Beguine Mystics: Hadewich of Brabant, Mechthild of Magdeburg, and Marguerite Porete*, ed. Bernard McGinn (New York: Continuum, 1994).

29. Marco Ariani, *Lux inaccessibilis: Metafore e teologia della luce nel Paradiso di Dante* (Rome: Aracne, 2010), reads Dante's use of metaphor in precisely this way. See also Marco Ariani, ed., *La metafora in Dante* (Florence: Olschki, 2009), 1–58, 193–220. A powerful reflection on the use of metaphor in expression of theological transcendence more generally is proffered by Sallie McFague in *Speaking in Parables: A Study in Metaphor and Theology* (Philadelphia: Fortress Press, 1975) or, again, condensed, in McFague, "Intimations of Transcendence: Praise and Compassion," in Caputo and Scanlon, eds., *Transcendence and Beyond*, 154–59.

presumable author of the *Zohar*, Abraham Abulafia (1240–92), active in Rome contemporarily with the formative phase of Dante's work, and Jalal al-Din Rumi (1207–73), father figure of the Mevlevi Sufi order of whirling dervishes.[30] Apophaticism crops up consistently at historical junctures where culture has taken a sharply secular turn. It represents a way for religious aspirations to preserve themselves even where the official or conventional *language* of religion has been undermined. This is the case in postmodern culture today, and it was the case in the late-medieval culture of Dante's time and milieu. Dante reflects this culture and shows himself to be perfectly well aware of the doctrines of negative theology already from the time of the *Convivio*, where, concerning things of Paradise spoken of in the Book of Wisdom, he writes:

> When it then says: They surpass our intellect, I am excused for being able to say little about them on account of their transcendence. Whence it must be realized that in a way these things blind our intellect, in that certain things are affirmed that our intellect cannot contemplate, that is, God and eternity and primal matter; which certainly are seen and with complete faith are believed to be, yet we are not able to understand what they are; and in no way except by negating things is it possible to approach knowledge of them, and not otherwise.

> Poi, quando si dice: Elle soverchian lo nostro intelletto, escuso me di ciò, che poco parlar posso di quelle, per la loro soperchianza. Dove è da sapere che in alcuno modo queste cose nostro intelletto abbagliano, in quanto certe cose [si] affermano essere che lo intelletto nostro guardare non può, cioè Dio e la etternitade e la prima materia; che certissimamente si veggiono, e con tutta fede se credono essere, e per quello che sono intendere noi non potemo; [e nullo] se non cose negando si può appressare a la sua conoscienza, e non altrimenti. (*Convivio* III.xv, 6)

It is this awareness of the limits of human intellect and speech that actually opens the (negative) way to an imaginative experience of the divine, which occurs in worldly, metaphorical terms.

---

30. See Michael A. Sells, *Mystical Languages of Unsaying* (Chicago: University of Chicago Press, 1994), for a focus on this historical period as one of a blossoming of apophatic thought. Elliot R. Wolfson, *Language, Eros, Being: Kabbalistic Hermeneutics and Poetic Imagination* (New York: Fordham University Press, 2005) pursues parallels in specifically Kabbalah mysticism across ages and cultures and genres.

III. Apophatic Theology as Secularized Prophetic Discourse in the *Paradiso*

Especially important, then, for illuminating the secularizing impulse of Christian revelation is the negative or apophatic theology that Dante pursues with matchless passion in the *Paradiso*. Negative theology—with its teaching that we can know only what God is not—is based on a self-reflexive critique of all positive, dogmatic formulations regarding divinity, beginning with the traditional expressions of religious myth. Dante accepts myth in its essential truth-content and as a necessary and inevitable mode of expression, but he corrects for its misleading representations and often dangerously misguided implications. He constantly invokes the myths of classical antiquity and uses them as *exempla* alongside and in parallel with Old Testament figures and stories in order to prefigure the truths of Christian revelation. These myths are poetic figures for theological truths and realities. In this hermeneutic practice, Dante is continuing in the Neoplatonist tradition of philosophical commentary on literary texts that runs from Macrobius (fifth century) and Fulgentius (sixth century) to Bernard Silvestris (twelfth century), all of whom build negative theological premises into their readings of pagan literature. They are themselves following Porphyry and an originally Greek tradition of philosophical and allegorical exegesis of pagan poets, especially Homer. They extend this tradition of allegorical interpretation of epic poetry as revealing philosophical and religious truth to Virgil.[31]

Negative theology, in the form known to Dante, derives from the Neoplatonic tradition of Christian fathers and theologians and especially from Dionysius the Areopagite (fifth–sixth century).[32] While negative theology is best known for recoiling into a passive posture of mysticism and muteness, it can also have another side, a prophetic, messianic side turned toward a newly emancipated world.[33] This is at least as strong in

---

31. I pursue these continuities in "On the Poetic Truth That Is Higher than History: Porphyry and the Philosophical Interpretation of Literature," *International Philosophical Quarterly* 50/4 (2010): 415–30.

32. Diego Sbacchi, *La presenza di Dionigi l'Areopagita nel 'Paradiso' di Dante* (Florence: Olschki, 2006), and Antonio Rossini, *Il Dante sapienziale: Dionigi e la bellezza di Beatrice* (Pisa: F. Serra, 2009), bring this derivation into focus.

33. This other side binds the apophatic inseparably to the kataphatic theology that is postulated already by its founding father, Dionysius the Areopagite, and never completely disappears in the ensuing tradition. See Denys Turner, *The Darkness of God: Negativity in Christian Mysticism* (Cambridge: Cambridge University Press, 1995).

the poetry of the *Paradiso* as any mystical inclination.[34] The ineffability of the vision of God, in which the poem culminates and on which it is predicated from its outset, thanks to the ineffability topos, does not lead Dante simply into silence. It leads him rather to "speak out" ("pro-phates") with the voice of a prophet, straining in every way to set the world, *this* world, to rights. Dante writes expressly "on behalf of the world that lives ill" ("in pro del mondo che mal vive," *Purgatorio* XXXII.103). And in this missionary undertaking, he finds himself authorized to use all available, worldly forms of representation freely, for it is, in any case, not possible to represent divinity in objectively accurate terms. Representation of a transcendent God can, under any circumstances, be only metaphorical and poetic. Realizing this, Dante discovers something that might be called "*prophetic license*" in analogy to—and, in fact, as indivisible from—poetic license.[35]

Although in principle God is inaccessible to representation, Dante's poem in effect is implicitly suggesting that he can best be contemplated—and can perhaps only be revealed—through the creative inventions of the imagination. A kind of equivalence between poetic representation and divine vision, the contemplation of God, emerges from Dante's poetic endeavor, in spite of—and really on account of—its incorporation of constant disclaimers concerning the very possibility of any adequate representation. Representation of divinity is impossible, and it is paradoxically *as* impossible, as an inevitably failed attempt, that the *endeavor* of constructing representations may attain its end of authentically communicating an experience of the divine.[36]

Thus Dante does not renounce poetic representation, even though he has accepted, in accordance with the insights of negative theology, the

34. Dante is, of course, also often read in this mystical key, for example, by Giuliana Carugati, *Dalla menzogna al silenzio: La scrittura mistica della "Commedia" di Dante* (Bologna: Il Mulino, 1991), and by Manuela Colombo, *Dai mistici a Dante: Il linguaggio dell'ineffabilità* (Firenze: La Nuova Italia, 1987).

35. On the basis of his own negative theology, Maimonides is led to formulate the notion of "prophetic license." See *RAMBAM: Readings in the Philosophy of Moses Maimonides*, ed. and trans. Lenn Evan Goodman (New York: Viking, 1976).

36. In this sense, "the impossible" has again become an obsession of postmodern forms of apophasis like deconstruction in the attempt to think without or beyond concepts. A good discussion of this pervasive theme can be found, for example, in John D. Caputo, *The Prayers and Tears of Jacques Derrida* (Bloomington: Indiana University Press, 1997), 20–25. A compendium of related approaches can be found in Hent de Vries, ed., *Religion: Beyond a Concept* (New York: Fordham University Press, 2008). See also Caputo's "Apostles of the Impossible: On God and the Gift in Derrida and Marion," in *God, the Gift, and Postmodernism*, eds. John D. Caputo and Michael J. Scanlon (Bloomington: Indiana University Press, 1999), 185-223.

impossibility of producing any adequate representation of the divine. Instead, this very impossibility frees representation in its worldliness to become the absolute embodiment of divine vision. It is not a matter of representing an objective truth but rather of witness to ineffable personal experience conveyed by inevitably metaphorical formulations.

Representation of divinity discovers itself in Dante to be necessarily, and by its own nature, poetic. It is, in effect, no longer beholden to any higher, originally theological authority but is itself absolute.[37] This does not mean that Dante does not feel himself bound by any higher authority, for he certainly did feel this, as every page of his poetry, as well as of his other writings, unequivocally attests. But he realizes that he has no direct means of apprehending and communicating this authority and must rather bear witness to its power over him by the way he wields a medium—linguistic, imaginative, metaphorical—that he recognizes as irrevocably secular. His pursuit of poetry to the limits of the capacity of human words to bear and render meaning enlightened him about the intrinsic limitations of human language and about the ineliminable admixture of the worldly in whatever truth, be it ever so heavenly, he might undertake to convey. The secular itself becomes the revelation of the divine, the only truly valid revelation. Yet this is a secularity that has become possible only because of Christian revelation: such secularization is the emancipation of specifically Christian revelation from the enveloping myths in which it first came enshrouded.

Dante is a great myth-maker, but he is also an *un*maker of myths. Negative theology is born of rational reflection upon the pitfalls and structural inadequacy of any human, inevitably mythic language for divinity, and exactly this kind of reflection is, in fact, far advanced in Dante's poem. An incidental hint of this can be found, for example, at the beginning of *Paradiso* VIII ("Solea creder lo mondo in suo periclo . . .") with its reference to the "ancient error," "believed by the world in its peril," that the stars or planets, like Venus, were gods or goddesses sending down their influences upon humans. And yet the fact that Dante apostrophizes Apollo and Minerva and the Muses at the outset of the *Paradiso* indicates that he is comfortable with evoking pagan divinities even in his programmatically Christian poem, since they can be read

---

37. In this respect, Dante anticipates the modern "phenomenological turn" and its effect of absolutizing perception. John Took, *Dante's Phenomenology of Being* (Glasgow: University of Glasgow Press, 2000), integrates modern with medieval approaches to the issue of grounding aesthetics in ontology but thereby also phenomenalizing and aestheticizing being.

transparently as metaphorical figures. When every possible representation of God is relativized as metaphorical—if it is not outright rejected as just some form of idolatrous reification—the status of representation itself changes. It can no longer be an objectively valid denotation of independently real things. Conspicuously metaphorical language is a reminder of this fact. Dante's obviously metaphorical description of Paradise—and it is programmatically so, being designed simply to "make a sign" ("far segno"), according to *Paradiso* IV.37–39—thereby becomes the most effective sort of witness and testimony to divinity as the unrepresentable.

Dante's poem is based on the hypothesis of a final moment of disclosure in aesthetic and theological vision. His narrative fiction is the story of a journey to a direct encounter with God. The journey culminates in mystical union with the divine by a fusion of his vision with "the infinite value" ("i' giunsi / l'aspetto mio col valore infinito," XXXIII.80–81). Yet these representations of union and vision are always only approximate. Even here at the poem's end, at the most direct the vision will ever be, there is nevertheless the displacement from God and his Being or Essence to the aura of "value" (or "power") that emanates from him. It is clear even here in the last canto that Dante's unmediated vision and union with God can still be described only in terms of its felt meaning for him and only by way of approach and as an endless nearing, an "ending" or "finishing," that also has the sense of an endless process of perfecting:

> E io ch'al fine di tutt'i disii
> > appropinquava, sì com'io dovea,
> > l'ardor del desiderio in me finii.
> > (XXXIII.46–48)

> And I who to the end of all desires
> > was drawing near, even as I had to do,
> > the ardor of desire in me finished/was perfected.

The hypothesis of unmediated vision is the point on which the whole poem pivots. But this point cannot itself be represented and so become a moment within the poem—not if it is going to serve, rather, to anchor the poem to something that is presumably other than and outside it. The vision of God itself, which is miraculously given in a moment of grace—as opposed to its literary projection and elaboration by Dante—grounds the poem. How could the vision of God itself be exhaustively expressed in the poem? Presumably, an absolute lyric intensity would be the mode of expression corresponding to the absolute ecstasy and plenum of this experience. Dante does strive after this lyric plenum in the *Paradiso* in some uniquely intensive ways. Yet his lyricism is embedded in narrative, just as his vision of eternity is embedded in history. In Dante's secularizing of theological vision, history *is* the revelation of eternity, and his poetry in its lyrical rapture is itself the experience of the delights of paradise. At least the poetry is a foretaste or the "first fruits" thereof. Christianity is, after all, incarnate revelation, and in this respect Dante makes its deepest and most distinguishing drives manifest.

Dante's lyric poetry in the *Paradiso* creates a linguistic density that concentrates experience and attention within language, even while this language remains a metaphor for what lies beyond language and representation altogether. It is not that the experience in question is a discrete experience of something other than all articulable experience or different from any experience whatsoever. It is rather that the ineffable is in—or at least can be experienced in—everything.[38] The *Paradiso* often focuses on language as the vehicle of experience in general rather than only on particular objects of experience. Of course, Dante reviews and inventories all culture, the whole store of human knowledge as it is available to him, in this endeavor. Yet all this is his content only obliquely, in order to point toward another sort of content—or rather a contentless "vision."[39]

Dante's lyric language in the *Paradiso* calls attention to itself as language. The sonic and graphic material of language moves into the foreground. Canto XVIII, for example, stages a kind of fireworks display in the Heaven of Jove, in which speech literally sparks and letters become a combustible material in the ether of the paradisiacal firmament. Language itself becomes a spectacle and revelation in its own right rather than only serving a utilitarian purpose of vehiculating an immaterial sense, while disappearing itself in its materiality. Yet neither is this material vehicle as such the only end and final purpose of the poem. It is present only as an allegory for something else entirely, something indeed unsayable and even unsignifiable, except by improper, metaphorical means: the Deity. The concrete language of lyric here is taken as paradigmatically about what cannot be said within the rules of language but only by means of their

---

38. Ludwig Wittgenstein, particularly in his "Lecture on Ethics," in *Philosophical Occasions 1912–1951*, eds. James C. Klagge and Alfred Nordmann (Indianapolis and Cambridge: Hackett, 1993), 37–44, places the experience of the mystical not outside but within the center of the most ordinary experience.

39. Cf. Marguerite Mills Chiarenza, "The Imageless Vision and Dante's *Paradiso*," *Dante Studies* 90 (1972): 109–24.

violation. Modern poets have understood the function of the lyrical especially in terms of freeing language from its instrumental use in order that its own intrinsic nature might be made manifest.[40]

Particularly the Russian school of Formalism was the standard bearer of this insight, which finds a widely influential formulation in Roman Jakobson's essay "Linguistics and Poetics."[41] The nature of language itself, as opposed to its value in communication, is also in a different way the central concern of Martin Heidegger's meditations on the "essence" of poetic language ("Das Wesen der Sprache"). Language reveals its own nature when it ceases to function smoothly and becomes problematic. It becomes an indicator of Being itself or "as such," as distinct from any and every particular being. Thus, from their very different types of insight into the nature of language, semiotic and hermeneutic thought both approach the ineffable as the source of language and of all its sense.[42]

For Dante, the naturally revelatory vocation of language makes it apt to reveal something transcendent. Dante treats language as a divinely created and bestowed faculty. Moreover, Dante's language in the *Paradiso* is poetic language declaring itself ever more clearly to be constituted by the lack of any articulable object. The history it presents is represented as depending on what does not appear and cannot become historical: the Transcendent. This is, in fact, essential to Christian revelation at a certain (negative theological) stage of reflection upon its own conditions and limits. All that is revealed in history and language is revealed as different from the true object or ultimate source of revelation—transcendent divinity—which is thus not an object at all, nor even possibly an object.

Paradiso is different from the other parts of the poem in that its object is programmatically designated as ineffable. This is perhaps only a

---

40. This is demonstrated for French poetry from Baudelaire to Mallarmé, with emphasis on Rimbaud, but with constant comparison to medieval, especially Thomistic, theological and aesthetic sensibilities, by Olivier-Thomas Venard, *Littérature et théologie: Une saison en enfer* (Geneva: Ad Solem, 2002).

41. Jakobson, "Closing Statement: Linguistics and Poetics," in *Style in Language*, ed. T. Sebeok (Cambridge: MIT Press, 1960), takes his cue in turn from Paul Valéry's description of poetry as a sustained hesitation between sound and sense ("Le poème, hésitation prolongée entre le son et le sens"), in "Rhumbs," *Œuvres II* (Paris: Gallimard [Bibliothèque de la Pléiade], 1960 [1941]), 637. For the pertinence of the semiotic model to Dante, see Raffaele De Benedictis, *Worldly Wise: The Semiotics of Discourse in Dante's 'Commedia'* (New York: Peter Lang, 2012).

42. I follow out this line of analysis, with bibliographical references to Heidegger and Agamben, in "Language and Transcendence in Dante's *Paradiso*," in *Poetics of Transcendence*, eds. Elisa Heinämäki, P. M. Mehtonen, and Antti Salminen (Amsterdam: Rodopi: 2014).

difference of degree, since in some sense all three eschatological realms—
Hell, Purgatory, and Heaven—are beyond mortal language and understanding. But the *Paradiso* expressly dwells upon its lack of any object
that can be said and represented. Whereas certain limits to representation
are encountered occasionally in the preceding *cantiche,* in the *Paradiso*
this impossibility of expression becomes the major premise of the very
discourse of the poem. At its deepest level, the poem is about precisely
this impossibility. Of course, Dante does, even in the *Paradiso*, represent
abundantly: he manages to represent a whole civilization—in some sense,
civilization in its entirety as it could be imagined at his particular historical juncture and from his Christian conviction and point of view. But
the source and focus of it all, nevertheless, escapes representation. The
representations of history reveal a sense transcending history and representation. The presence of God would be this ultimate instance of sense.
The fiction on which the whole poem is erected is that its itinerary leads
finally into the fully unobstructed vision of God. If God could be directly
contemplated in his essential being and total presence, the vision would
be beyond representation, but as an enabling fiction this postulate orga-
nizes the whole journey of the poem.

Perhaps all major, truly epochal poets have felt the imperative to
pursue to its limits the means of expression inherent in their chosen art
form. Goethe in his exploration of the ultimate potentialities of his poetic
medium in the second part of his *Faust* becomes for many of the admir-
ers of his earlier work virtually unintelligible.[43] Mallarmé's pursuit of the
Absolute of verbal signification drives him ineluctably to a rupture with
sense in the pure poetry of scintillating silence. Joyce's characteristic verbal play is carried to such an extreme in *Finnegans Wake* that it is no longer possible to say definitively in what language, dead or alive, any given
word or expression is written: there are any number of radically different
linguistic codes in which each phrase solicits interpretation.[44]

Analogously, Dante in the *Paradiso* pushes to their extreme consequences his own aesthetic principles and technical innovations and
employs his poetic talents upon uncharted seas that will leave readers,

43. Wolfgang von Goethe's 1805 masterpiece *Faust. Eine Tragödie* became the object
of intensive further elaboration by the author from 1825 to 1831. *Faust. Der Tragödie
zweiter Teil in fünf Akten* was published in 1832, a year after Goethe's death.

44. I develop this thesis in detail in *Poetry and Apocalypse: Theological Disclosures
of Poetic Language* (Stanford: Stanford University Press: 2009). Part 2 presents *Finnegans
Wake* as the culmination of Christian epic and of the theological revelation inherent in
poetic language.

all except the elect few ("Voi altri pochi"), lost and bewildered (*Paradiso* II.1–15). His talents for poetic representation carry him to the furthest limits of the possibility of representation, and he discovers there the Unrepresentable as his ultimate non-object. Such is the burden of Dante's last and greatest project, the *Paradiso*. It is illuminated by being understood within the framework of a pervasive, millenary culture of negative or apophatic theology. Apophatic discourse, in its inherent anti-authoritarianism and undermining of definitive doctrine, takes on revolutionary overtones in certain contemporary movements, including radical Franciscanism or, as previously mentioned, the new women's vernacular mysticism of the beguines fostered by Meister Eckhart. Such analogues fill in the background for rendering fully intelligible the specifically prophetic turn of Dante's culminating work.

IV. Poetic Language as Secular Theological Revelation

The *Paradiso*'s negative theology, like negative theology in many of its historical incarnations, is highly secularizing. Negative theology (the doctrine that we can know only what God is *not*) is reflective and critical by its very nature. It involves rational critique of all of theology's positive representations. It leads away not only from positive dogmatic formulas but even from all supposedly positive contents of mystical experience. The bare, worldly fact of language is left stripped of any articulable object and of the transcendence of meaning through a voiding, or at least suspending, of semantic content. The consequence is a confrontation with radical emptiness, at least at the level of what is represented. To really imagine negative theology is to contemplate divine presence and plenitude as not representable—not even, except provisionally, by the modes and forms of emptiness and absence. This non-vision of negative theology reaches one of its peaks in Catholic tradition in Dante's own time with Meister Eckhart and continues down to our times in numerous revivals, for example, with Stanislas Breton and his philosophy of nothing.[45] It also develops in forms of thought more akin to Judaism and even radical Protestantism, issuing in the deconstructive styles of Emmanuel Levinas, Maurice Blanchot, and Jacques Derrida.[46]

---

45. See Rubina Giorgi, *Dante e Meister Eckhart: Letture peril tempo della fine* (Salerno: Ripostes, 1987), and Stanislas Breton, *La pensée du rien* (Kampen, Netherlands: Kok Pharos, 1992).

46. See chapters on each in Franke, *On What Cannot Be Said*, vol. 2, as well as Franke, *Dante and the Sense of Transgression*.

The plenitude that the poem so rapturously sings is that of passion, pure passion without any definable object, for the God it celebrates is not and cannot be any objective being. This God can be designated in finite terms only inadequately and in the form of privations. In lieu of giving us God's presence represented as any objective kind of being, the *Paradiso* conveys a passion for poetry itself and a celebration of forms of aspiration and desire.[47] Pure form becomes its element, although this is not divorced from political motivation and the detailed representation of history. Yet the vision of God per se turns out not to be a vision of any discrete object at all. How could it be, since God is not an object? Dante displaces divine vision rather to the universe, the visible dimension in which God is mysteriously manifest as what is not objectively known or grasped. This becomes explicit in the final vision, which veers from God himself as "infinite value" to "that which is unfolded through the universe" ("ciò che per l'universo si squaderna," *Paradiso* XXXIII.87). The idea of an unmediated vision of God himself, which motivates and directs Dante's entire journey, is exposed in the end as functioning somewhat in the manner of an enabling fiction. Such vision cannot as such be proved in any discourse or even be represented in poetry. Dante describes, rather, the "passion impressed" on him, as if by a dream, once all objective memory of his experience has been erased and no longer returns to mind ("la passion impressa / rimane, e l'altro a la mente non riede," *Paradiso* XXXIII.59–60).

The vision of God has been achieved all along the way, so far as it can be, in and through the vision of a world in which God's order is manifest. As also for Nicolas Cusanus, in his 1453 treatise on the subject, the *visio Dei* is the vision of the universe as God sees it: "vision *of* God" becomes a subjective genitive, God's own seeing. The promise of the unmediated vision of God himself as a discrete something, distinct from the universe, guides Dante to the avowal of its final impossibility. Nonetheless, the hypothesis of such a vision proves necessary as a postulate that enables the performance of the poem as a worldly simulation of the otherworldly.

In this way, Dante's language is not so much mystical revelation as historically incarnate revelation of God. God is present, or rather effective, not as an object of language but rather right within the dynamism of language and history—as what can never be objectified and yet motivates and guides language in its engagement with history, thereby revealing an ethical and perhaps also a metaphysical transcendence. The images

47. Lino Pertile, *La punta del disio: Semantica del desiderio nella Commedia* (Florence: Cadmo, 2005), especially chapter V: "Desderio di Paradiso," 137–61.

of scintillating and sparking persistently mark the language of the *Paradiso*. Dante repeatedly employs the invented word *sfavillar* (XVIII.71), which combines and fuses words for sparking (*favillare*) and speaking (*favellare*). This image of speaking as sparking is apt to suggest the conspicuous display of language released from or exceeding the conceptual constraints of the Logos and its objective mode of reference. This is thus language rather as a spontaneous combustion and explosion or "sparking" of sense.

A sense of direct encounter with God and especially with Christ has been found traditionally by commentators to be conspicuously missing from the *Paradiso*. One does not necessarily feel, as with other great mystics, an intimacy with the divine person of Christ encountered in prayer. Dante's mystic vision strikes its most powerful and characteristic notes in a kind of expression far different from that of the intimate experience of an individual turned exclusively toward what is inwardly present. It expresses itself in a passion for the world, *this* world, a passion that remains, nevertheless, otherworldly in its origin and intensity.[48] The prophetic and messianic burden of the *Paradiso* is the realization of its mystic vision, for the mystical as such cannot be represented: it is, for Wittgenstein, "the inexpressible" ("das Unaussprechliche," *Tractatus* 6.522). Dante finds that he can express his mystical vision and passion for what transcends the world perhaps best in ways turned toward the world.

With the Incarnation of God that constitutes the central proclamation and the shattering novelty of Christian revelation, the body and specifically the flesh become the crucial site of revelation. This revelation in the flesh is crucial in Christian tradition right from John the Evangelist's declaration that the divine Word "was made flesh and dwelt among us, and we beheld his glory, the glory as of the only begotten of the father, full of grace and truth" (Gospel According to John 1:14). It is still today the source of novel philosophical insight, for instance, in the phenomenological investigations of Michel Henry.[49] Henry's Christian phenomenology, centered on the divine mystery of the flesh, is presently being developed further by Emmanuel Falque specifically in the terms established by the patristic and medieval fathers and doctors of the Church.[50] In our own postmodern cultural context, expressions of the apophatic reach even to the bodily and carnal as centers of revelation. This was

48. See, for example, Jaroslav Pelikan, "The Otherworldly World of the Paradiso," in *Eternal Feminines: Three Theological Allegories in Dante's Paradiso* (New Brunswick: Rutgers University Press, 1990).

49. Henry, *Incarnation: Une philosophie de la chair* (Paris: Seuil, 2000).

50. Emmanuel Falque, *Dieu, la chair et l'autre: d'Irénée à Duns Scot* (Paris: Presses Universitaires de France, 2008).

already the case in premodern times and notably in patristic writers. Signally Tertullian (*De carne Christi*), Athanasius (*De Incarnatione*), and
St. Augustine (*De Incarnatione Verbi*) wrote on the flesh as the ineluctable and ineffaceable locus of Christian revelation. This lesson was never
quite forgotten even in the highly spiritualizing Middle Ages and all the
way to Scholasticism: indeed, Dante mightily exploits all the physical
senses in his spiritual ascent. Again today, in postmodern times, there
is a widespread revival of such worldly approaches to this traditionally
mystical topic of incarnation, and the new approaches often stress particularly the body.[51] Similarly, aesthetic approaches root apophatic experience in the senses. The apophatic vocation especially of modern art has
been the subject of intense exploration.[52] The indispensable role of the
senses in the sacraments revealing a mystery beyond words has also been
brought out, for example, in relation specifically to seventeenth-century
English literature.[53]

These are all sensory, worldly expressions of the spiritual, and thus
they can be most easily annexed by a secular outlook. Still, in order to
preserve also the otherworldly perspective that originates from beyond the
manifest, it is necessary to prevent secularism from becoming reductive,
from defining everything in terms of itself and of its own immediately perceptible world. The world must also be appreciated as Other, as originating in the otherness that no terms are adequate to express. This is where
Dante can join (and in a certain sense cannot help joining) hands with as
unlikely an ally as Jacques Derrida (and, behind him, Walter Benjamin),
another sort of prophet of messianic otherness. Derrida, moreover, is one
who clearly perceives how, in the perspective of Western philosophy, modern secular culture is the result of specifically Judeo-Christian tradition
and its basis in revelation: "The opposition sacred/secular is very naive,
it raises many deconstructive questions. Contrary to received wisdom,
we have never entered into a secular era. The very idea of the secular is
through and through religious, Christian in truth."[54]

51. See *Apophatic Bodies: Negative Theology, Incarnation, and Relationality*, eds.
Chris Boesel and Catherine Keller (New York: Fordham University Press, 2009), and
Wolfson, *Language, Eros, Being*.

52. Amador Vega, *Arte y santidad. Cuatro lecciones de estética apofática* (Pamplona: Universidad Pública de Navarra, 2005), or, in summary form, "Estética apofática
y hermenéutica del misterio: elementos para una crítica de la visibilidad," *Diánoia* 54,
no. 62 (2009): 1–25. See, further, Mark Taylor, *Disfiguring: Art, Architecture, Religion*
(Chicago: University of Chicago Press, 1992).

53. Regina Schwartz, *Sacramental Poetics at the Dawn of Secularism: When God
Left the World* (New York: Routledge, 2004).

54. Jacques Derrida and Antoine Spire, *Au-delà des apparences* (Latresne, Bordeaux:
Le bord de l'eau, 2002): "L'opposition sacrée/séculière est bien naïve, elle appelle bien

Christianity is a religion of revelation, and in Christian revelation the secular world, history itself, becomes theophany. But history is a linguistic phenomenon, at least insofar as it articulates its meaning, and not least its theological meaning. Augustine understood it as such in the *Confessions,* where he figured all history as one long sentence being recited like the verses of a song (XI.xxviii, xxxviii). In the New Testament, as we have recalled, in the prologue to the Gospel of John, the Incarnation is understood linguistically as a revelation of the divine Word, the Word become flesh (1:14). Dante as poet is fascinated by this power of disclosure inherent in language and particularly in language's historical embodiment in the temporally evolving vernacular. His book *De vulgari eloquentia* (*On the Vulgar Tongue*) is devoted to theoretical speculation on this head.

In the *Paradiso,* Dante seems to be carried off into direct transcendence toward the vision of God vehiculated by language. Yet the sense of this transcendence is actually realized only by historical representation in and through language. Dante asserts a ground for historical revelation in God and in the direct intuition of God—a God, however, who cannot be represented. This moment of total presence is a fiction within the representation of his poem—the fiction that enables representation of history to metamorphose into revelation and apocalypse.

For Dante, history is the disclosure of theological truth. It is a history that is not complete or objectified but rather in process of becoming. Its true significance is revealed only eschatologically. The poem continually appeals to what *will* happen in history for vindication. A messianic event is imminently expected, for example, in *Paradiso* XXVII.148, which announces that "true fruit will come after the flower" ("e vero frutto verrà dopo il fiore"), not to mention the enigmatic messianic prophecies of the Veltro and the DXV, in the *Inferno* and the *Purgatorio* respectively, that frame the *Paradiso* and look to it for their fulfillment. However, history is all a linguistic construction. Language, therefore, as Dante creates it in the *Paradiso,* is historical revelation. He creates an historical language for the Italian people, creating them as historical thereby, and he grounds this language in divine revelation. At the same time, by artistically and poetically synthesizing a theological grounding for language, Dante in effect reveals this grounding as historical and as a human construction.

Dante's testament (like that of Western civilization as a whole) is

des questions déconstructrices. Contrairement à ce qu'on croit savoir, nous ne sommes jamais entrés dans une ère séculière. L'idée même du séculier est de part en part religieuse, chrétienne en vérité" (28).

peculiarly complicated and difficult to interpret because it entails at once a secularization of language and a sacralization of the "beyond" of language. Dante both invents a language of realistic representation that opens a genuinely secularized perspective on the world and also de-realizes this language, exposes it as incapable of adhering to the truly and ultimately real, thereby opening a dimension of transcendence beyond language and representation, a dimension where the divine can insinuate itself and presumably be encountered in spirit and in truth. Thus Dante's work gives us both sides of a two-way movement pivoting first toward and then away from realistic representation as the motor of secularizing religion. Such religion redefines itself as ultimately concerned with God or the Transcendent, but as more immediately about the limitations of language itself—and of every worldly form employed for apprehending intimations of divinity. Whereas Dante initially gives an impulse to secularization by his realistic representation of an otherworldly reality, it is finally by breaking away from representation as the primary and revelatory function of language that his poetic-prophetic mission is fulfilled. In this way, the very secularizing force of Dante's vision leads finally to a reopening of the realm of the sacred.

In a baffling paradox, both representation and its negation prove to be instrumental and indeed equally indispensable to this momentous project of translating religion into worldly terms, of transmuting revelation into literature, and vice versa. Religious myth is secularized by literary representation, and then, in a further step, literary representation is itself demythified by a negative poetics that is, in reality, negative theology at work in the poetic text. At this point, the religious opens up again as the most vital and urgent of questions from beyond the death of representation. The death of God proves to have been only the death of *representations* of God, and consequently the *question* of God comes back as alive as ever. As Wallace Stevens, in the implicitly Dantesque *terza rima* of his *Notes toward a Supreme Fiction,* divined:

> Phoebus is dead, ephebe. But Phoebus was
> A name for something that never could be named.
> There was a project for the sun and is.

The sun remains in its fully sensual intensity. Although the names and myths placed upon it die, as a project or eternal ideal the sun shines only the more brightly. It does so even in its "difficulty"—the negativity of its being unnamable due to the inadequacy of every name:

There is a project for the sun. The sun
Must bear no name, gold flourisher, but be
In the difficulty of what it is to be.

This is how a secular, negatively theological outlook releases the mystery of the divine once again into circulation. Here is Dante's *luce nuova, sole nuovo* (new light, new sun) dawning again beyond all his (and any possible) imaginings. Uncannily, he addresses us from a distance through Steven's injunction:

You must become an ignorant man again
And see the sun again with an ignorant eye
And see it clearly in the idea of it.

The ignorant man rediscovers the dimension of the unknowable, which is discernible only in a self-critical gaze turned on his own ignorance. In effect, he becomes an ephebe, a youthful, naive seeker after knowledge. Only in the incompleteness of the ephebe does the idea of Phoebus, implying the perfection of effulgent divinity, the sun god, become clearly visible. The god "Phoebus" is to this extent himself a reflection and projection of the "ephebe," as the juxtaposition of their nearly homophonous names subtly insinuates.

Still for Stevens, following in Dante's train, poetry is a negative theology directing us to the question of the source and ground—or groundlessness, so far as all articulable terms are concerned—of our secular world. The mediating powers of language have functioned as the engine for this whole movement in both directions—the movement toward representation and back away from it again. It is in literature that these capabilities and limits of language are revealed most strikingly, and they are explored and exploited and exposed by none more influentially and ingeniously than by Dante Alighieri.

V. Addendum on the Rise of Dante Studies in the University[55]

So far, this chapter has presented and illustrated a chiefly philosophical

---

55. A version of this chapter, beginning with the reflections at the heart of this section, was written for and presented at the 2003 Modern Language Association (MLA) National Convention in San Diego in the Division on Literature and Religion organized by Dayton Haskins on the topic of "Religion and the Rise of Literary Studies."

thesis about literature as the secularization of religious revelation. This thesis was originally deployed in opposition to Terry Eagleton's argument that the academic study of literature arose because of "the failure of religion."[56] Taking Dante's *Divine Comedy* and the history of its insertion into the university curriculum as an eminent example, I attempt here to interpret the rise of literary studies rather as religion's greatest success, namely, its translation of itself into secular idioms and institutions. The irony is that I am near to Eagleton's perception of the close relation between religion and literary study as one of succession, though not necessarily of supersession. In fact, I would argue that Marxism (Eagleton's religion, in effect) is itself essentially a translation of Christian humanism, plus biblical apocalypticism and its utopian vision, into a secular language. But where Eagleton reads the failure of the precedent culture (religious cult and worship), I see religion's power demonstrated in its having transformed—indeed converted—itself into new kinds of cultivation (signally poetic creation and literary education) that do not definitively replace so much as supplement it, creating new opportunities for religious expression and reflection.

In this perspective, Christianity itself appears as a far-reaching, historically revolutionary deconstruction of religion. Just such a view is being developed by a number of contemporary thinkers, including Jean-Luc Nancy and Gianni Vattimo, who were anticipated in this respect especially by Michel de Certeau.[57] For all these thinkers of religion, Christianity takes the lead in undermining the metaphysical bases of traditional religions and opening them to the dynamism of history as kenotically revealing an eschatological truth in the death (and resurrection) of Christ. Even the old cultic institutions of sacrifice to gods located in some supposedly other world are transformed by Christian secularization into ethical and social action for redeeming *this* world and into aesthetic works for beautifying it.

In order to gain historical perspective on the secular study of literature, which is often alleged to be a compensation for the loss of religion, perceived as being in decline, as by Eagleton, we can hardly do better

---

56. Eagleton makes an argument to this effect in chapter 1, "The Rise of English," of *Literary Theory: An Introduction* (Minneapolis: University of Minnesota Press, 1983). He continues his reflections in *After Theory* (London: Allen Lane, 2003).

57. Jean-Luc Nancy, *Déconstruction du christianisme*, vol. 1: *La Déclosion* (Paris: Galilée, 2005), vol. 2: *L'adoration* (Paris: Galilée, 2010); Gianni Vattimo, *Dopo la cristianità: Per un cristianesimo non religioso* (Milan: Garzanti, 2002), trans. L. D'Santo as *After Christianity* (New York: Columbia University Press, 2002); and Michel de Certeau, "Penser le Christianisme," in *La faiblesse de croire* (Paris: Seuil, 1987).

than to take as our focus the history of teaching the *Divine Comedy* in our institutions of higher learning in the English-speaking world, which can be set alongside its inculcation principally in secondary schools in Italy. As a great exponent of theological poetics, or of translating religious truth into poetic and personal experience, Dante Alighieri is capable, like perhaps no other, of shedding light on this issue. The translation of religion into literature is at work in an extraordinary and yet exemplary manner in his writings. Specifically concerning the history of the *Divine Comedy* in the university curriculum, moreover, there is a fascinating story that has received extended novelistic treatment and best-seller attention, thanks to Matthew Pearl's popular murder mystery, *The Dante Club* (2003). In this fiction, resistance from university authorities to the attempt of Boston intellectuals, including Henry Wadsworth Longfellow, Oliver Wendell Holmes, and James Russell Lowell, to introduce the study of the *Divine Comedy* in English translation into the curriculum at Harvard in the mid-nineteenth century leads to gruesome murders modeled on some of the grisly punishments in Dante's *Inferno*.

The novel indirectly suggests that the academic teaching of literature with a religious message may not always be easy or innocent. It spurs us to ask: What have been the difficulties posed by the literary use of a religiously committed work such as the *Divine Comedy* for humanities studies in the university? It even prompts us to speculate a little on how these difficulties devolve from tensions within society between religious and secular culture. I will comment briefly on how these tensions have been manifest in the scholarly study of Dante in Italy and in America respectively in the last century.

In Italy there have been strong pressures to read Dante as purely literary, to separate the poetry from the non-poetry, the lyrical content from the theological structure with which it is in fact indissolubly fused together. Enforcing just such a separation was something of a mission for Benedetto Croce, programmatically in *La poesia di Dante* (1921). He extended such a program broadly to reading modern European literature in *Poesia e non poesia* (1955). And even later generations of critics who rejected Croce very often attempted to neutralize and work around the poem's theological pretensions in order to concentrate on the purely literary aspects of the work. Its theology is thereby bracketed as not relevant to the poem as a work of literature.

In North America, on the other hand, starting with Charles Singleton, there was a strong tendency to redress this bias and to stress the vitally theological character of the poem in its central meaning and message. However, as reported by his student John Freccero, Singleton was scorned and ridiculed by Italian scholars, the Dante studies barons of the day, when he presented his theological reading of the *Vita nuova*, interpreting Beatrice as a Christ figure. Some more recent American critics, including Robert Hollander and Teodolinda Barolini, have continued to insist that the theological claims of Dante's work are crucial at least to its working as poetry. And Christian Moevs, for one, has offered a powerful new articulation of the religious and metaphysical vision that inspires the entire poem. Similarly, Giuseppe Mazzotta, Steven Botterill, and Peter Hawkins, to name just a few more leading voices, are representative of the theologically oriented styles of criticism that have been particularly rife in the American academy.

Nevertheless, the history of Dante in America places into evidence the secular nature of the religiosity that Dante's vision has, in effect, fostered historically. Dante was ushered into the curriculum at Harvard in the middle of the nineteenth century by "Transcendentalists" and "Boston Brahmins."[58] The association with Emersonian mysticism in particular would already suggest that interest in Dante may belong to the ambience of a strongly secularized, nature-based, mystical—and not ecclesiastical—religiosity. Of course, the flourishing American Dantism of recent decades, say, since 1966, with the beginning of the journal *Dante Studies* (formerly the *Annual Report of the Dante Society*, founded in 1881), can be characterized as largely exegetical rather than philosophical in nature: and to that extent, it is modeled on interpretation of the Bible. Criticism, accordingly, emphasizes the poem's theological contents and purposes.[59] Nonetheless, the approach to theology through Dante's poetic text as outlining a "poetics of conversion" (to echo the title of the collected essays of John Freccero) is already a secularized way of treating its religious content and inspiration. Thus the theological bias of American Dante criticism can itself suggest how secularization is a way of preserving and even of divulgating religion, spreading it to a larger public through a wider diffusion of general culture unconfined by confession or creed.

The rise of literary studies, which is often taken to correlate with the demise of religion, in this case presents itself rather as a somewhat indi-

---

58. These labels are used by Glauco Cambon, "Dante's Presence in American Literature," *Dante Studies* 118 (2000): 217–42. See also Matthew Pearl, "'Colossal Cipher': Emerson as America's Lost Dantean," *Dante Studies* 117 (1999): 171–94.

59. A summary of this tendency can be found in Giuseppe Mazzotta, "Reflections on Dante Studies in America," *Dante Studies* 118 (2000): 323–30.

rect route for the revival of religion, its metamorphosis into new forms of revelation. We can observe in this process an interesting illustration of the power of historical distance. Dante's Catholic medieval worldview and its implications for society are still somehow too dangerously close in Italy, where towering medieval cathedrals dominate the public squares—the piazze—of city centers, and the popes are still sensed as being imposingly present, physically and politically, as well as spiritually. Near the precincts of the Vatican, a need is felt by many, especially among the ruling intellectual elite, to keep Dante, as one of Italy's most potent cultural icons, from having an apparently self-evident valence as legitimating the established powers and official organs of political and cultural hegemony—and potentially oppression. At a greater historical distance from Dante's own cultural home ground, in twentieth- and twenty-first-century America, the stronger need is to recuperate the lost power and passion of a spiritual vision such as the *Divine Comedy* embodies and derives to a considerable extent from its investment in the world of Catholic medieval Christendom. At such a historical remove, this heritage has by and large ceased to be threatening and beckons instead with the enchanting voice of a nearly forgotten age of mystery and imagination, sometimes even of esoterism, that scholars and the public alike thrill to recover.

So my hypothesis concerning the adoption of religious matter into the academic curriculum via literature is that this happens most readily at a safe distance. The university, true to its name, aspires to be in some sense "universal" and neutral in its teaching, and to that extent it may be hesitant about matters with too direct an ideological stake in the burning controversies and crises of the present; for, in such cases, there is a risk of destabilizing society's institutions and of upsetting the delicate equilibrium among competing claims to authority and allegiance within a secular, lay democracy or republic. The potentially revolutionary ferment of religion, as displayed all over the globe in recent decades, and not entirely unsuspected even by Matthew Arnold in *Culture and Anarchy: An Essay in Political and Social Criticism* (1869), is underestimated by Eagleton when he aligns religion too unilaterally with the conservative forces that cement society.

Even within its constraints of ideological neutrality, the university, nevertheless, has a role to play in fostering an at least generic religious sensibility, and this, I believe, is very pertinent to the special value that study of the *Divine Comedy* can have in our academies today. Religion freed from confessional and doctrinal boundaries has to do with contemplation of the Infinite and the Open, with totality and universality too vast to be grasped by representations, or to be closed within concepts. Of course, religion also concerns fragmentation and finitude too elusive and singular to be susceptible of adequate articulation: this, too, entails transcendence of all our schemas of comprehension and issues in evocation of what surpasses them. In both of these registers, Dante is exemplary in showing how literature and the poetic can take over and continue to perform, even within the context of secular culture and education, the essential function of religion—that of somehow tying all things together and of gesturing toward the larger whole beyond all that can be represented and comprehended by any particular system of ideas. Such is the enabling frame and context of all our endeavors, but it eludes our attempts to definitively formulate and grasp it. Poetic works perform a "religious" function especially on the basis of their potentially negative capability—their receptivity to intimations of what inevitably evades positive definition and objective reality altogether.

This zone of ineffability and the indefinable, although invisible, is crucial to everything in human life and society. Of course, one might wish to have no religion whatever, and certainly atheism, too, is a position and tradition that must be included and honored within the overall study of the humanities. However, when it takes itself to be the only truth and militates against religion, then secularism has become a religion in its own right—and an intolerant one.

My perspective on this perennial issue derives from a negatively theological reading of Dante that admits its own necessary ignorance of what God is and claims to be able to know only what he is not.[60] In this negative theological perspective, literature is part of a process of religious revelation that nevertheless dissolves (or infinitizes) the definition of whatever divinity is being revealed, making it rather the inexpressible object or intent of inexhaustible metaphorical expression. I believe, however, that this is a fundamental dimension of all culture and that liberal education should aim at awakening and cultivating this sensibility for what is beyond any possibility of rational calculation and yet insinuates itself in the margin between the definable meanings of words. This sensibility, which poetic literature arouses and refines, is indeed akin to and perhaps identical with religious awareness and might be welcomed and

---

60. I work out this perspective on Dante more fully in *Dante and the Sense of Transgression* and in a number of published articles on the *Paradiso*. I present it in general philosophical terms in *A Philosophy of the Unsayable* (Notre Dame: University of Notre Dame Press, 2014). I reconstruct the tradition in which it is embedded in the two volumes of *On What Cannot Be Said*.

celebrated as its realization in a secularized culture. Literature and literary study can thus become key to enabling religious revelation to occur anew as a genuine event of truth by teaching us how to understand the language of our religious traditions in a more open and searching and, withal, unassuming way.

chapter 2

"enditynges of worldly vanitees"

truth and poetry in chaucer as compared with dante

I. The Contextual Frame: A Paradigm Shift

The question of the truth of poetry subtends Chaucer's entire oeuvre. The "retracciouns" of the "makere of this book" at the end of the *Canterbury Tales* cast all of Chaucer's most significant poetic achievements into a shadow of doubt, indicting them as "translacions and enditynges of worldly vanitees" and as outside the sanction of "oure doctrine." A similar rejection of poetry, accompanied by a turning to the other world, occurs in the middle of his works at arguably the most crucial juncture in the Chaucer canon, the last stanzas of *Troilus and Criseyde*. Here a litany of pagan vanities condemned with vehement religiousness climaxes in the stigmatization of poetry: "the forme of olde clerkis speche / In poetrie. . . ." ("old scholars' manner of speech / In poetry").[1]

These stanzas have been treated by some, for example, Tatlock, as an outright contradiction of both the sense and sensibility of the poem and as required only to make a shockingly realistic portrayal of human pas-

---

[1]. Citations of Chaucer's works are from *The Riverside Chaucer*, gen. ed. Larry D. Benson, 3rd ed. (New York: Houghton Mifflin, 1987). Translations (where deemed necessary) are my own.

sion palatable to Chaucer's medieval audience.[2] Others, like Robertson, find the palinode already planted in the poem from its beginning in the form of an ironic undercutting of the erotic, human love that is ostensibly celebrated.[3] Even within the first view, which assumes that the "epilogue" constitutes a sharp turning, a disjunction, indeed a contradiction, widely divergent paths of interpretation open up. We need to ask whether the narrator is finally coming to see the truth about the vain love he has nurtured throughout his equally vain poem or is rather refusing to accept the truth of his tale, jerking it back into line with Christian orthodoxy by moralizing wholly inadequate to its profound human beauty and meaning. In other words, once we admit the contradiction between the poem and its conclusion, we still have the question of which view of poetry is being presented as true.

These interpretations might not prove to be as irreconcilable as they seem, however, if we can manage to understand the rather complex, paradoxical sort of truth value that Chaucer's poetry embodies.[4] In preliminary terms, my hypothesis is the following: as a man of medieval faith, Chaucer believed that truth belonged properly only to a transcendent realm of Being that he understood in a Platonic-Boethian sense and to another world, the world to come, as revealed in Christian Scripture and dogma. Moreover, unlike Dante, he believed this truth to be beyond the reach of poetry. Nevertheless, poetry for him seems to have played a crucial role in gaining perspective on the whole motley gamut of human folly and its thoroughgoing travesty of truth—in fact, its inevitable *un*truth. And this sort of knowledge may be taken as a first step toward orienting him to what emerges in the end—beyond all human *poiesis* or "making"—as true. Unmasking human falsehood rather than revealing divine verities would thus turn out to be the didactic burden, the "truth" of the poems that Chaucer wrote. For Chaucer himself, the infinite disproportion of such human "truth" to Truth in the proper and theological sense seems to have loomed large at moments of final reckoning, as his

---

2. John S. P. Tatlock, "The Epilog of Chaucer's Troilus," *Modern Philology* 18 (1920): 625–59.

3. D. W. Robertson, Jr., "Chaucerian Tragedy," *English Literary History* 19 (1952): 1–37.

4. Barbara Newman, in *Medieval Crossovers: Reading the Secular against the Sacred* (Notre Dame: University of Notre Dame Press, 2013), ix, characterizes this "jarring Christian turn" in a poem that "for most of its gorgeous length is humanistic, classical, and pagan" as an example of the dialectical "crossing over" of sacred and profane genres or codes. She suggests that double-coding calls for "double judgment" according to a "both/and" logic (56).

retractions poignantly testify. In saying this, I assume that Chaucer, by devoting himself to poetry, aimed at more than just distraction for himself and others. In any case, he certainly achieved more.

Dante's and Chaucer's creative peaks are separated by little more than seventy years, a relatively short span of time from the early to the late decades of the fourteenth century. Yet their intellectual frameworks, particularly at the level of the epistemological assumptions that are operative in their poetry, lie on oppositely inclined slopes of a watershed. However disputed the details, we may take it as common knowledge in medieval studies that Dante thought largely within—or at least in relation to—the parameters of the so-called medieval synthesis of faith and reason that was rigorously worked out by Thomas Aquinas. Thomas was himself building on the work of Albert the Great of Cologne, his teacher, among others. Chaucer's England, in contrast, was imbued with a skeptical philosophy, the tradition of Duns Scotus and William of Ockham, which radically dissociated these two faculties or modalities of knowledge.[5] Skepticism regarding the human intellect's power to discern truth beyond the realm of the senses (and the senses, of course, for a Boethian were a changing realm of untruth) was complemented by blind faith in the truths received by revelation. Instead of the continuity of natural reason and faith that permitted Dante to imagine Virgil (symbolically, human reason) as leading him directly to Beatrice (symbolically, theology or divine revelation) in *Purgatorio* XXX, Chaucer was faced with a radical divorce between a positivistic theology derived hermetically from Holy Writ and an empirical philosophy that restricted the application of human reason to earthly matters. In the succinct phrase of Gordon Leff: "a growing empiricism was giving rise to a growing fideism."[6]

---

5. Lawrence Eldredge, in "Boethian Epistemology and Chaucer's *Troilus* in the Light of Fourteenth Century Thought," *Mediaevalia* 2 (1976): 49–75, cites the Condemnation in 1277 of propositions stemming from Aristotle and Arab commentators that were held to compromise God's free will as a turning point after which "theologians, in order to show that their doctrines lay beyond philosophical realms, launched a critique of human knowledge to show that theology could be neither established nor refuted by philosophy. This in turn inevitably led philosophy away from metaphysics and toward empiricism . . ." (50). This philosophical sea change is presented as the beginning of modernity and all its calamities by the Radical Orthodoxy movement. Their narrative is outlined, for example, in Catherine Pickstock, "Duns Scotus: His Historical and Contemporary Significance," *Modern Theology* 21/4 (2005): 543–74.

6. Gordon Leff, *Medieval Thought from St. Augustine to Ockham* (Baltimore: Penguin Books, 1958), 291, quoted in Robert Burlin, *Chaucerian Fiction* (Princeton: Princeton University Press, 1977), 12. The philosophy in question, generally known as nominalism, is recognized as marking a divide between Dante and Chaucer, particularly in terms

Faith being potentially reasonable, Dante took upon himself the task of demonstrating its truth in the medium of poetry. Since classical times, poetry had been recognized for its special merit of combining and sweetening doctrine with delight: "omne tulit punctum qui miscuit utile dulci / Lectorem delectando, pariterque monendo" ("whoever mingles the useful with the pleasing gains points, delighting and likewise instructing the reader"), in the canonical formula from Horace's *Ars poetica* (lines 343–44). The power of poetry to move emotionally, to stimulate the imagination, and to arouse the senses could be exploited for prophetic and for paraenetic purposes, as in impassioned preaching. As Marcia Colish noted, "For Dante, the poet is a prophet and a teacher. Poetic beauty becomes the means whereby he communicates God to man."[7] Dante's poetry relies willingly on similes and metaphors taken from the most common experiences of ordinary life as terms of comparison for the phenomena of heaven, hell, and purgatory. Bees in flight, for example, are used to describe the choreographic movement of the angels on the paradisiacal rose. The presupposition of such a method is that the sensible world from which poetic imagery is drawn is capable of offering signs by which the human intellect may apprehend divine reality. The theoretical foundation for Dante's use of poetry as an "epistemic method" can be traced to St. Augustine. The idea that it is possible for human language to represent things divine, to signify God, albeit only in part and indirectly ("per speculum in aenigmate"—I Corinthians 13:12), passes from Augustine through Anselm of Canterbury and Thomas Aquinas to Dante. In Colish's streamlined summary of this complex tradition: "They all hold that human powers of speech and conceptualization are capable of signifying divine truths accurately though incompletely" (206). The general warrant for believing that divine significance could somehow attach to human signs for all these thinkers was the doctrine of the Incarna-

---

of their epistemological "confidence," by Holly Wallace Boucher, "Nominalism: The Difference for Chaucer and Boccaccio," *The Chaucer Review* 20 (1986): 213–20. Of course, that Chaucer was affected by nominalism does not necessarily mean that he subscribed to it, as is pointed out by John Michael Crafton, "Emptying the Vessel: Chaucer's Humanistic Critique of Nominalism," in *Literary Nominalism and the Theory of Rereading Late Medieval Texts: A New Research Paradigm,* ed. Richard J. Utz (Lewiston: Edwin Mellen Press, 1995). See review of the issue by Rodney Delasanta, "Nominalism and the *Clerk's Tale* Revisited," *The Chaucer Review* 31 (1997): 209–31, and Stephen Penn, "Literary Nominalism and Medieval Sign Theory: Problems and Perspectives," in *Nominalism and Literary Discourse: New Perspectives,* eds. Hugo Keiper, Christoph Bode, and Richard J. Utz (Amsterdam: Rodopi, 1997), 180–82.

7. Marcia Colish, *The Mirror of Language: A Study in the Medieval Theory of Knowledge,* rev. ed. (Lincoln: University of Nebraska Press, 1983), 152.

tion. "Dante aims at expressing the strange and wondrous things which he experiences in the other world of the spirit in terms of this world so that they will be immediately recognizable to his audience. His motive is didactic, and the underlying rationale of his imagery is Incarnational typology" (Colish, 217).

But this rationale was no longer valid for Chaucer. The bifurcation of philosophy and theology intervening between Dante and Chaucer meant that human reason was no longer viewed as capable of discovering God incarnate in the world and that faith alone in dogma could assure human beings that revelation was true. It was no longer deemed reasonable to believe that, since God had given himself to be humanly known in the body of Jesus Christ, he would likewise, by his grace, give himself to be known by human intellect applied to sensible signs. This requires illuminating reason from within, in order that its apprehension of the significance of signs might be true, but such illumination could no longer be taken for granted as part of the natural endowment of human reason. Human faculties, including poetic faculties, were no longer considered to be naturally competent to complement the knowledge gained by faith. For Augustinian sign theory, with its tenet that signs signify real things and even divine things, had been shaken to its foundations by the nominalist controversy. It is not surprising, then, that Chaucer never demonstrated any confidence that poetry could in any way represent the reality of the divine. This might simply be ascribed to interests different from those of Dante. However, the utter lack of any reliable instruments for knowing supersensible reality surfaces as a crucial issue repeatedly in Chaucer's poetry. That all such knowledge can be only hearsay is thematized, for instance, in the Prologue to *The Legend of Good Women*:

> . . . ther nis noon dwellyng in this contree,
> That eyther hath in heaven or in helle ybe,
> Nay may of his noon other weyes witen,
> But as he hath herd seyd, or founde it writen;
> For by assay ther may no man it preve.
>
> (Text F, 5–9)

> . . . there is no one dwelling in this land,
> That has been in either heaven or in hell,
> Nor may know of them by any other means
> Than by what he has heard said or found written;
> For by experience can no man test his knowledge.

One of the essential premises of Augustinian sign theory, deriving from Aristotle, is that being is prior to knowing, and, for this reason, "the subjective function of signs in helping to communicate knowledge depends on the knower's previous relationship with the object" (Colish, 223). But Chaucer has categorically excluded the possibility of previous acquaintance in this life with the transcendental world. And yet he enjoins his reader, on God's authority, to believe anyway:

> But God forbede but men shulde leve
> Wel more thing then men han seen with ye!
> (F 10–11)

> But God forbid but that men should believe
> Much more than what their eyes have seen!

We are urged (not, perhaps, without irony) to believe on the authority of unspecified "bokes," even though all that such books really authenticate are

> ... olde appreved stories
> Of holynesse, of regnes, of victories,
> Of love, of hate, of other sundrey thynges. . . .
> (F 20–24)

The narrator has shifted from facts about the afterlife to history and fable as the sort of knowledge that "the doctrine of these olde wyse" can verify, and even so his reverence for these written authorities is eclipsed by his contemplation of a natural object, the daisy, when the month of May comes round.

In a different but related vein, in the proem to the *House of Fame*, Book I, Chaucer discusses authorities for the knowledge of the supernatural, this time through dream experience. Again, however, no reliable grounds for such knowledge are found. "Why that is an avisoun / And this a revelacioun" is beyond the narrator's comprehension. In the voice of a good-humored but confused, intellectually modest seeker, Chaucer turns fideistically to God, petitioning that every dream be for the good: "God turne us every drem to goode!" (1; cf. 58). The very fact that the question of authority is treated *within* Chaucer's *poems* rather than shaping them from without means that we are dealing with positions and postures set up within a framework of fiction. Moreover, the excessive "profusion of authorities" cancels authority out, and the status of the poem, by implication, degenerates to rumor by the end.[8] Rumor's house, perpetually whirling ("that never no hyte stille stente") and perforated with "[a] thousand holes, and wel moo" in which "tydynges" proliferate by a process of false reporting, is a vivid and witty indictment of the authority of poetic tradition.

Mainly, of course, Chaucer is not, like Dante, writing about the other world. Yet this fact itself nevertheless conditions all that he does write. And when in early works such as the *House of Fame* he ostensibly addresses himself to transcendent subjects, he resorts to a parodic mode, spoofing the solemn, spiritually serious treatment of Dante. This is evident, for example, in the way that his invocations of various sources of authority (Memory, Apollo, etc.) renders them in effect completely nonauthoritative. Dante's noble summons—

> . . . o mente che scrivesti ciò ch'io vidi,
> qui si parrà la tua nobilitate
> (*Inferno* II.8–9)[9]

> . . . o memory that wrote that which I saw,
> here your nobility will appear

—is debased practically to a dare in the voice of a spunky character from comedy putting his ingenuity to the test:

> O Thought, that wrot al that I mette,
> And in the tresorye hyt shette
> Of my brayn, now shall men se
> If any vertu in the be
> To tellen al my drem aright.
> Now kythe thyn engyn and myght!
> (523–29; cf. 1091–1109)

> O Thought that wrote all that I dreamt
> And shut it in the treasury of my brain,
> Now shall men see whether there be

---

8. Cf. Sheila Delany, *Chaucer's* House of Fame: *The Poetics of Skeptical Fideism* (Chicago: University of Chicago Press, 1972); quotation, 46.

9. *The Divine Comedy* is quoted and translated from *La Divina Commedia secondo l'antica vulgata*, ed. G. Petrocchi. 4 vols. (Milan: Mondadori, 1966–67).

Any virtue in you
To rightly tell of my dream.
Now make known your ingenuity and power.

Even when transported to extraterrestrial realms by the eagle from *Purgatorio* IX, Geffrey perceives reality in a fantastical, flamboyant style bearing more in common with the French romance tradition than with Dante's representations of the world beyond the grave by comparisons to the commonplace and familiar.[10] The eagle's lengthy excursus on the physics of sound in Book II indicates, in the sort of knowledge it is capable of giving Geffrey, another difference from Dante. In the realm to which the eagle transports Geffrey, we are actually nearer to experimental knowledge of the physical world, "experience," than to spiritual truths and contemplation of the divine:

I preve hyt thus—take hede now—
Be experience; for yf that thow
Throwe on water now a stoon. . . .
                    (787–89)

I prove it thus—pay attention now—
By experiment; for if you
Throw a stone now into water. . . .

According to one interpreter, after his escape from the temple of love tradition in Book I, Geffrey is brought by the eagle to a "new vision of the whole art of poetry." He has discovered that "poems are made not out of love but out of sound" and that they are "'of fals and soth compounded.'"[11] But if the pandemonium of *House of Fame*, Book III, is Chaucer's account of the art of poetry, it is a very disturbed view indeed. It reflects a sense of crisis in the tradition of poetry that seems to have no way of distinguishing true from false. All such discernment is portrayed as arbitrary—as tossed up into the air and as coming down simply to the wild caprices of Fame. The sudden breaking off of the fragment with the mysterious appearance of one who "semed for to be / A man of gret auctorite . . ." (2157–58) suggests that the authority the poem cries out for at

---

10. See Charles Muscatine, *Chaucer and the French Tradition* (Berkeley: University of California Press, 1957), 114ff.

11. Lawrence K. Shook, "The *House of Fame*," in *Companion to Chaucer Studies*, ed. Beryl Rowland, rev. ed. (Oxford: Oxford University Press, 1979), 420.

the same time renders its continuation impossible. It reads as a last witty gesture implying the impossibility of establishing genuine authority in this world of only seeming knowledge.[12]

Indeed the authority of man generically is in crisis, as is intimated by the accusations of Dido, to whom Chaucer gives a voice of her own, declaring, "Non other auctor allege I" ("I cite no other author," 314). Yet the strongly feminized figure of Fame only crowns the abuses of authority exposed by the poem as a whole. Fame travesties an authority which is ultimately the authority of Revelation:

> For as feele eyen hadde she
> As featheres upon foules be,
> Or weeren on the bestes foure
> That Goddis tronne gunne honoure,
> As John writ in th'Apocalips.
> (1381–85)

> For she had as many eyes
> As there are feathers upon fowls,
> Or as were on the four beasts
> That gave honor to God's throne,
> As John writes in the Apocalypse.

The image of parodic apocalypse is completed by Eolus with his "blake trumpe of bras, / That fouler than the devel was" ("black trumpet of brass / That was fouler than the devil") blowing abroad Fame's judgments, as fickle as those of her sister Fortune, "As al the world shulde overthrowe" (1637–40), puffing and blasting "[t]il hyt was at the worlde's end" (1867). This is not Chaucer's discovery of a new poetic so much as his despair over the state of poetical tradition and authority in his age of skepticism—a despair expressed most creatively by comic response. His works following the *House of Fame* will all grapple with the situation here declared, in which there is no adequate poetic—no theoretical basis for legitimating poetry as an authoritative kind of knowledge or channel to truth.

---

12. Katherine H. Terrell, "Reallocation of Hermeneutic Authority in Chaucer's *House of Fame*," *The Chaucer Review* 31/3 (1997): 279–89, suggests how this transfers hermeneutic authority to the reader. Yet there is no indication that the reader will be able to find—or perhaps forge—the truth, as is indeed presupposed by Dante's addresses to the reader, as I undertake to show in chapter 1 of *Dante's Interpretive Journey* (Chicago: University of Chicago Press, 1996).

II. Textual Interpretation Focused on *Troilus and Criseyde* and *The Canterbury Tales*

In the dream visions, accordingly, poetry is seen to be woefully inadequate as a hermeneutic method for deciphering higher-order reality. Moreover, by the time we get to *Troilus and Criseyde*, it is no longer representing the true world, as Dante had done, that is in question, but rather poetically representing earthly love in a way that is consistent with true Christian knowledge. *Troilus and Criseyde* purports to place into a Christian perspective a pagan love tragedy that is quintessentially poetic. The world of romance is visited not for its intrinsic value but as an *exemplum* to be given a Christian significance and thereby be made true and edifying. The Christianization of pagan fables was a familiar procedure of exegetes like St. Jerome and a standard practice for medieval writers, including Dante, who deployed a distinction between the literal and several levels of allegorical meaning in order to uncover and excavate from these narratives their hidden Christian significances. The impeccably Christian purpose of the narrator of *Troilus* is announced in the proem to Book I in terms of several Christian watchwords:

> For so hope I my sowle best avaunce,
> To prey for hem that Loves servauntz be,
> And write hire wo, and lyve in charite,
>
> And for to have of hem compassioun,
> As though I were hire owne brother dere.
> (I. 47–51)

> For so I hope best to profit my soul
> By praying for them who are Love's servants
> Writing their woe, and living in charity,
>
> And having compassion on them,
> As though I were their own dear brother.

Writing the woe of his ill-stared lovers will be for the narrator an exercise in such Christian virtues as charity and compassion, promoting the advancement of his soul toward the goal of salvation. The implicit assumption of this attitude is that one can, even as a Christian, be interested in pagan love. The narrator describes his role as that of being "the sorrowful instrument, / That helpeth loveres, as I kan, to pleyne" (I.10–11) and considers it conducive to truth that he involve himself, to the extent of putting on a sad face so as better to companion his sad subject:

> For wel sit it, the sothe for to seyne,
> A woful wight to han a drery feere,
> And to a sorwful tale, a sory chere.
> (I.12–14)

> For it is suiting, truth to tell,
> For a woeful creature to have a dreary companion,
> And for a sorrowful tale to have a sorry manner.

Seeking to extend his fraternal solicitude by encouraging others to share it, the narrator appeals to the "pyte" (pity) of happy lovers, bidding them to pray for despairing lovers, specifically beseeching that God may "So graunte hem soone out of this world to pace" (I.41) and bring them, perhaps like Troilus, to solace in heaven ("hem brynge in heaven to solas," I.31). This appeal is made to happy lovers on the basis of their presumed personal experience of love and its pains—

> Remembreth yow on passed hevynesse
> That ye han felt . . .
> (I.24–25)

> Remember your past heaviness
> That you have felt . . .

—which is supposed to enable them to feel for the suffering lover, that is, to have compassion.

The adoption of this Christian perspective by narrator and reader as a frame for the story, however, will be undermined systematically throughout the whole course of the poem, beginning within this very first proem to Book I. The invocation of Tesiphone to help endite (write) "Thise woful vers, that wepen as I write" (I.7) is a first hint that the narrator's involvement might not be completely circumscribed by the perspective from above, the standpoint of Christian compassion, but may perhaps have something to do, instead, with infernal forces. It is also telling that when the narrator denies having any direct involvement in love of the erotic kind, saying that he would sooner die, this detachment is not described as blessedness but rather as darkness and so as exactly the opposite of what would or should be dictated by the Christian auspices of the proem.

> For I, that God of Loves servantz serve,
> Ne dare to Love, for myn unliklynesse,
> Preyen for speed, al sholde I therefore sterve,
> So fer am I from his help in derknesse.
>
> (I.15–18)

> For I, who serve the servants of the God of Love
> Dare not pray, because of my uncomeliness,
> To Love, though I should therefore die,
> Since I am so far from his help in darkness.

Such hints of motivations and feelings not strictly Christian in character adumbrate a role that is passionately involved for the narrator, as the sequel will demonstrate in great psychological detail. By the end of Book I the narrator's role will have taken on the same odor as Pandarus's, with verbal echoes of the proem turning up in Pandarus's desirousness to "serve" his lover as friend and his consequent dwelling upon his "matere." Indeed at this point it is plain that the narrator had cast himself unwittingly as a pander at the service of his readers in that very proem:

> . . . if this may don gladnesse
> To any lovere, and his cause availle,
> Have he my thonk, and myn be his travaille!
>
> (I.20–21)

> . . . if this [work] may bring gladness
> To any lover, and help his cause,
> Let the thanks go to Love and to me the labor.

To the extent that the narrator's attachment to his story parallels Pandarus's attachment to his plot, it stinks of everything false and meretricious in the world. Pandarus is a rhetor: all skill and no moral purpose. Whatever Troilus's love of Criseyde has of truth and the ideal is corrupted precisely by Pandarus's influence, to such a degree that at one point Troilus offers to pander his own sisters to Pandarus. Without Pandarus, romantic love might remain pure and idealistic. Presumably Troilus would have suffered and died for love, like a Christian martyr, had he not been pushed into bed by Pandarus. By Pandarus's acting as catalyst, this sublime love becomes a matter of times and places, of physical acts rather than noble and eloquent sentiments. Pandarus can change in his sentiments with every new situation and indeed "hates" Criseyde when that is what the situation demands, whereas Troilus irrevocably avows:

> . . . Yow, that doon me al this wo endure,
> Yet love I best of any creature.
> > (V.1700–1701)

> . . . You, who make me endure all this woe
> I still love more than any other creature.

The narrator, like Pandarus, is strictly bound to time and place in realizing and scripturally materializing his story, for his, too, is a merely external view on love. He takes Troilus's universal lyric about love's contradictoriness and localizes it "here / Loo, next this vers . . . here" (I.398–99). Like Pandarus's horning in, that they may be "gladed alle thre," on a relationship where by rights he does not belong, so poetry, which is also vicarious love, takes illegitimate liberties in having fully its "entente," that is, in going beyond a Christian to an erotic meaning.

The pretense of being disengaged is kept up in the proem to Book II ("of no sentiment I this endite," II.13). And yet, the poetry of the narrator's statements informs us otherwise. The opening strophe translates the first lines of *Purgatorio* I, in which Dante finds himself in "miglior acque," the calmer waters lapping the shores of salvation, the penitential slopes of the mountain of Purgatory. But what is most noticeable in Chaucer's lines is the sense of the "boot" ("boat") of the narrator's "connyng" or skill being nearly capsized by the "tempestuous matere" of Troilus's despair. The narrator seems, at least as much as Dante, to have been through hell and to have recovered considerably less. Winthrop Wetherbee astutely notes how the gasping stutter "O wynd, o wynd" and the calculatedly clumsy effort of the stanza to allegorically gloss itself betray the narrator's uncertainty and emotional imbalance.[13] Clearly the narrator's serene view from above, comprehending the whole arc and circuit of his hero's adventures in love, "Fro wo to wele, and after out of joie," has been shaken.

---

13. Winthrop Wetherbee, *Chaucer and the Poets* (Ithaca: Cornell University Press, 1984), 147–48.

Whereas he clearly knew the whole story, including how it ends, right from the beginning of the poem, Book II ends with an expression of anxiousness that shows the narrator to be so involved that the tension is killing him as he contemplates along with Troilus himself what Troilus should say to Criseyde: "O myghty God, what shall he seye?" (II.617–18).[14] The thinly disguised feeling of the narrator for Criseyde has been described, with good reason, in terms of his being "in love" with her, too.[15]

The fact of the narrator's emotional involvement is too plain to need more insisting upon. His expressions and exclamations of enthusiasm, regret, voluptuous delight, and pain punctuate the drama and direct our responses all throughout. But the moral evaluation to be made of this involvement is a more complicated matter, and one that bears directly on the question of truth. On the one hand, a long epistemological tradition of Platonic cast made impersonal rationality and detached objectivity an essential quality, indeed the indispensable criterion of true knowledge. On the other hand, poetry had been advocated at least since Aristotle as a uniquely powerful mode of knowledge precisely because of its capacity to engage the knower personally, to involve the emotions, and thus to provoke a catharsis. In this way, poetry can pierce through blindness and lead toward that virtue which is knowledge, as Plato, too, would have it. But in which light does vicarious involvement appear in the poem?

Perhaps the best gloss on the narrator's involvement in *Troilus and Criseyde* is Dante's response to Paulo and Francesca in *Inferno* V.[16] Newly arrived in Hell, the pilgrim is seduced by the story of their passion. Francesca quotes clichés from the poetic tradition of *amor cortese*. Most conspicuously, her "Amor, ch'al cor gentil ratto s'apprende" echoes Guinizelli's sonnet "Al cor gentil rempaira sempre amore," already imitated by Dante in his *Vita nuova*, chapter XX. Francesca's high-flown rhetoric for what we see punished as an ignoble sin may be understood to constitute a self-deceiving propaganda speech for which Dante literally falls:

> Mentre che l'uno spirto questo disse,
>   l'altro piangea, sì che di pietade

———

14. Donald W. Rowe, *O Love O Charite! Contraries Harmonized in Chaucer's "Troilus"* (Carbondale: Southern Illinois University Press, 1976), 158.

15. E. Talbot Donaldson, *Speaking of Chaucer* (London: Athlone Press, 1970), 68.

16. Karla Taylor, in her chapter "A Text and Its Afterlife: *Inferno* V and *Troilus and Criseyde*," *Chaucer Reads 'The Divine Comedy'* (Stanford: Stanford University Press, 1989), has made this connection all the more evident.

io venni men così com'io morisse;
e caddi come corpo morto cade.

$$(139–42)$$

While one spirit said this
    the other wept, in such manner that from pity
    I fainted just as if I were dying;
and I fell as a dead body falls.

Earlier in the scene, Dante's anxious curiosity about circumstantial details, about when and how it all happened, put him directly in line with Pandarus's practical understanding of and approach to love as a matter of arranging the times and places for furtive opportunities on the sly:

"Ma dimmi: al tempo de' dolci sospiri,
    a che e come concedette amore
    che conosceste i dubbiosi desiri?"

$$(118–20)$$

"But tell me: at the time of the sweet sighings
    at what and how did love concede
    that you should know the dubious desires?"

The answer is that a *book* and its author played the part of intermediary between the illicit lovers: "Galeotto fu 'l libro e chi lo scrisse" ("Gallehault was the book and the one who wrote it," v.137). Virgil attempts to call Dante back to himself from this sympathetic and even pathological involvement, but he is so fervid in his pity that he has already descended beyond the point of no return, across the threshold of possible recall, into the depths to which passion sinks on its tragic course:

Quand'io intesi quell'anime offense,
    china' il viso, e tanto il tenni basso,
    fin che 'l poeta mi disse: "Che pense?"

$$(109–11)$$

When I heard those hurt souls,
    I looked down and kept my face down
    until the poet asked me: "What are you thinking?"

The gestural iconography of bowing in reverence here takes on connotations of abasing oneself. Of course, Dante believes that his commotion is Christian or pious ("pio"):

"Francesca, i tuoi martiri
a lacrimar mi fanno tristo e *pio*."
(116–17)

"Francesca, your sufferings
bring me, sad and full of pity [or pious], to tears."

But he will learn in the course of his journey through Hell that pity for the damned is not holy and can only be self-deception. It comes from a lack of understanding of the "Giustizia" (Justice) which moved the "Alto Fattore" (High Maker) to create hell in the first place, as the inscription on Hell's gate peremptorily declares, though Dante had difficulty understanding the words: "Maestro, il senso lor m'è duro" ("Master, their sense is difficult for me," III.12). Later on, in Canto XXXII of the *Inferno*, Dante will be seen as still involved but in a very different way: he will be seen to be actively participating in meting out punishment, even to the point of kicking faces and pulling hair, and "courteously" betraying Frate Alberigo in Canto XXXIII.

As pointed out by Winthrop Wetherbee (*Chaucer and the Poets*, 38), the elencation of the damned in the circle of the lustful is sentimentalized by Dante's own unconscious desire into a procession of the "conventional knights and ladies of courtly romance." Hence Dante's description:

Poscia ch'io ebbi il mio dottore udito
nomar le donne antiche e' cavalieri,
pietà mi giunse, e fui quasi smarrito.
(70–72)

After I had heard my teacher
name the ancient ladies and knights,
pity [or piety] came over me and I was nearly lost.

According to Wetherbee, Dante the pilgrim, like the narrator of *Troilus and Criseyde*, loses his perspective on the universal values of human life, such values as constitute the profounder meaning of classical epic, through the fault of his romanticized reactions. For Wetherbee, *Troilus and Criseyde* is about "the poet-narrator's evolution from a writer of romance who views his material in the idealizing light of the courtly love tradition to a disciple of the *poetae,* capable of realizing the tragic and finally the spiritual implications of his story" (10).

Wetherbee convincingly shows how thoroughly Chaucer's conception of poetry was dependent on the prestige and authority of the classical epic tradition, with the proviso that this engagement with pagan poetry issues finally in a Christian perspective essentially distinguished from it, as in Dante. But Wetherbee attenuates and effaces the condemnation under which poetry as such is placed by *Troilus and Criseyde.* The spiritual implications, the "religious perspective that surfaces in the final stanzas of the poem" (9), constitute no harmonious resolution and sublimation. This religiousness entails, rather, a rejection of pagan poetry because it is poetry, and the idea of a redeemed poetry from a Christian perspective has been refuted by the poem's analysis of empathetic poetic involvement. The Christian perspective surfaced even in the proem to Book I, but that did not make the poem religiously edifying. On the contrary, it is just the narrator's religiosity that makes his stooping to Pandarus's level, as the poem works its seduction even on him, such an indictment of poetry.

When Wetherbee writes that "it is through a sympathetic sharing of the errors and aspirations of his characters that Chaucer's narrator gains the knowledge that enables him, finally and at great emotional cost, to withdraw himself from the world of the poem and view the love of Troilus from a Christian perspective" (22), he seems to suggest that this is a true perspective reached in and through poetry. He is very explicit about this later in his book: "To be a poet, then, is to participate in a continuum of imaginative experience which transmits the essential truths of human life from one generation to another" (233). Yet this states exactly what Chaucer, in his very own eyes, fails to achieve as a poet, so far as we can infer from his poetry, particularly from its pivot point in the epilogue to *Troilus and Criseyde.*

This conclusion has been borne out by extensive study of *Troilus* in relation to Dante by Karla Taylor. In the final chapter of *Chaucer Reads 'The Divine Comedy,'* which is focused on the ending of *Troilus,* Taylor finds similarly that for Chaucer religious truth proves to be beyond the parameters of poetry and, furthermore, that Chaucer implicitly critiques Dante's claims by implying the impossibility of any authentic rendering of transcendent experience in human poetry.[17] For Chaucer, poetry is not a

---

17. Taylor, *Chaucer Reads 'The Divine Comedy,'* 200–202. In the earlier chapter on

positive program for authoritatively delivering the truth to humanity. As becomes increasingly clear in the *Canterbury Tales,* truth begins for Chaucer where poetry ends. Why did Chaucer go on writing poetry if this is the conclusion that he had reached already in *Troilus and Criseyde?* Why the *Canterbury Tales?* This is a question Chaucer seems to have asked himself many times, indeed one that he dwelt upon obsessively and with increasing intensity toward the end of his life. In particular the Pardoner's, the Canon's Yeoman's, and the Manciple's Tales problematize this very phenomenon of continuing to say something even when you know it is false.

Dante was personally involved in his poem both as poet and as protagonist in the highest degree. Such visceral, emotional involvement risked betraying him into error, as in *Inferno* V, but it was not per se fallacious. Dante works through a progressive series of attachments purging his desire by degrees. The process is one of gradually revealing that all desire is really desire for God by letting what is false in every other attachment fall away. Thus on the whole, for Dante, affective involvement is positive, although, as with all things adhering to earth, it has a portion of dross and error. Chaucer did not share Dante's confidence in the partnership and synergism between poetry and faith. He doubted poetry's capacity for eliciting sympathetic participation that would induce to apprehending and enacting the Christian truth. For him, there is no continuum between earthly and divine love. Earthly love cannot be purged: it can only be placed in perspective. For Chaucer, true knowledge comes not from erotic love but from doctrine. The final word is left to "moral Gower" or the Parson, and it is conspicuously *not* poetic. This divides Chaucer from Augustine as well as from Dante and the whole tradition in between these two great Christian writers, for whom to know God was to love. Chaucer has lost the confidence that love can be rational and thereby redeeming. This is what becomes apparent in the undermining in *Troilus and Criseyde* of the narrator's alleged reasons for caring about his lovers: such "reasons" are unmasked as mere rationalizations.

This narrator is supposed to tell his story as an exposure of the truth about pagan folly, but the truth of the story is that he is involved in it with erotic passion. As a result, the story is not unattractive, as Christian doctrine would require, not apparently "false worldes brotelnesse"

Inferno V and *Troilus and Criseyde,* Taylor adduces Troilus's borrowings from the *Paradiso* as evidence of Chaucer's opposing Dante's authority as interpreter of transcendent truth, warning against illusory transcendence in the context of the poet in paradise no less than of the lover in hell (76–77).

(V.1832).[18] The truth that this love is false is not found in the story. The poem is as much a seductively false appearance as the pagan rites and world it professes to condemn. What we get from the poem is not a demonstration that worldly values are empty and treacherous. They prove rather to be seductive and to subjugate us irresistibly. Poetry, like Pandarus, leads us not to truth but to tragedy, after which we can only start over in the opposite direction to seek truth.

Dante's poetry, on the other hand, functions, like Beatrice, as a mediator. Beatrice is the truth—theology, according to a common allegorical interpretation—but in a form not yet wholly sublimated, one which works, rather, by appealing to man's lower faculties so that the higher may be awakened to the perception of the spiritual truth she represents in embodied form. The pilgrim draws ever nearer the truth by following her attractions, as does the reader by relishing Dante's poetry. This movement of drawing ever closer to union and thus to truth is reversed by Chaucer. For Chaucer, poetry works instead by placing its worldly contents into perspective, which is a form of distancing. Affective involvement may be a prelude to this movement of detachment but is not integral to it. The involvement is precisely what is left behind when the perspective on passion and its folly is gained. We can play out our worldly attachments to the limits, which are infernal, as the imagery of *Troilus and Criseyde* insists, and by that means gain a perspective on what otherwise remains unconscious and governs us according to false principles. But the authentic movement toward truth is a movement of withdrawal, as in Chaucer's lyric "Truth," which begins, "Flee fro the prees, and dwelle with sothfastnesse. . . ." ("Flee from the crowd, and dwell in truthfullness . . .").

There are false objects of love for Dante, too, like the Siren, and false kinds of loving, like pity for the damned. But Dante the poet never even bothers to give Dante the pilgrim a perspective on his error in *Inferno* V. The error shows that he is still far from truth, but he pursues nevertheless his course guided by Virgil toward closer union with truth, confident that such false attachments will fall aside as mere accidents along the way. His love as such is good, however much it may be misdirected. He simply needs to straighten its course. It is not by drawing away from his love, distancing it through a perspective, but by centering more intensely upon it, that he will follow a continuous path "straight to the happy mark"— "drizza in segno lieto" (*Paradiso* I.126). What was loved erroneously

18. Middle English "brotelnesse" is cognate with "brittleness" and implies fragility and mutability, often with moral implications.

turns out to have been unreal (the Siren), and so to have been no love at all.

For Chaucer there is no such continuity. Earthly and heavenly love lie in different directions. When Troilus finally sees his earthly love for Criseyde in perspective, he damns it: and "al oure work," which falls within the purview of this damnation, includes the poem itself. The narrator's charity and compassion, announced in the opening proem, that is, his Christian involvement, do not lead him to truth, as if with this attitude earthly love in its inadequacy could be instructive and edifying and could advance the narrator's soul in perfection. The narrator's "Christian" involvement leads only to rejection of this very involvement, to rejection of his poem. Indeed, poetry *tout court*, as a modality of knowledge that is involved in the world, must be rejected. One does not progress by poetry toward more direct apprehension of the truth, as Dante does. Instead, one distances poetry by placing it in perspective—"Lo swich the fyn of olde clerkis speche / In poetrie . . ." ("Lo, such is the end of old scholars speech in poetry . . .")—and turns to another sort of discourse, that of "moral Gower" or "philosophical Stroude," or more finally and definitively yet, to the Way and Truth Himself, Christ, the "Uncircumscript" Word that is unmediated by any discourse whatsoever.

At this most revealing of moments within Chaucer's oeuvre, it is possible to glimpse in their generality the assumptions as to how poetry mediates or is related to divine truth that underlie Chaucer's work as a poet and make it contrast in certain crucial respects with Dante's understanding of this relationship. R. A. Shoaf finds at first a similar theory of mediation to be operative in both Chaucer and Dante, albeit in different ways suited respectively to the human particular and to divine transcendence. For both Dante and Chaucer, artistic self-consciousness acts to neutralize the distorting effects of mediation. For both, awareness of the artificiality of their aesthetic medium of poetry constitutes true consciousness of falsehood. This consciousness of the inevitable falsehood introduced by human mediation of divine truth is the only way to save the truth, and this is where Dante and Chaucer are able to meet. Nevertheless, the capital difference between them is also given lapidary formulation by Shoaf in his observation that "what for Dante is a problem of the expression of transcendence is for Chaucer a problem of the transcendence of expression."[19] It seems necessary to conclude that, for Chaucer,

19. R. A. Shoaf, in *Dante, Chaucer, and the Currency of the Word* (Norman, OK: Pilgrim Books, 1983), 234.

as for T. S. Eliot, in the end the poetry does not matter anymore ("East Coker," II, *Four Quartets*).

Still, even if poetry is no help in positively approaching truth, Chaucer recognizes that neither he nor his narrator will as a consequence disengage himself from it. There is an interest expressed for the "litel myn tragedye," that it assume its place in the tradition of poetry, which is pagan and unredeemed, and hence tragic, the tradition of "Virgile, Ovide, Omer, Lucan, and Stace," as well as a hint of a comedy to come. The narrator has also expressed anxiety lest his text be corrupted, since "ther is so gret diversite / In Englissh" and commended it to Gower and Stroude to "correcte," not to shred. Placing in perspective and distancing is not effacing or forgetting. What Chaucer's poem offers us, since it cannot help our salvation, is precisely this perspective. Though we should know that it will not advance our souls, we may nevertheless, all too humanly, be interested in poetry and love as they are realized in the poem. The perspective remains focused on *this* world. Where the soul of Troilus, escorted by Mercury, is going is left vague, but what he sees, looking down to the exact spot, "Ther he was slayn," which must mean in love as well as in war, is intensely focused. Vividly realized as well are the "yong, freshe folks," and the last reference to "love of moder and mayde," directs us down earthward from the Trinity with a gesture toward the Incarnation. The Incarnation of God in the virgin mother, Mary, however, has become purely an article of faith, no longer a visible fact permeating the world and permitting poetry to represent the divine as a radiance manifest in the sensuous.

Chaucer still had a distance to go on earth, but the poetic pilgrimage to Canterbury does not lead to Canterbury; nor is it a pilgrimage. As becomes increasingly obvious as the stories run their course, it is rather a going to hell on horseback. Yet stories that put this damned humanity in perspective still serve in important ways for recognition of human falseness. The positive truth value of the poetry of the *Canterbury Tales* can only be the material it provides to be put in perspective in the end by the "Parson's Tale," which utterly rejects poetry, as the Parson announces in his prologue. Precisely the recognition of "false worldes brotelnesse," which Chaucer's poetry ineluctably leads to, can turn us toward the Truth that no poetry as such can vouchsafe.[20]

---

20. The abysmal distance from Dante is made only the more dramatic by the thesis of Richard Neuse, *Chaucer's Dante: Allegory and Epic Theater in "The Canterbury Tales"* (Berkeley: University of California Press, 1991), that the generic model for Chaucer's *Canterbury Tales* is the medieval epic, as an extension of the classical Greco-Roman

III. Speculative Reflection: Truth and the Lyrical

Poetry proved inadequate as a hermeneutic for interpreting the other world already in the dream visions, especially in the *House of Fame.* The specifically linguistic grounds of this inadequacy were analyzed more deeply, then, in *Troilus and Criseyde* and the *Canterbury Tales.* Whether the poet is attempting to represent the transcendent order or not, there is, in the Augustinian tradition, a certain transcendence already inherent in the structure of language itself as the hermeneutic condition of any order of significances such as constitutes a world. But this becomes dubious in the age of Chaucer, contextualized as it is by the new philosophies of nominalism, which will usher in the new epistemological paradigm of experimental science. Chaucer's doubts about knowledge of a divine order of transcendence, accordingly, are fused with doubts about the nature and capacities of language. A strongly demystifying view of language had been expressed already in the *House of Fame,* as we saw, in the eagle's affirmation that sound (and therefore, consequently, also voice and speech) is nothing but broken air ("Soun ys noght but eyr ybroken," 765). This leads to doubts about language as a disclosure of truth. Chaucer's mistrust specifically of poetry as a vehicle to truth of a religious order can be brought to perhaps its sharpest focus with respect particularly to the language of lyric. But the full significance of this form of language for Chaucer emerges only against the background of basic medieval conceptions about the epistemological and ontological status of language.

Language, in a certain medieval, specifically Platonized, perspective, was taken to belong to the intellectual order and could be recognized, therefore, as higher than the material world and closer to God. This proximity was sometimes taken to constitute a reason why language should not imitate the sensible order. Instead, language should translate into its own purer, less material and distorting, medium the very Word by which all things were made (John 1:3). Thus, truth was to be sought out by searching directly into the meanings of words, by exegesis and hermeneutics, especially of the Word of God, that is, the Bible, rather than by looking out upon a mute, inarticulate order of nature. Isidore of Seville, for instance, in his *Etymologiarum sive Originum,* found the key to the inner nature of all things in their names and in the etymologies that excavate and expose the significances of these names. This orientation toward

---

epic, specifically in its Dantesque form. See especially chapter 2 on "*The Canterbury Tales* as Dantean Epic."

linguistic immanence, of course, in which the word is effectively inhabited by its meaning, is strongest in the language of poetry, especially poetry in a lyric mode. The preeminent exemplar here, Dante's *Paradiso,* is a sustained rapture upon the formal structures and the intrinsic symmetries of language as themselves revelatory of the divine essence. God, in his Trinitarian self-reflexiveness, is perfectly imaged by the self-reflexive structures of lyric language. Such reflexivity is concentrated into the culminating verses at the height of the Dante's final *visio Dei:*

O luce etterna che sola in te sidi,
    sola t'intendi, e da te intelletta
    e intendente te ami e arridi.
        (Paradiso XXXIII.124–26)

O eternal light, who in yourself alone reside,
    yourself alone comprehend, and by yourself contemplated
    and contemplating smile on and love yourself.

It has already been pointed out, however, that the originally Aristotelian principle that "being precedes knowing" was a cardinal tenet of epistemology and, consequently, also of semiology in the Middle Ages. Saint Augustine particularly insisted that we know the meanings of signs only by virtue of our direct acquaintance with the things that they signify.[21] Knowledge and hence its formulation in language must conform to how things are. Chaucer enunciates this notion in the "General Prologue" in the adage—"The wordes moote be cosyn to the dede" ("The word should be the cousin to the deed")—and again in the "Manciple's Tale" (IX.207–10). This is in crucial respects a more skeptical attitude. Language is divested of its preordained affinity with the divine. Thus language is constantly suspected of falsehood precisely because of its detachment from a concrete world of objects.

Chaucer obviously no longer believes himself to have access to a language that is naturally invested with divinity. Despite his pose as a mere translator, as if poetry were to be educed more or less directly from *the* Word, via the words of "authorities," it is evident that his "translations" do anything but respect the authority of the words they translate. The "Wife of Bath's Prologue," with its citations of St. Paul's sexual moral-

---

21. Augustine, *De doctrina christiana.* See reflections of Margaret W. Ferguson, "Saint Augustine's Region of Unlikeness: The Crossing of Exile and Language," *The Georgia Review* 29 (1975): 842–64.

ity *inter alia,* shows how authoritative words can be recontextualized and thereby be given almost any significance whatever. Not revelation, but only confusion, can be expected to come of the words of tradition, as we see all too clearly in the house of Rumor. "Adam Scriveyn," with its indictment of copyists' errors in transmission, in a similar vein, might be interpreted as reflecting the loss of prelapsarian adherence to the true Word, a loss in effect perhaps ever since Man first wrote.[22]

The inevitable flaws in any human and conventional language, given this loss of adherence to an extra-linguistic ground, are especially concentrated in the case of lyric language—that is, in language that focuses attention on its own verbal form rather than on any extra-linguistic content. In this regard, it is possible to read *Troilus and Criseyde* as the tragedy of the lyric as a form of knowing. According to Eugene Vance, lyric per se in *Troilus and Criseyde* is revealed as tragic. Vance claims that the lyric cores of the poem generate the narrative, in accordance with commonly accepted medieval onto-aesthetic notions that he finds articulated by Dante:

> Reality in a poem such as the *Troilus* does not derive primarily from the nonlinguistic world of created things to which its language seems to refer—for these are mere accidents—but more properly from the less tangible order of phonetic structures in which the universal laws of the cosmos are embodied. Narrative events are generated, then, less by life than by lyric, and this is perhaps the sense of Dante's insistence that prose writers (*prosaicantes*) derive both their language and their examples from poets.[23]

Lyric can be said to generate narrative not in the sense of an efficient cause but rather in that it renders transparent the universal structures that predetermine all that can and does happen in the field of events. The structures of language, which lyric self-reflexively throws into relief, directly

---

22. See detailed analysis along this line of interpretation, emphasizing the materiality and the corporeality of writing, by Carolyn Dinshaw, in *Chaucer's Sexual Poetics* (Madison: University of Wisconsin Press, 1989), 4–7. I had the immense privilege of studying Chaucer with Professor Dinshaw, whose wider influence on my Chaucerian interpretations I gratefully acknowledge. For further suggestions concerning the instabilities of Troilus's lyric language with constant comparison to Dante, see Thomas Clifford Stillinger, *The Song of Troilus: Lyric Authority in the Medieval Book* (Philadelphia: University of Pennsylvania Press, 1992), especially chapter 6.

23. Eugene Vance, "Mervelous Signals: Poetics, Sign Theory, and Politics in Chaucer's *Troilus*," *New Literary History* 10 (1979): 310.

translate the cosmic principles by which all things are made and come to pass. At their source and origin, these principles are simply the Word, the divine Logos. For instance, the condition of desire, which motivates human actions, as first lodged in a lover's mind or heart, is conceived of as a law or letter that is expressed in lyric outpourings. These effusions enact lyrical aptitudes and templates that are conventional, suprasubjective, and transpersonal: indeed the case of the "Canticus Troili" of Book I of *Troilus and Criseyde* presents a Petrarchan sonnet outright. That is to say, these verbal structures concentrated in lyrical language determine the personalities through which they are expressed rather than vice versa. Thus Troilus is given a passion by the words he wields. In this sense, Vance maintains that "reality . . . 'imitates' language," which is precisely the inverse of the word's being "cousin to the deed"—to echo once more the standard litmus test for ethically acceptable, legitimate language that is repeatedly evoked in the *Canterbury Tales*.

The fact that lyric and poetic language generally are revealed as tragic in *Troilus and Criseyde* depends on a view of figuration as a kind of original sin, a treacherous substitution of the improper for the proper. This substitution mirrors in the order of language a transgressive social order that brings in its train, by a kind of necessity, all the violence of history. The departure from the true, original values of words is taken as the paradigmatic case of betrayal of the social contract or system of conventions that binds society harmoniously together, if scrupulously observed. But without proper grounding in a referential reality, lyric language becomes a vain circle of self-adulation and mere appearance. Chaucer, on Vance's account, would have perceived that this lyric-based poetic inscribed the tragedy of Troy into a cyclical nutshell. Troy's language, in its movement from noble origins with referential foundations to a decadent phase of purely lyrical speech that empties language of objective truth and correspondence to external reality, prefigured the pattern of Troy's decline and fall. This same pattern was being repeated again in the general decline of medieval civilization and most particularly in the flagrant turpitude of London in Chaucer's own day. Sexual delinquency, the favorite bogey of medieval morality, and the great sin of Troy, emblematized by Paris and Helen, is construed as a substitution of the erotic for the martial, of a lover's dalliance for a hero's deeds. Thus not only does it have the structure of metaphor; it is also first and fatefully realized at the linguistic level in Troilus's tragically lyrical speech.[24]

24. See also Adrienne R. Lockhart, "Semantic, Moral, and Aesthetic Degeneration in *Troilus and Criseyde*," *The Chaucer Review* 8 (1973): 100–117, and Shoaf, *Dante,*

By this account, *Troilus and Criseyde* is a systematic indictment and rejection of the lyric impulse and its ecstasy because they transgress pragmatic linguistic norms and transcend the normal statutes of proper expression. This parallels and emblematizes, moreover, loss of uprightness in ethics and action. Lyric, as the least referential, most purely formal sort of language, might appear to bear affinities to the divine. Dante's most intensely and sublimely lyrical work, the *Paradiso*, celebrates the purely formal, self-reflexive properties of language in which an immaterial, Trinitarian deity is reflected and dynamically imitated. But, for Chaucer, the lyric, as a closed, self-referential form lacking correspondence to a world, and therefore not matching the deed, must be taken rather to epitomize the essential falseness of poetry. Lyric, moreover, represents the loss of objective detachment and intellectual perspective; it tends toward a modality of pure feeling, a mystic merging with the object, toward union with God. Paradigmatic exemplars here are the Ambrosian hymns, which remained such powerful models of lyric language throughout the Middle Ages, thanks to their familiar recitation in the Latin liturgy.[25] In pure lyrical rapture, poetry aspires to transcend all representational structures, which are but perspectives, toward ecstatic union with the ultimate reality in a musical mode. Lyric does so by embodying the cosmic harmonies that most immediately imitate the Creator in creation. But, for Chaucer, all this is counterproductive to the one and only positive, yet critical, purpose—the disillusioning function—that poetry is competent to fulfill.

Chaucer does not believe that poetry is intrinsically prophetic and truth-disclosing. The empirical criterion of verification that has dominated English thought from his day to our own already becomes discernible in Chaucer's poetic works. It is diversely expressed but remains constant from medieval nominalism to modern British empiricism to contemporary analytic philosophy. Language must be "cousin to the deed" to be true, and Chaucer shows how impossible this is, owing, among other things, to the intrinsic lack of representational integrity that is inherent to language as such. Lyric only exacerbates extravagantly this tendency of language toward representational failure or inadequacy. This condemnation of lyric for its dislocation of meaning points up Chaucer's profound skepticism about the capacity of poetry to tell the truth. For him, there is no

---

Chaucer, and the Currency of the Word, Part Two: "*Troilus and Criseyde* and the 'Falsing' of the Referent."

25. Cf. C. S. Baldwin, *Medieval Rhetoric and Poetic to 1400* (Gloucester, MA: Macmillan, 1928), 123ff.

"dritto parlar," no "straight" or "upright" speech in poetry, as there is, or presumably can be, for Dante. All that poetry can do is to undeceive us by showing all our language to be devoid of truth—at least from the perspective of the final judgment that alone, in Chaucer's estimation, matters in the end.

prophecy eclipsed

hamlet as a tragedy of knowledge

I. From Prophetic Revelation to the New Epistemology

Science, as the dominant paradigm of knowledge in our secular culture, has had a decisive impact on the possibility and even on the very intelligibility of religious revelation. In order to sound this aspect of the impact of science in the modern world, it is instructive to consider *Hamlet* as a tragedy of knowledge. The play was written probably in 1600 and at any rate near the opening of the seventeenth century, an age that saw the rise of empirical, experimental science. Its language and imagery are tinged with this new vocabulary and embody the new sensibility and outlook together—and in tension—with an older vision and language. Thematically, moreover, *Hamlet* wrestles with the incalculably far-reaching meaning of this transition from a more traditional *épistémè*, or general framework for knowledge, one based on revelation, to the new scientific epistemology. Revelation, particularly biblical revelation, envisages the ultimate ends and context of human life as resting upon a metaphysical order of invisible beings including angels, demons, and divinity. But in the scientific worldview, knowledge lacks all transcendent foundation and is grounded at bottom on the physical senses and their perceptions of the material world. The tragic loss involved in this transition is made palpable and poignant in the overarching conception of Shakespeare's *Hamlet,* as well as in filigree in the imaginative and expressive textures of the play.

Shakespeare transmitted and also concocted some of the most compelling representations of what has been dubbed "the Elizabethan world-picture" featuring a three-tiered universe that reaches both above and below the world accessible to mortal sight into the otherworldly realms of heaven and hell.[1] This outlook is represented in *Hamlet* as having fallen into crisis and as tragically unable to endure the strain under which it is placed in the emerging culture of the Renaissance propelled to a considerable degree by impulses imparted by the new scientific methods of investigation and verification. At issue in *Hamlet,* at the very heart of the play's significance, is an epochal turning from what we may call the age of prophecy—in which a whole world-order and a future destiny, including an afterlife, were accepted as revealed—to an age of science, in which what is real is equated with what can be proved by empirical evidence, "the sensible and true avouch / Of mine own eyes," as Horatio so vividly and pithily puts it near the play's outset (I.i.55–56).[2]

In the age of prophecy, the most authoritative knowledge was supposed to come from sources higher than the physical senses. A vision or a spirit could reveal truths that were incapable of being proved by empirical means. The impetus to the action of revenge, which is the central business of *Hamlet* at the level of plot, comes from just such a prophetic revelation—an apparition hailing from the other world. Hamlet's murdered father comes back from the dead, from the world of eternity, to tell Hamlet the truth about how he died and to demand that his son avenge his death by executing justice upon the usurper, his treacherous brother, for this most ancient and heinous of crimes (Cain's murder of Abel being the primordial archetype). When Hamlet first hears this disclosure, he exclaims: "O my prophetic soul!" (I.v.40). He is apparently saying that he had already inwardly divined the criminal course of events and their concealed guilt—as if by some kind of supernatural prompting from a higher source. With the ghost's confirmation of what he already himself suspects, the kind of knowledge he holds in connection with his father's death can

1. E. M. W. Tillyard, *The Elizabethan World Picture* (New York: Macmillan, 1944). See also Arthur O. Lovejoy, *The Great Chain of Being: A Study of the History of an Idea* (New York: Harper & Row, 1960; William James lecture at Harvard, 1936).

2. Quotations of *Hamlet* are from the Norton Critical Edition, ed. Cyrus Hoy (New York, 1963), with consultation of the text in *The Riverside Shakespeare,* text ed. G. Blackmore Evans (Boston: Houghton Mifflin Co., 1974).

aptly be said to be "prophetic" in nature. There is, in any case, something paranormal about it.

And yet this prophetic revelation—his own father come back from the dead in order to directly inform young Hamlet of how he was killed—becomes enmeshed in a web of doubts and eventually even in play-acting generated by attempts to test and prove its authenticity. Hamlet is later heard saying, "I'll have grounds more relative than this" (II.ii.570), which seems to mean even more relevant, or pertinent and convincing, circumstantial evidence than he has already. But this statement also ironically suggests that all the grounds that Hamlet is seeking to establish can at best be only relative, not absolute. By failing to embrace the certainty offered him by the actual presence of the father speaking directly to him as a voice of revelation from the other side of death, from the divine world, he condemns himself to having not fully sufficient but only "relative" grounds, no matter how far he carries out his investigation.[3] Of course, the uncertainty is deeply rooted in Hamlet's character and even more deeply in the emerging character of the new Renaissance individual as grounded in an objective, material world and as losing all bearings in a transcendent, spiritual reality. By these means, *Hamlet* dramatizes far-reaching shifts in the nature and foundation of knowledge that are beginning to be acutely felt in Shakespeare's time.

Closely connected with the issue of the foundation of knowledge is that of the grounding of morality and of other types of value. *Hamlet* still shows many signs of the will to venerate the sacred values of the medieval world, but now in a new age of skepticism these values and the ground beneath them are shifting: they are being questioned and even under-

---

3. At least the word suggests this to our ears, even though such a use was probably not current in Shakespeare's time. It is nevertheless a semantic potential inherent in the word that comes out in the course of the evolution of the English language. Historical dictionaries indicate that the word was not used in the sense that makes it contrast with "absolute" until 1818, or, at the earliest, 1642. However, the transhistorical reading I pursue here takes account also of the enrichment of an artwork's meaning over time by ineluctable "misinterpretation" as belonging to its larger significance within the evolving history of language and culture. Such a hermeneutic method is expounded by Hans-Georg Gadamer in *Truth and Method* (*Wahrheit und Methode*, 1960) and is applied to aesthetics by Gadamer in *Die Aktualität des Schönen* (Stuttgart: Reclam, 1977), translated by Nicholas Walker as *The Relevance of the Beautiful* (London: Cambridge University Press, 1986). As with the foregoing interpretation of "O my *prophetic* soul," my aim is not to delimit exactly what the word meant in its original historical context (as if it necessarily meant only one thing to all even then) but to discern the perhaps unsuspected nuances of possible meaning that such terms take on in the wider context of an ongoing, open-ended linguistic history that includes especially poetic tradition.

mined. Young Hamlet has studied in Wittenberg, where he has presumably learned about the latest scientific discoveries and has been exposed to stirring new cultural currents. He is a youth and, as such, represents the future. But the play focuses just as intensely on his relation to the past as embodied in the form of his father—or, rather, not quite as embodied, since his father has become a ghost. Hamlet is not sure he believes in the revelatory word he receives as coming to him from his father. He loses touch, consequently, with the transcendent ground of his existence and with the noble past communicated through the tradition of his ancestors. His father recedes into a past that is in the process of becoming inaccessible: it is rapidly turning into a remote age of medieval mystery and myth.

The eclipse of prophetic vision ushers in a present age of skepticism that is expressed from the play's outset especially by Horatio, who is unbelieving with regard to "this thing," the "apparition" of the dead King Hamlet reported by Bernardus and Marcellus: he holds it to be nothing more than their "fantasy" (I.i.23ff). Horatio's rational suspicion of superstition is but one expression of a crisis of traditional belief in all sectors, not only religious but also political and social. The general cultural predicament in Denmark (as a metonymy for Europe and for the whole modern world) is that of a defunct moral and spiritual order. On a political plane, this condition translates into the crisis of the Danish state remarked at the outset of the play as ensuing upon the death of the king—the indispensable ground of authority and order. This situation obtains in Denmark and in Norway alike. The deceased kings Hamlet and Fortinbras are chivalric figures who had engaged in a noble duel "by a sealed compact / Well ratified by law and heraldry" (I.i). They are succeeded respectively by the usurper scorned by Hamlet as "a king of shreds and patches" (III.iv.104) and by the "young Fortinbras" who has "Sharked up a list of lawless resolutes" (I.i.98). In contrast to the purportedly lawful and valiant warring that distinguished the previous generation of kings, the present marshal maneuvers of their successors are seen either as immoral opportunism or as the unruly marauding of an ignoble horde. These are among the earliest signals of the general moral degeneration that upsets Hamlet and that provokes him to scathing denunciations which in some ways recall the eloquent jeremiads of the biblical prophets.

The hierarchy of value in the traditional medieval worldview depended upon a supreme and divine Good, namely, God, and on an animate universe of angelically guided spheres. Without this scaffolding, the whole structure of the moral order and of the social world, no less than of the

physical cosmos, would presumably collapse. "The world is out of joint."
"It is the times." "The times now give it proof." *Hamlet* shows extreme
sensitivity to its own time as a time of crisis. Formerly this world, both
natural and social, fit into and was supported by a total cosmic system.
Hamlet evokes this old world-picture—which has, however, become of
late tarnished and tacky, like discarded theater scenery—in expressing his
sense of the rottenness and corruption of life as he experiences it in the
present:

> This goodly frame, the earth, seems to me a sterile promontory, this most
> excellent canopy, the air, look you, this brave o'er-hanging firmament, this
> majestical roof fretted with golden fire, why it appeareth nothing to me
> but a foul and pestilent congregation of vapors. What a piece of work is
> a man, how noble in reason, how infinite in faculties, in form and moving
> how express and admirable, in action how like an angel, in apprehension
> how like a god: the beauty of the world, the paragon of animals. And
> yet to me, what is this quintessence of dust? Man delights not me. (II.
> ii.287–97)

Man here is no longer "crowned with glory and honor," as in Psalm
8:5. Although conceived as an endlessly wondrous creation, precisely as
in the same biblical text, where he is "a little lower than the angels,"
with "all things under his feet," here man, this "piece of work" (echoing ironically the psalmist's phrase "the work of thy fingers"), is reducible to his material substance, and that substance itself to mere ashes and
"dust." The "goodly frame of earth" and "excellent canopy" of the air
are likewise reducible to mere mechanisms and inert elements, indeed
the makeshift constructions of a stage. They no longer make up a throb-
bing, animate universe suffused with divine light and life. The majesty of
the creation has fled. Its material reduction has undermined the spiritual
vision of transcendent being and value that was formerly inscribed everywhere in the visible universe. The excellence of God's Name no longer
resounds in all the earth, as the psalmist had proclaimed ("O Lord, our
Lord, how excellent is thy name in all the earth," Psalm 8:1, 9). Hamlet
frames his discourse within the old order of earth and sky and man—the
last with his place of special prominence in the hierarchy—but the magi-
cal aura of it is gone. It depended upon a transcendent order that con-
ferred a radiance from above. When taken in and for themselves rather
than as a manifestation of divinity, the physical phenomena of the heavens are just "a foul and pestilent congregation of vapors," and in exactly

the same way man without relation to immortal being—as no longer the visible image of God—is but "this quintessence of dust."

Demonstrably, Hamlet still has one foot in the former, nobler world of theological revelation and chivalric tradition, as his very intolerance of the present mean and evil age symptomatically indicates. He is possessed by the vision of a prophetic past that still haunts him in the shape of his father's ghost. Indeed, the fact that this sensibility is no longer commensurate to the wider world in which he lives, given its decadence and corruption, determines his demise. Such a nature as his cannot survive, either psychically or physically, in the Denmark that Hamlet himself depicts and bitterly deplores. Although Hamlet has a spiritual revelation (a direct disclosure from a spirit), and to this extent remains in touch with the older, spiritually grounded order, he is nevertheless not able to sustain his belief in it. He, too, is complicit in the degenerate new order, as his unsparing self-deprecation vehemently acknowledges, for example, in the soliloquy beginning, "O, what a rogue and peasant slave am I!" (II.ii.516). The immediate presence of his father's spirit fades to a spectrous apparition of a ghost because Hamlet himself, being inescapably conditioned by the skeptical consciousness of the new age, ceases almost to believe in all but material reality.

Correspondingly, all of Hamlet's nobler values are shaken. He falls tragically into a world of sheer materiality, brute fact, rough manners, and political Machiavellianism. He does still have a hold on an ideal vision of love; it is expressed, for example, in his statement that his father was

so loving to my mother,
That he might not beteem the winds of heaven
Visit her face too roughly.
(I.ii.140–42)

But even this very tender tone of filial reverence and courtly delicacy vis-à-vis the gentler sex eventually sinks, in the course of the crisis that he is represented as undergoing, to the level of raw sexual innuendo concerning "c(o)untry matters" (III.ii.105).

In this harsh, new, disenchanted perspective, everything that was able once to give clear purpose to life turns obscure. Even the overwhelming presence of the father, at first observed by all together on the watch and galvanizing Hamlet to seemingly implacable resolve and firmness of purpose, becomes dubious and apocryphal. Hamlet moves thenceforth in a limbo of doubt, where clear, unambiguous revelations are a thing that can only be imagined as having existed in the past—or else as staged precisely in the process of their disappearance.

The presence of the father internally to Hamlet's spirit is fundamentally troubled and becomes vulnerable to being declared an illusion. Hamlet has to *write down* the command enunciated by the ghost of his father, thus giving it the form of an external, material entity: "My tables—meet it is I set it down" (I.iv.107). This gesture substitutes for the unmediated spiritual presence of the father a concrete empirical object, a positive existence, a "thing." Hamlet can be sure of what he has himself written, but this medium of the written word is no longer the bearer of an unequivocal testimony, no longer the immediate presence of the father's spirit. By the same token, the father's spirit may be doubted and suspected of having been in truth only a "sheeted" ghost, a blatant artifice. The notorious problems of doubt and delay are in this way shown to derive from epistemological conditions enacted in the opening scenes: the new conditions of the now skeptical worldview set in motion the actions and—even more tellingly—the *hesitations* that fatefully inflect the plot of the play.

Hamlet's world as a whole is turned to irreality by its being out of joint with the metaphysical order that alone was able to guarantee and found moral ideals no less than epistemological certainties. Hamlet's heart is still disposed to believe in these noble values, but his intellect, like that of his fellow-student, Horatio, has become skeptical.[4] This disunity within him, and the disintegration of the moral universe to which he ideally belongs, engender a split that becomes virtually madness—whether literally so or not. Given the constraints of a corrupt social universe, only in madness can the pure dictates of the heart and the immediate truth perceived by the soul be authentically expressed. It is the "prophetic soul" within him and its incompatibility with the world around him that, at least incipiently, drive Hamlet mad. This is so irrespective of the hints that he is, at least sometimes, in control of this madness, as when he says that he is mad but "north northwest" and again "mad but in craft." In fact, his "madness" is a necessary adaptation in this world that is out of joint: he opts to "put an antic disposition on" (I.v.172) as a strategy for survival.

---

4. For subtle analysis of how the forms of thought typical of skepticism are played out especially in Shakespeare's *Hamlet* and in some other tragedies, see Stanley Cavell, *Disowning Knowledge: In Seven Plays of Shakespeare*, updated ed. (Cambridge: Cambridge University Press, 2001).

Despite all his innate idealism, Hamlet is, after all, deeply submerged in a material vision of the world—as is the whole modern age that is here seen raw in its birth and infancy. Among the many incidental, apparently innocuous indications of his falling under the influence of the new, mechanistic, scientific outlook that was replacing the spiritual vision of the Middle Ages is the closing formula of his letter to Ophelia: "Thine evermore, most dear lady, whilst this machine is to him" (II.ii.22–23). The machine metaphor that shows up here expresses a whole new understanding of bodily existence in the world. It was coming into vogue to describe what formerly were considered sacrosanct mysteries of divine creation sealed by the conferral of a living bond between body and soul. Now, however, not only the body, but the universe itself, can be viewed as a mere machine. A similarly telling sign, this time specifically of Hamlet's infection by the moral relativism that follows from the collapse of the metaphysical worldview, is his remark: "there is nothing either good or bad, but thinking makes it so" (II.ii.243–44). Likewise the emphasis on the times, on the changing fashions of London theater, for example, indirectly indexes the demise of stable, inherited customs and antique ceremony now as a newer, crasser age, with its logic of commerce and expediency, devoid of morality, usurps upon the hallowed usages of old.[5]

The traditional model of the epic, such as it is realized in the *Odyssey,* the *Aeneid,* and the *Divine Comedy,* consistently leads to an encounter with the father as a necessary passage for establishing the true identity of the hero and as a means of authoritatively legitimating his quest. Hamlet, however, encounters his father in the guise of a ghost for whose word he must seek the supporting corroboration of empirical proof. The revelation of the father becomes a problem for him, the theme of a drama of play-acting, rather than standing unshakably as the foundation for his life and action. Being dramatized, it loses its unquestioned, unconscious authority, just as epic, with specific motifs from the *Aeneid,* is turned into mock-epic by being "put on." The work rehearsed by the players at Hamlet's instigation, when they first arrive at Elsinore, is a staging of a civilization's demise and of its patriarch's death: Hamlet asks to hear the tale of "Priam's slaughter" from Virgil's *Aeneid,* Book II, which recounts the fall of Troy. But this great epic and prophetic poem is turned into

5. The crisis of values at issue here is described by David Shalkwyk, *Shakespeare, Love and Service* (Cambridge: University of Cambridge Press, 2008), in terms of a lost world of love interlocking with service as the crucial organizing concept for social relations.

melodrama by the troupe's recitation. It loses its tragic elevation through a crudely overdone, sometimes virtually comic language, with many a heavy, cumbersome, and even grotesquely alliterated line like: "But with the whiff and wind of his fell sword" (II.ii.444), which undercuts itself.

The slaughter wrought by Pyrrhus, bloody son of the noble warrior Achilles, and specifically the atrocities of his killing of "old grandsire Priam," are so fulsomely acted out that the tragic demise of this noble patriarch and his ancient empire falls from high seriousness to the wooden and ridiculous, and the attempt to recreate their greatness seems forced. The story, moreover, is one of regicide, the "lord's murder" (II.ii.432), and of how the "father falls" (445)—indeed the very story underlying *Hamlet* itself! Even Hamlet's own nemesis, his fatal state of hesitation, is reflected into "Pyrrhus' pause" (458), as he inexplicably suspends action:

> So as a painted tyrant Pyrrhus stood,
> And like a neutral to his will and matter,
> Did nothing.

The mock-heroic style represented by this preliminary play-within-the-play conceals a key to the world of *Hamlet:* just such a mockery of his heroic forbears is the painful predicament under which Hamlet himself labors, playing out his "part."

II. Play-Acting and the Ground of Action

The doubtfulness into which all cognizance of life after death has slipped in the new age of skepticism interferes with the possibility of decisive action. This is brought out dramatically by Hamlet's meditation in the famous soliloquy: "To be or not to be" (III.i.56ff). Only the prospect of judgment in the life to come gives sense and consequence enough to the struggles of humans on this earth to make them patiently endure and bear their burdens. Curiously, the *certain* lack of an afterlife would be felt as freedom and relief, yet the *un*certainty of it paralyzes or "puzzles the will" and "does make cowards of us all." Such uncertainty had formerly been unthinkable, since the other world seemed constantly to be attested and revealed by priest, prophet, and poet-seer, not to mention many more common and homely superstitious sources. Only on such a basis were positive purpose and resolute action even in this world possible, and, without it, Hamlet languishes in impotence. It is particularly the disastrous consequences *for action* of the eclipse of the metaphysical worldview that the play develops as the central tragedy of modernity. Hamlet himself both embodies and expounds this paralysis, in which

> the native hue of resolution
> Is sicklied o'er with the pale cast of thought,
> And enterprises of great pitch and moment
> . . . lose the name of action.
> (III.i.84–88)

Prophetic revelation is in principle an authoritative message needing no proof and demanding simply unquestioning belief. But in *Hamlet* we see this prophetic dimension eclipsed by this-worldly concerns and contradictions in a new mindset which admits only empirical knowledge to be possible or, at least, authoritative. Hamlet's tragedy is that he still has a connection with that prophetic dimension and with the noble world of spiritual ideals that it opens upon, but he finds himself acting pragmatically, according to the dictates not of a prophetic word but of a degenerate world, where only immediate physical reality counts. The noble world revealed by prophecy fades from Hamlet's view, and he is rendered incapable of acting effectively in the fallen universe of power politics because he loses touch with the transcendental ground of ultimately purposeful action. He himself understands his predicament of impotence to achieve any action whatsoever—even to end his own life, if not to avenge his father's death—as following from his uncertainty about the other world. The possibility of that other world and its afterlife continues to hold him in check, even while his resolution is infirmed by reflection, and so issues in no act:

> Who would fardels bear
> To grunt and sweat under a weary life,
> But that the dread of something after death,
> The undiscovered country, from whose bourn
> No traveller returns, puzzles the will,
> And makes us rather bear those ills we have
> Than fly to others that we know not of?
> Thus conscience does make cowards of us all . . .
> (III.i.87)

The lack of a confident relation to a transcendent order that can ground action in purposes transcending one's own always only relative impulses and labile resolution is brought out explicitly and is accurately analyzed in the play-within-the-play. Our own will can always be altered at will and so is never imposed as a simple imperative.

Precisely the necessity of a higher command and an authoritatively given rationale for action, in place of merely positing one's own ends and aims, is acutely made a theme in this *mise-en-abîme* of the play itself. The resolutions of the Player Queen, inasmuch as they are made simply to herself, lack what would ensure their being kept. There is need for a transcendent ground for action; otherwise, this sort of merely self-referential motivation necessarily collapses upon itself, as the player King explains:

> I do believe you think what now you speak,
> But what we do determine oft we break.
> Purpose is but the slave to memory,
> Of violent birth, but poor validity;
> Which now, the fruit unripe, sticks on the tree,
> But fall unshaken when they mellow be.
> Most necessary 'tis that we forget
> To pay ourselves what to ourselves is debt.
> What to ourselves in passion we propose,
> The passion ending, doth the purpose lose.
>
> (III.ii.170–79)

All this applies to Hamlet's own effort to give himself a purpose on the basis of his own passion rather than standing firmly on the transcendent ground of the command from the father immediately embraced and obeyed without need of any mediation by self-conscious reflection. His own "almost blunted purpose" (III.iv.113) seems almost to be directly envisaged by the Player King's concluding aphorism: "What to ourselves in passion we propose, / The passion ending, doth the purpose lose" (III.ii.178–79). Hypertrophied self-consciousness is here individuated as a handicap of the now crippled predicament of the new, modern individual. The stage lends itself to becoming the privileged venue for this rude realization, and Shakespeare does not fail to use it as an analogy for life.

The same predicament of inauthenticity, which Hamlet lives authentically by virtue only of his despair, is seen in his penchant for and inner bond with the players. He attempts to correct their excessive artifice in the precepts he gives for play-acting. He warns against overplaying passion and prescribes rather acting marked by "a temperance that may give it smoothness" (III.ii.6). In line with classical mimetic theory, he affirms that nature must be the guide to art:

> Suit the action to the word, the word to the action, with this special observance, that you o'erstep not the modesty of nature; for anything so o'erdone is from the purpose of playing, whose end both at the first, and now, was and is, to hold as 'twere the mirror up to nature, to show virtue her own feature, scorn her own image, and the very ages and body of the time his form and pressure. (III.ii.15–21)

Language and art in this theory interpret the outer world of nature rather than any higher realm. One of the results is that words per se are empty. They have no intrinsic revelatory capacity; they have meaning only by contrived associations with concrete entities through demonstrative reference. Hamlet's theory of drama emphasizes the mimetic relation between language and nature, but this underscores the degree of their removal from the perspective of a prophetic language of revelation. Language, so conceived, does not translate a higher reality vertically downward; instead, it only mirrors an external reality on a horizontal plane.

Words, words, words, such as Hamlet says he is reading, have become basically empty signs without inherent worth or transcendent reference and grounding. A similar sense of their vanity is expressed when Claudius confesses to himself:

> My words fly up, my thoughts remain below.
> Words without thoughts never to heaven go.
>   (III.iii.96–97)

Although Claudius's intention is simply to admit his frustration at being unable to direct and control his thoughts by the discipline of uttering pious words, his imagery is suggestive of the general predicament of language as revealed in the play. Words no longer have any natural connection with a higher reality; they are no longer inhabited by an aura making them powers in their own right. Claudius is all too acutely conscious of their becoming *mere* words through their disassociation from the inner life of his mind.

The extreme prostration of language, as emptied out into ineffectual form, is epitomized by Polonius's rhetoric. He comically exacerbates language's liability to spin itself into empty webs of merely formal rhetoric, provoking the Queen's demand for "more matter and less art." Hamlet takes the "tedious old fool" of a counselor, so grave and silent in death, to task for having been a "foolish prating knave" in life (III.iv.219–21), but he chastises himself as well for "unpacking his heart," like a whore, "with words" (II.ii.552). He is all too painfully aware of the verbally generated possibilities of hypocrisy whereby "sweet religion makes / A rhapsody of words" (III.iv.48–49). And, of course, the larger issue is that of action itself. Words are just one form of action that is shown to be undergoing a loss of potency, since they are liable to degenerate into a species of impotent inaction.

Hamlet's own ineluctable assignment, as if by fate, to merely play-act is manifest all through the play, even, for example, in his playfulness with Ophelia during the Mousetrap performance. He is condemned to play-act, since there is no place anymore for truly efficacious action by noble spirits in the real world. That this should be the case is only the more poignant, given Hamlet's opening protestation to his mother that he "knows not seems":

> Seems, madam? Nay, it is. I know not 'seems.'
> 'Tis not alone my inky cloak, good mother,
> Nor the customary suits of solemn black,
> Nor windy suspiration of forced breath,
> No, nor the fruitful river in the eye,
> Nor the dejected haviour of the visage,
> Together with all forms, moods, shapes of grief,
> That can denote me truly. These indeed seem,
> For they are actions that a man might play,
> But I have that within which passes show—
> These but the trappings and the suits of woe.
>
> (I.ii.76–86)

The elegantly rhyming couplet at the end even of this speech betrays an incongruous artfulness that is mischievously at odds with what Hamlet is saying about himself.

Hamlet's tragedy is that he cannot act because he can only "act"—in the theatrical sense of the word. This predicament is brought over the threshold of consciousness when Hamlet, in his second soliloquy, contrasts himself, unfavorably, with the player whose merely pretended grief rouses him to such purportedly great, or at least passionate, acting:

O, what a rogue and peasant slave am I!
Is it not monstrous that this player here,
But in a fiction, in a dream of passion,
Could force his soul so to his own conceit
That from her working all his visage wanned;
Tears in his eyes, distraction in his aspect,
A broken voice, and his whole function suiting
with forms to his conceit? And all for nothing,
For Hecuba!
What's Hecuba to him or he to her,
That he should weep for her? What would he do
Had he the motive and the cue for passion
That I have? He would drown the stage with tears,
And cleave the general ear with horrid speech,
Make mad the guilty, and appal the free,
Confound the ignorant, and amaze indeed
The very faculties of eyes and ears.

(II.ii.516–32)

Hamlet's inaction costs him his own most basic self-respect. This is true even when he has motives for it in reality, or at least in what he believes (though not quite wholly, nor free from all doubt) has been disclosed to him as true. Ironically, however, Hamlet accuses himself of a lack of *passion*, whereas it is rather *action* in which he is deficient: his problem is hardly too little theatrical expression of emotion but rather uncertainty in the convictions that ground it and, consequently, a lack of resoluteness in following them through with the appropriate action. He is only too good at tempestuous speeches. He does that superbly, even in berating himself in this very passage. But such histrionics are only the confirmation of what he really lacks, namely: potency that reaches beyond the virtual sphere of mere representation and enters into the realm of the real. He is lacking in effectual power to transform the situation.

Hamlet can only "play-act" in a self-conscious, soliloquizing style because the reality that is worthy of total self-sacrifice in action, the heroic reality that his father stands for, has now receded into *un*reality. It is dependent upon an otherworldly dimension that cannot be verified by the methods newly reigning in the world in which Hamlet lives and attempts really to act. The truth and moral standards of the noble world of values grounded in a metaphysical order such as is revealed through prophecy are incommensurable with the factual, contemporary world of lust and flattery at the court, and this reduces Hamlet, the would-be noble prince, to inconsequential play-acting. In his self-conscious soliloquies, he himself explains how, through hesitation, the noble deeds that he should enact "lose the name of action." What perversely becomes important for Hamlet—and this is tragic—is not achieving the act commanded by his father but rather the play-acting, the dramatization of the process of self-reflection and self-examination in which this task involves him: "To be or not to be, that is the question." Depending on how we hear this sentence, it may ring with melodramatic pretentiousness. The transitive accomplishing of the act gives place to the immanent dramatization of "acting." The acting becomes an end in itself rather than a means to an end. The immanent process of self-questioning—not arriving at an end result that transcends the instrumental interplay of means and methods—is what in effect "interests" Hamlet. This at least is the only conclusion we can draw from the evidence of his (in)action.

Fundamentally, as comes out later in Laertes's comparatively conventional speeches invoking heaven's pity, it is the eclipse of the viewpoint of the heavens that makes *us* only observers of our own "acting"—we become self-conscious actors: "Do you see this, O God?" (IV.vi.194). The gods are also invoked by the player who interprets Hecuba ("But if the gods themselves did see her then"). "Unless things mortal move them not at all," he is sure that heaven itself would weep (II.ii.483–89). Yet this "passion in the gods" smacks more of theatricality than of action proper to divinity, and the whole scene tends to transform this metaphysical framework, in which the gods preside, into the artifice of a proscenium. The older epic tradition tends to turn into a parody of itself when trotted out onto the stage. Its potentially tragic elevation is undermined by the verbal awkwardness and exaggerated alliteration—the purple poetry—of the player's speech.

Claudius too, having lost all authentic relation with higher powers, is shown in the throes of a vain attempt to pray: "My words fly up, my thoughts remain below." He is incapable of reaching any reality beyond himself and therefore is incapable of sincerely repenting for his crime. His acting as if he is really praying fools only Hamlet. Claudius, like Hamlet, is paralyzed and unable to truly act, being divided within himself:

> My stronger guilt defeats my strong intent,
> And like a man to double business bound,
> I stand in pause where I shall first begin,
> And both neglect.
> (III.iii.40–43)

Claudius recognizes that he cannot "shove by justice" in the other world the way he can "in the corrupted currents of this world" (III.iii.57). He acts consequentially and adroitly to avert what menaces him politically, but he is impotent vis-à-vis the other world, powerless to convert his corrupt heart to sincere repentance. He is even lucidly aware that this would require heavenly grace, hence his "Help angels! Make assay" (l.69). But his soul is trapped like a bird in lime, bound fast to earth. He is quite incapable of it, and nevertheless, for all that, he sees the need of connection to another, higher, yet now inaccessible, reality.

III. The King's Two Bodies

The correspondence between this world and another higher world is inscribed capillary-wise into the imagery of *Hamlet*. The idea of the human individual as a microcosm corresponding to the macrocosm of the universe is invoked repeatedly to describe physiological processes as analogous to the fluctuating motions of the universe. But in the Elizabethan world-picture, there was, beyond the visible universe, a metaphysical order, one that was known by revelation, that is, by prophecy, and this realm, in which God was the king reigning in glory with the angels and saints, was ideally mirrored by the human sphere in the social order—with all its components hierarchically ranged under the supreme authority of the king. This image of the king's authority as cosmically grounded, a divine right, is invoked with insistence in *Hamlet*. It forms the cornerstone of the imagery of correspondences between earthly things and that higher order that had once been prophetically revealed. The complex of imagery revolving around kingship thus becomes another way of representing the fall of the real world away from the ideal metaphysical order based on prophetic revelation and deposited in a language that has now become calamitously hollow.[6]

Accordingly, a central image of the metaphysical worldview that *Hamlet* stages in its demise is that of the king as supreme authority on earth bearing an analogous relation to the authority of God in Heaven, the "kingpin," so to speak, in the social universe. Much of what *Hamlet* has

---

6. Ernst H. Kantorowicz, *The King's Two Bodies: A Study in Mediaeval Political Theology* (Princeton: Princeton University Press, 1997 [1957]), chapter 2, 22–41, presents especially Shakespeare's *Richard II* as the tragedy of the king's two bodies leading to the undermining of transcendent value: "The Universal called 'Kingship' begins to disintegrate; its transcendental 'Reality,' its objective truth and god-like existence, so brilliant shortly before, pales into a nothing, a *nomen*" (29).

to say about its tragic world is woven into the recurrences of this pervasive image.[7] The perversity of Claudius is expressed in the way he inverts this relation of dependency between heavenly and earthly glory, making his own glory absolute and using heaven in order to reflect and magnify it. In commending the drunken celebrations that for Hamlet display the depravity of the nation, he impiously proclaims:

> No jocund health that Denmark drinks to-day
> But the great cannon to the clouds shall tell,
> And the king's rouse the heaven shall bruit again,
> Respeaking earthly thunder.
> (I.ii.125–29)

Indeed this king would have heaven reverberate his own earthly glory, even though the king, according to the doctrine of the divine right of kings, really possessed only a delegated authority: he was himself but a viceroy of the supreme deity. Yet here we have a king who, so far from being anointed by God to the holy office of shepherding the nation, has actually usurped his throne by means of an offense that "hath the primal eldest curse upon it, / A brother's murder" (III.iii.37–38). Claudius traduces the ideal so egregiously that Hamlet can say riddlingly, "the body is with the king but the king is not with the body" (IV.i.27–28), insinuating the king's negligence of the body politic. While his own biological body is with him, he does not abide with the body of the state—nor even, in a veiled reference, with the dead body of his slain minister, Polonius.[8]

The medieval theory of kingship and its sanctity was coded into the idea of the king's two bodies. Not only his own biological body but also the body politic lives from him and receives from him its direction, as from the head. This theory surfaces for the first time in the play in Laertes's advice to Ophelia with reference to Prince Hamlet, pointing out

---

7. My reading is, in effect, a reversal of Franco Moretti's in *Signs Taken as Wonders: On the Sociology of Literary Forms* (London: Verso, 2005 [1983]). Moretti contends, "At bottom, English tragedy is nothing less than the negation and dismantling of the Elizabethan world picture" (48), and he celebrates the violent overthrow of theology by secularism, which culminates in the decapitation of the king, Charles I, under Cromwell. What Moretti's reading misses in the historical transition that he himself dubs "The Great Eclipse" is precisely the tragedy of this history that Shakespeare's play so dramatically renders.

8. Benjamin Parris, "'The Body is with the King, but the King is not with the Body': Sovereign Sleep and *Hamlet* and *Macbeth*," *Shakespeare Studies* 40 (2012): 101–42, sifts the impact of this image in recent Shakespeare study (especially since Agamben's *Homo sacer*, 1995).

that as head of the body politic, he is not free to choose his spouse: "on his choice depends / The safety and health of this whole state," which is "that body / Whereof he is the head" (I.iii.20–24). The image is present again in Guildenstern's statement to King Claudius:

> Most holy and religious fear it is
> To keep those many bodies safe
> That live and feed upon your majesty.
>
> (III.iii.8–10)

The image of the king's two bodies figures the higher life, that of the community as a whole, that is invested in the king. This image is employed obsequiously by Claudius's courtiers as a self-evident truth that justifies all the means that the king wishes to use to protect his own interests, while the events and antecedent facts of the play, especially Claudius's own murder of King Hamlet and his taking possession of his wife, flagrantly belie all such sanctity as is enshrined in the theory of the king's two bodies. Rosencrantz elaborates the theory, together with the implication of a morality of practical, rational egotism that he draws from it, for Claudius: he brings the image of the wheel of fortune, around the hub of which all spokes revolve, into the picture to express the dependency of all lives in a society upon the king's life at its center:

> The single and peculiar life is bound
> With all the strength and armor of the mind
> To keep itself from noyance, but much more
> That spirit upon whose weal depends and rests
> The lives of many. The cess of majesty
> Dies not alone, but like a gulf doth draw
> What's near it with it. It is a massy wheel
> Fixed on the summit of the highest mount,
> To whose huge spokes ten thousand lesser things
> Are mortised and adjoined, which when it falls,
> Each small annexment, petty consequence,
> Attends the boist'rous ruin. Never alone
> Did the king sigh, but with a general groan.
>
> (III.iii.10–23)

But, of course, Claudius exploits this ideal of symbiosis in unscrupulous fashion for his own selfish interests. It serves as a pretext that enables him to identify the general weal with his own self-aggrandizing and treacherous schemings. His courtiers obligingly articulate whatever reasons of state he wants to hear. Himself a regicide, he hypocritically affects to be shielded by divine immunity: "There's such divinity doth hedge a king / That treason can but peep to what it would, / Acts little of his will" (IV.v.121–23)—even while, at the same time, he plots death for the legitimate heir. He identifies his own acts with "providence": "It will be laid to us, whose providence / Should have kept short, restrained, and out of haunt, / This mad young man" (IV.i.16–18), implying a shameless usurping of even heavenly sovereignty. The other world, in which legitimate kingly authority could be grounded, has been completely travestied by Claudius's criminal acts, as his words and actions repeatedly betray.

Under these conditions Hamlet has every right and, furthermore, every reason to say, "The king is a thing . . . Of nothing" (IV.iii.24). He is stripped of his divine halo, of all his mantels of cosmic significance. Kingship is indeed a thing "of nothing," for the connotations of the word *king* are but human conventions, whereas by nature a king is nothing beyond what any man is. Just this disillusioned natural viewpoint feeds Hamlet's black imagination in its extreme reduction of all the divine dignity pertaining to kings. He plays on the theme with his—at least feignedly—diseased wit, as he shows King Claudius "how a king may go a progress through the guts of a beggar" (IV.iii.28–29), since "A man may fish with the worm that hath eat of a king, and eat of the fish that hath fed of that worm" (IV.iii.26–27). So considered, a king is but the same wretched food for worms as is any beggar: "Your fat king and your lean beggar is but variable service—two dishes, but to one table. That's the end" (IV.iii.20–24).

IV. From Reduction by Death to Providence in Place of Prophecy

The reduction of human life to nothing by death is dwelt upon with pathos, but also with black comedy, especially in the grave-digging scene with which act V opens. A comic handling of this scene plays eerily with its tragic theme and tenor. The logic-chopping wit of the clowns treats death farcically, but with the arrival of Hamlet and Horatio, the discussion of life from the point of view of the grave grows serious and suggests how death represents a total reduction of life to material fragments unable to sustain and bear significant meaning. Human acts and artifacts in their

worldliness are revealed as vanities. All human reckonings, the legal bind-
ings and "fines" (or ends) of men, are naught as measured against this
end, "the fine of his fines" (V.i.95). Death is felt to be the supreme insult
against human dignity in a line like Hamlet's, "Horatio! Why may not
imagination trace the noble dust of Alexander till 'a find it stopping a
bung-hole?" (V.i.180–81). In Yorick's skull, Hamlet stares death in the
face, and this dumb fragment replaces the father's ghost in bringing tid-
ings from the other side of life, from death. In this case, not a prophetic
revelation but a cruel, lipless laugh or gasp is the last word that points to
what lies beyond the threshold of the tomb.

The other world, the dominion of the dead, has become no longer
a living spiritual presence but only a dried bone, a relic. Nevertheless,
a sense of providence, of being in God's hands, of life being directed
toward a goal and leading toward some purpose beyond itself, though
invisible, is not all lost, not even in the often despairing outlook projected
by the play. A scaled-back, skeptically fideistic sort of belief in providence
expresses itself beyond the crisis of knowledge determined by the eclipse
of revelation and the effacing of immediate insight even into divinity by
prophetic disclosure. In their place, Hamlet affirms a mysterious, indirect working of divinity in human affairs and action. Although he is now
without knowledge that is clairvoyant and prophetic, yet in a rough and
approximate way, he can still discern and affirm a consonance between
heavenly purpose and human history: "There's a divinity that shapes our
ends, / Rough-hew them how we may" (V.ii.10–11). Hamlet interprets
his adventures at sea and his escaping from the king's plot against his
life in this key. With regard particularly to his having his father's signet
with him, enabling him to exchange his own death warrant with those
he composes for Rosencrantz and Guildenstern, he exclaims, "Why even
in this was heaven ordinant . . ." (V.ii.48). This vision is not fatalistic; it
is rather the vision of a shaping to perfection by providence of what we
ourselves design. Yet most important from our side is the readiness to
respond nimbly to chance and circumstance rather than just inflexibly following out our own grand schemes:

> Rashly,
> And praised be rashness for it—let us know,
> Our indiscretion sometime serves us well,
> When our deep plots do pall.
> (V.ii.6–9)

This spontaneity is far removed from the ethic of steadfastness to one's first purpose that belongs to the heroic code voiced, for example, by the Player Queen's protestations calling down curses upon herself: "If once a widow, ever I be wife!" (III.ii.207). Hamlet has suffered severe disillusion over the briefness of woman's love (III.ii.137), and he has prized Horatio's indifference to—or at least inflexibility in the face of—"Fortune's buffets and rewards" (III.ii.59). He is dismayed and driven to despair by the rampant opportunism and the general forsaking of ethics that he sees mushrooming like cancer all around him. Nevertheless, in the play's latter movement, he shows himself to have learned to act in a less purely and rigidly idealistic way so as to be more responsive to circumstance. This readiness is a humbler sort of waiting upon the powers that be and that so consistently cross human will but that, nevertheless, have their own kind of providential design for those who can accept and work along with the grain of events.

This sort of sense of providence is a far cry from prophetic vision in the conventional, vernacular sense. In fact, Hamlet says, "we defy augury" (V.ii.199). The word *augury* expresses the low, material understanding of prophecy—no longer as an inspired interpretation of history—that becomes current when prophecy is thought of positivistically as foretelling objective events, as is inevitably the case once it is misunderstood in terms of the scientific paradigm of knowledge. And yet a certain readiness of attunement to the inscrutable purpose of heaven is still convincingly embraced. It entails a vision that is no longer necessarily prophetic of a higher reality but one that is, nonetheless, still providential:

> There's a special providence in the fall of a sparrow. If it be now, 'tis not to come; if it be not to come, it will be now; if it be not now, yet it will come. The readiness is all. Since no man of aught he leaves knows, what is 't to leave betimes? Let be. (V.ii.199–203)

The sparrow here is reminiscent of the imagery of the gospels: "Are not two sparrows sold for a farthing? And one of them shall not fall on the ground without your Father" (Matthew 10:29). The spirit of letting be and acceptance, of faith in a higher purpose and order controlling human life, can be based precisely on insuperable ignorance, just as once it was based on indubitable revelation. In this way, the reality of eternity is affirmed even as unrevealed, as concealed behind the veil of time.

Before beginning the fatal fencing match with Laertes, Hamlet confesses a deep sense of foreboding: "how ill all's here about my heart"

(V.ii.193). But rather than shrinking back from action, as before, at this point he commends himself to the higher powers and acts in a time-transcending "now" that is unconditioned by temporizing calculation: "ready; now or whensoever" (V.ii.183), simply accepting that what will be will be. He no longer seeks any prophetic revelation of the secret of the future. In fact, this is precisely the point at which he says, "We defy augury." A sense of providence at work in whatever happens, however dangerous, and a resolve to accept it, however difficult, replace all attempts to foresee and manipulate the course of events. Without prophetic revelation, man gropes his way along, yet still trusting as best he can in the postulate of providence. This may come down simply to wishful thinking, but it may also be more. It opens to and invites a divine counterpart of grace. As a disposition of hopeful engagement and trust, it is recognizable as the live ember and remnant of what formerly was expressed in the fire of full-blown prophetic visions revealing the final apocalyptic purpose of collective human endeavor in history. This scaled-back belief in providence now orients and animates only individual destinies.[9]

V. Language and Time

This revision or reversion to a different type of grounding in a transcendent order is worked out by Hamlet in the very new relationship that he learns to take up particularly to language and time. The dialogue between Hamlet and Osric, very much like the one earlier between Hamlet and Polonius, points out, in the first place, the radical devaluation of language in the court. Hamlet parodies the courtiers' overrefined deformations of language, in which formalities become so inflated that they obscure sense. The vocabulary of weapons (rapier, dagger, poniard, sword, foil) and other apparatus (carriages, hangers, etc.) for the tournament with Laertes is shown to be redundant and unwieldy, and so only empty and confusing. Horatio mocks Osric for having recited canned flourishes of eloquence and so being incapable of extending his speech or inventing further responses: "All's golden words are spent" (V.ii.124). The criticism of such language turns on the criterion of a phrase's being "germane to the matter" (V.ii.1148), of its congruity with nature, mak-

9. On the original sort of "faith" informing Shakespeare's plays and on how it redefines the relation between skepticism and religion, see John D. Cox, *Seeming Knowledge: Shakespeare and Skeptical Faith* (Waco: Baylor University Press, 2007).

ing this norm analogous to what is demanded also in dramatic language according to Hamlet's precepts for play-acting.

Hamlet shows, furthermore, how courtiers like Polonius and Osric can be made to say anything that is expedient or ingratiating. They twist language to serve what they take to be their own interests, for it has lost all real integrity for them. Language for them is completely malleable to time and occasion. Though Hamlet despises this spineless temporizing, he, too, conversely, needs to abandon his inflexible adherence to timeless ideals. He must learn to speak and act in a timely way. He manages to shift from a moral to a more pragmatic ground without, however, completely abandoning all relation to some higher purpose.[10] His margin of action at the end of the play is circumscribed by the *time* it will take for news of Rosencrantz and Guildenstern's execution to arrive from England. And his control over this reality of time, moreover, is fundamentally *linguistic:* "It will be short; the interim is mine. / And a man's life's no more than to say 'one'" (V.ii.73–74). Time is here defined by language; its unity or oneness is grasped as man's utterance of one word. In language, then, we still have a power, however limited, for shaping our lives.

When linguistic ritual is no longer truly religious and revelatory but has become merely social artifice, then language can be redeemed from vanity only by adhering to the matter—just as a man without any direct vision of eternity, unable to be true to changeless ideals, must live in synchrony with time: this is what Hamlet is seen to learn. Our language must adhere to the matter, as is shown time and again, especially in the ridiculing of those, like Polonius and Osric, who egregiously violate this principle. As a possible exception, the language of art redeems language by enabling it to be apt in terms of larger patterns of significance. In this

---

10. This is the point from which Carl Schmitt's work of interpretation elucidates *Hamlet* as a fascinating allegory of timeliness in the service of fixed and even of eternal purpose. His *Hamlet oder Hekuba: Der Einbruch der Zeit in das Spiel* (Stuttgart: Klett-Cotta, 1985 [1956]), trans. David Pan and Jennifer Rust as *Hamlet or Hecuba: The Intrusion of Time into the Play* (New York: Telos Press, 2009), firmly anchors the play to events contemporaneous with its writing, in particular those leading up to James I's accession to the throne in 1603. James Stuart is the model for Hamlet, and his mother, Mary of Scotts, who married the presumptive murderer of her husband a few months later, is the model for Gertrude. Schmitt's text, in turn, is a catalyst to the recent flurry of scholarship, incorporating also Agamben, on Shakespeare's registering of the transition from medieval political theology to the secularized nation-state, notably in the work of Julia Reinhard Lupton, *Thinking with Shakespeare: Essays on Politics and Life* (Chicago: University of Chicago Press, 2011) and *Citizen-Saints: Shakespeare and Political Theology* (Chicago: University of Chicago Press, 2005).

case, language is not just a tool for practical use, although it can also become perverse by seriously claiming (rather than only artistically pretending) to be something more than this. The language of *Hamlet* subtly suggests some kind of higher, metaphysical values and meanings, even in unmasking the collapse of just such a system of values as the merely linguistic conventions that are commonly used and traduced by unscrupulous human beings.

Language and time are deeply connected in another speech that expresses language's unique capability of projecting past and future and thereby of liberating human beings from limitation to the immediate, sensuous present that circumscribes the life and consciousness of brute beasts. However, the same speech also implies Hamlet's gnawing despair over the catastrophic fall from the biblical ideal of a rationally endowed humanity made in the image of the divine Word:

> What is a man,
> If his chief good and market of his time
> Be but to sleep and feed? A beast, no more.
> Sure he that made us with such large discourse,
> Looking before and after, gave us not
> That capability and godlike reason
> To fust in us unused.
> (IV.iv.33–38)

The king, too, even from his own position as Hamlet's antagonist, is nevertheless aware of the mutual dependence of time and language and of the fact that if language is to be more than mere words it must be sensitive to changes in events:

> That we would do,
> We should do when we would; for this 'would' changes
> And hath abatements and delays as many
> As there are tongues, are hands, are accidents,
> And then this 'should' is like a spendthrift's sigh
> That hurts by easing. But to the quick of th' ulcer—
> Hamlet comes back; what would you undertake
> To show yourself in deed your father's son
> More than in words?
> (IV.vii.116–23)

Temporal modes can be grasped only in language. Here time and language, specifically the conditional tense, break down willful resolution: their mediation threatens to make action abortive. Language that is not grounded in a reality beyond itself becomes just arbitrary manipulation. The imperative becomes the conditional. Without some external anchor, the order of language and time disintegrates, and the mind is exposed to madness.

VI. Madness and Mantic Vision

As befits tragedy, it is especially the language of madness that, in a world out of joint, retains some capacity for intimating a higher order, the invisible reality of things. Madness is treated as a revelation from beyond the range of reason and, in this regard, as closely akin to prophecy. Accordingly, in *Hamlet* it is most conspicuously the discourse of madness that replaces prophetic discourse. The latter is no longer accepted by a society that believes to be real only what is positively and objectively perceived and dismisses the dimension of the infinite and indefinable. But madness reveals what cannot fit into the grid of rational understanding that delimits "normal" experience. The person who cracks up gives a glimpse into a deeper—and vitally true—reality. Ophelia's madness serves this purpose, and Hamlet himself strews words of revelatory madness throughout his speeches. The clowns also, in another way, break out of the courtly decorum of reasoned, socially acceptable discourse and into a disturbing language that is more deeply veracious and revealing.

In madness, with the derangement of reason, particularly language and the sense of time are directly affected. What madness does so clearly in Ophelia is to break down tense barriers. All time becomes strangely accessible. Past and future are unveiled in the delirium of madness: all dimensions of time, including what is not present, can then be lived simultaneously and with heightened intensity. Normally, consciousness of time—and the division of consciousness from itself in time—is what weakens resolution, undermines action, and reduces to meaninglessness all human efforts to achieve permanent significance. This is what happens when time is no longer grounded in a vision of eternity that reveals the final significances of things. But the mad return to a simultaneous presence of all time, as in Ophelia's songs "To-morrow is Saint Valentine's day" (IV.iv.47–48) and "And will 'a not come again?" (IV. vi.183ff), where all times merge, times of love and of loss, in an eternal return. Although the barriers of the tenses are dissolved, her gnomic pronouncement "Lord, we know what we are, but know not what we may be" (IV.v.42) is uncannily in touch with time and its intrinsic surprises; it opens to the inherent unknowing of temporal existence beyond all rational calculations and assurances.

As to Hamlet, whether his madness is real or feigned, he has a vision of another world besides the concretely and immediately real one, and this in any case brings his outlook very close to madness. Whatever view be taken of Hamlet's at least feigned madness, he does see things that other people cannot see. Not long after seeing the vision that his mother does not see, he implies that he can see into the king's purposes, saying, "I see a cherub sees them" (IV.iii.46). The point is that he does have some kind of extrasensory perception, an extra, imaginative or angelic, dimension of awareness that enables his dead father to speak with him. Yet the tragedy is that this higher vision is incommensurate with the present reality he lives in—and to such an extent that it can only haunt him as a ghost, while he in fact acts on the basis of another standard than that of this higher, spiritual reality. He acts in a sphere and according to a logic of political machinations, putting on even madness. Like Horatio, he makes judgments exclusively on the basis of physical fact and empirical evidence, and like Claudius he attempts to outmaneuver his enemies. Prophetic vision, measured by the standards of the ordinary view of reality, is madness—as indeed prophets, throughout history, have found out, most often the hard way. Prophetic vision is like real madness, as Shakespeare represents it, in revealing a truth that ordinary mortal vision misses and even precludes. Madness, as it is depicted in Ophelia and Hamlet, is a revelation of another world and thereby also an exposé of the hidden truth of this world—the shared, public world.

Madness goes together, throughout Shakespeare's works, with a special insight into reality—or rather with sight *beyond* the reality that is visible to normal people. And there is "method" in such madness (II.ii.202). The actual madness of Ophelia demonstrates this, even though the truth that is thereby revealed is in the highest degree unsettling:

> She speaks . . .
>   things in doubt
> That carry but half sense. Her speech is nothing,
> Yet the unshaped use of it doth move
> The hearers to collection . . .
>   (IV.v.6–9)

"Collection" or "recollection" is a meditative, religious frame of mind in which one gathers oneself together for silent reflection. Such is the pious awe inspired by Ophelia's words of madness. They point us toward the ultimate reality of our lives beyond the narrow focus of our day-to-day consciousness. This perspective of madness resembles that of eternity.

In the end, *Hamlet* makes its peace with the higher order of things. The play ends with Hamlet's reintegration as a "soldier' into the collectivity, with the irony that even this reconciliation has an ambiguously theatrical inflection in Horatio's words: "Bear Hamlet like a soldier to the stage" (V.ii.381). In IV.iv, Hamlet almost envied soldiers—though they be doomed to slaughter—for their unreflective promptness to act in humble, heroic self-sacrifice for a corporate purpose, even when this purpose has no objective worth whatsoever. It might be but the defense of an absolutely nugatory territory "that hath in it no profit but the name" (IV.Iv.19) and "which is not tomb enough and continent / To hide the slain" (IV.Iv.64–65). Still, buried with the dignity of the soldier, Hamlet is no longer destined only to stand all alone in splendid yet tragic isolation as the new individual of the modern age. The play endeavors finally to shield him from this dead end and thus to recover for him the comforts of community and of collective consciousness. The birth of the modern individual tragically cut off from any organic community grounded in transcendent value remains, nevertheless, Hamlet's indelible and searing significance for posterity.

VII. The Ghost of the Past

Paradoxically, the inaccessibility to mortal apprehension of the world from which the father's spirit hails is its most conspicuous characteristic. The ghost's first speech makes it clear that the other world, with its secrets regarding unearthly things, cannot be disclosed, in fact, "must not" be blazoned or revealed:

> But that I am forbid
> To tell the secrets of my prison house,
> I could a tale unfold whose lightest word
> Would harrow up thy soul, freeze thy young blood,
> Make thy two eyes like stars to start from their spheres,
> Thy knotted and combinèd locks to part,
> And each particular hair to stand an end,

Like quilles upon the fretful porpentine.
But this eternal blazon must not be
To ears of flesh and blood. List, list, O, list!

(I.v.13–22)

The ghost says enough to suggest how concrete and real the experience of the other world is, particularly its purgatorial fires, and he especially emphasizes the subjective reaction of fear to what *would* be seen by
Hamlet, if he were allowed to behold it. The other world is present here
only through the representation of subjective reactions because its own
contents themselves are withheld, forbidden, barred. This evokes a strong
sense of a most vividly experienced afterlife—and at the same time locks
it up in a remoteness from all familiar reality, rendering it simply incred-
ible. The logic of strong separation between the eternal world and the
world of mortal flesh presages their inevitable split and their eventually
becoming unintelligible to one another in a secular age.

Shakespeare hints, nonetheless, at a direct insight into the spirit world
on Hamlet's part. He does so, for example, through the ambiguous madness of Hamlet. And yet this, too, only dramatizes how Hamlet's doubt is
not just circumstantial, how his uncertainty is deeply rooted in his character and in the times themselves in which he lives. When he seems to let on,
in conversation with Horatio, that his father is present to him in vision
("My father—methinks I see my father"—I.ii.184), evidently startling his
friend, he brings his statement back into line with normalcy by explaining that he only *imagines* his father, only sees him "in my mind's eye"
(186). There is here, nevertheless, a suggestion that the father has become
a ghost for him even before the ghost appears on the stage. Hamlet is
haunted by the memory of his father. There could even be a hint here
that the ghost is in some measure a figment of his mind. At least there is a
strong correlation between the ghost's reality and the psychological intensity of Hamlet's memory and interior vision of his father.

The actual appearance of this apparition on the stage confirms dramatically that Hamlet is given some special access to knowledge beyond
the ken of ordinary mortals—that he has a superior, a prophetic apprehension of truth. This gift is the psychic counterpart to his moral supe-
riority, or at least discomfiture, vis-à-vis the unscrupulous world of the
court in Denmark, which he finds to be unbearably repugnant. At the
same time, the presence of the ghost is demystified for the audience in the
swearing scene in which, according to the stage directions, "*The Ghost
cries under the stage* 'Swear,'" and Hamlet mutters, "Ha, ha, boy, say'st

thou so? Art thou there, truepenny? Come on. You hear this fellow in the cellarage. Consent to swear" (I.v.149–51). By express reference to this fellow in the cellarage, Shakespeare draws attention to the apparition from the other world as being in reality only an effect of theatrical artifice.[11] In this way, the play's own dramatic technique and apparatus for creating special effects actually participate in the skeptical crisis that they represent. This does not, however, make the suggestion of a transcendent, supernatural reality any the less haunting. It does, on the other hand, make it inextricably literary—a production of art. It is, to this extent, an irrevocably secular kind of revelation of another world.[12]

VIII. *Hamlet* as Prologue to the Modern Age

Hamlet, perhaps more than any other text, deserves to be read as an inaugural work of the modern period. The pervasive influence of *Hamlet* upon the key nodal points in the development of modern literature can be gauged, for instance, from its central importance for French "architects" of the modern spirit such as Stéphane Mallarmé (particularly for his *Igitur ou la folie d'Elbehnon,* 1869) and Paul Valéry (for example, in "La crise de l'esprit," 1919). *Hamlet* had exemplary value for many other writers as well within the modern tradition, particularly for "high modernist" authors such as T. S. Eliot.[13] As the emblem of modern man, Hamlet is most commonly invoked for his famous flaw, his legendary hesitation, his failure to act when he has the chance and his self-consciously staging his own inner uncertainties instead. Hamlet expresses his own painful awareness of this flaw explicitly in the lines addressed to the ghost of his father, who appears to his procrastinating son again while the son is busy berating his mother:

> Do you not come your tardy son to chide,
> That lapsed in time and passion lets go by

---

11. Stephen Greenblatt, *Hamlet in Purgatory* (Princeton: Princeton University Press, 2001), emphasizes the anxiety occasioned by a transition from the Catholic ritual in the medieval order to an especially Protestant theatricality, and he focuses attention particularly on the theatrical intensity of the ghost.

12. This secular thrust of Shakespeare's "gospel" is grasped in its unity with his religious vision by Piero Boitani, *Il vangelo secondo Shakespeare* (Bologna: Mulino, 2009).

13. Specifically concerning the ghost, see Part I: "Modern Writers and the Ghosts of *Hamlet*" of Martin Scofield's *The Ghosts of Hamlet* (Cambridge: Cambridge University Press, 1980).

Th' important acting of your dread command?
                    (III.iv.108–10)

The same painful awareness of his tardiness registers in Hamlet's soliloquy provoked by the passage of young Fortinbras's army on the way to
war:

> Now, whether it be
> Bestial oblivion, or some craven scruple
> Of thinking too precisely on th' event—
> A thought which, quartered, hath but one part wisdom
> And ever three parts coward—I do not know
> Why yet I live to say 'This thing's to do,'
> Sith I have cause, and will, and strength, and means,
> To do't.
>   (IV.iv.39–46)

This is precisely the characteristically modern predicament that Eliot,
too, aims to describe in "The Hollow Men," for example, in these lines:

> Between the conception
> And the creation
> Between emotion
> And the response
> Falls the Shadow.

Hamlet first dramatizes the condition of hollowness that comes with
the loss of a certain groundedness in a metaphysical worldview, a loss that
is ushered in by the age of science and that leads to what Ortega y Gas-
set describes as the condition of the mass-man (*La rebelión de las masas*,
1930). But Hamlet is a prince and of noble character—enough so for his
character to be upset and profoundly shaken by the corruption of the
world which importunes him on all sides round. In "The Love Song of J.
Alfred Prufrock," Eliot's persona measures itself against Hamlet but measures up as decidedly inferior. Prufrock is a kind of Hamlet, though of a
much meaner sort. Hence the denial—

> No! I am not Prince Hamlet, nor was meant to be,
> Am an attendent lord, one that will do
> To swell a progress, start a scene or two,

Advise the prince; no doubt, an easy tool,
Deferential, glad to be of use,
Politic, cautious, and meticulous;
Full of high sentence, but a bit obtuse;
At times, indeed, almost ridiculous—
Almost, at times, the Fool.[14]

The irony here is that Prufrock, as a representative figure of the modern individual, *is* a Hamlet of sorts. He is no longer heroic, as Hamlet is, for over the centuries that noble, princely stature of the tragic hero has eroded to next to nothing. As Hamlet says of his father, affirming the nobility of his essential manhood independently of all social distinctions, "He was a man, take him for all and all, I shall not look upon his like again" (I.ii.187–88). Such dignity and authenticity are no longer to be seen in Hamlet's own world. Indeed, Prufrock represents the consequences of exactly what was begun with Hamlet and what Hamlet himself bitterly despaired over and lamented. The reduction of the status of man begins with his severance from a world of transcendent values. Prufrock's "I should have been a pair of ragged claws / Scuttling across the floors of silent seas" (6), as he drowns impotently in dreams of mermaids who will not sing to him, is surely another echo of Hamlet in his own damp dream soliloquy:

Yet I,
A dull and muddy-mettled rascal, peak
Like John a-dreams, unpregnant of my cause,
And can say nothing; . . .
        (II.ii.533–35)

This obsession with impotence and sterility reverberates all through Eliot's "The Hollow Men" as well:

Between the desire
And the Spasm
Between the potency
And the existence
Between the essence

---

14. T. S. Eliot, *The Waste Land and Other Poems* (New York: Harcourt, Brace & World, 1962), 8.

And the descent
Falls the Shadow.

Hamlet, in fact, already marks himself as unheroic by evoking the absurdity of any comparison of himself to Hercules (I.ii.153). It is this self-conscious fall from heroism that becomes only the more starkly evident and sharply mordant in distant scions like Prufrock. Of course, Hamlet does redeem himself in the end, and just before the last curtain, as we have seen, he is granted a soldier's death ("Bear Hamlet like a soldier to the stage," V.ii.381), the soldier being a man of action. Even though in life Hamlet suffered chronically from irresolution of the will, he died fighting. While making the supreme sacrifice, he avenged his father's murder in decisive action foiling the far more cynical and sinister stratagems of the fratricidal king.

Hamlet is a great work, like the *Divine Comedy* or *Faust*, not primarily because of its perfection as a play—Eliot pronounced it an artistic failure—but rather because of the way it raises the great philosophical, metaphysical questions—most explicitly in the famous meditation "To be or not to be"—that have sustained unending discussion among commentators in all fields and have made the play into an emblem of the modern era. The history of its effect (*Wirkungsgeschichte*) is still being played out in the impotencies of Prufrock (despite his "No! I am not Prince Hamlet") and of the Hollow Men. We have all been Hamlets plagued by the doubt that follows consequentially upon the collapse of a stable and securely grounded cosmic order. *Hamlet* brings us to the threshold of modernity as marked by the crisis of the metaphysical world picture. In it, we can descry the painful tension between a mythopoeic and a scientific worldview. The former was destined to become suspect as mere fiction once it was no longer credible as the revelation of our deepest destiny and truest reality. And this is so in spite of the great works of modern fiction that continue to demonstrate the creative shaping power of art. Hamlet is still restrained by his residual belief in the metaphysical world order, even though he has serious doubts about it. He illustrates, in its first emergence, the sort of doubt and delay vis-à-vis revealed reality and truth in the transcendent sense that will prove to be a major nemesis for those coming after him. Already at work in him against his most heartfelt instincts is a distancing and abstracting and objectivizing of reality that characterizes the new mentality of the Renaissance and that leads to the scientific and technological revolutions of modernity.

These remarks suggest that *Hamlet* itself begins recording the story of how, in the modern age, beginning with the Renaissance, all intellection of any reality higher than the mundane is endangered in ways relating to the rise of science as the dominant paradigm of knowledge. *Hamlet* illustrates with excruciating cogency the risk of losing traditional, unscientific forms of knowledge that are "prophetic" (in a large sense) and the tragedy that this entails. The play indirectly, without necessarily purposing to do so, calls us to our responsibility to resist this encroachment upon these supposedly "prescientific" forms of knowing to the point of obliterating them together with the wisdom that they embodied. We can do so by historically contextualizing and circumscribing scientific knowledge—and thereby rendering evident its limits as well as its powers. One important way to do this is by reinterpreting and renovating alternative models for human awareness and inquiry that have been handed down particularly in the traditions of prophetic poetry. Milton and Blake recognized Shakespeare as a crucial link in this transmission. Evidently, the power of Shakespeare's poetry to disclose our world at unseen depths made it for them per se prophetic, even without employment of any more specifically prophetic forms of discourse or properly religious modes of revelation. What in any case is plain is that Shakespeare already all too lucidly dramatizes the tragedy of prophecy's incipient demise at the dawning of the modern age.

blind prophecy

milton's figurative mode in *paradise lost* and in some early poems

Just Heav'n thee like Tiresias to requite
Rewards with Prophecy thy loss of sight.
—A. M. (Andrew Marvel)

I. *Paradise Lost* and the Prophetic Tradition

Paradise Lost presents itself as Christian prophetic poetry. By invoking the "Heav'nly Muse" that inspired Moses, and by endeavoring to soar above all the classical founts of poetic inspiration, Milton places his poem in a tradition of sacred poetry originating in the Bible and claiming to deliver not merely human wisdom but, more momentously, divine truth. Yet Milton's theological outlook made it by and large impossible for him to adopt the characteristic poetics of this tradition as it was handed down to him through such works as the *Divina Commedia*, the *Gerusalemme Liberata*, and the *Faerie Queene*. All of these works share in common the problem of representing a human story—or we might even say *the* human story—as having a wider and deeper significance, a higher truth, in the light of Christian revelation. If human affairs, by the aid of Christian revelation, can be seen in their ultimate meaning, then it is the pro-phetic poet's task precisely to find the means of figuring that meaning in the story he relates.

The methods of accomplishing this developed by *Paradise Lost*'s Christian prophetic forbears can generally be subsumed under various forms of allegory. Whether allegory is conceived Neoplatonically as relat-ing the visible world to "the invisible things" that are above "in heav-enly places in Christ" (Ephesians 1:3), as it generally was by Christian poets, or after the fashion of biblical typology, as establishing an analogy between what we *now* see in a glass darkly with what we *then* will see face to face (I Corinthians 13:12), Christian allegory constitutes a mode of externalizing spiritual truth, of giving it some intuitable shape that the human mind and imagination can grasp. Milton, however, for reasons of his own, or rather of his Reformed religion, was not able to accept, if not in strictly limited ways, such methods,[1] for the status of the image as a vehicle of truth had been undermined by the Reformation's ardent icono-clasm. Milton needed to redefine radically the status of imagery from that of being a gross embodiment or a shadowy type of invisible truth to that of being a heuristic device used and consumed in provoking an immediate, subjective, nonobjectifiable relation to a truth that could not be iconographically represented at all.[2]

In other words, Milton as a prophetic poet could surrender neither the image nor the truth, in spite of their presumptive incompatibility with one another. As a third alternative, he retained both but disconnected them, so that the image no longer functioned as an outward manifestation and rep-resentation of how things really are, but rather fed the reader's personal

---

1. More detailed consideration of Milton's stance vis-à-vis antecedent traditions of poetic allegory and prophecy can be found in Judith Kates, *Tasso and Milton: The Problem of Christian Epic* (Cranbury, NJ: Associated University Presses, 1983); Irene Samuel, *Milton and Dante: The "Commedia" and "Paradise Lost"* (Ithaca: Cornell University Press, 1966); and, more recently, Noam Reisner, *Milton and the Ineffable* (Oxford: Oxford University Press, 2009). Maureen Quilligan, in "Milton's Spenser: The Inheritance of Ineffability," in *Ineffability*, ed. Peter Hawkins and Anne Schatter (New York: AMS Press, 1984), explains that "Milton was able to dismiss the need for allegory in his approach to the ineffable being of God because, with what appears to be absolute certainty about his own inspiration, he did not need a language in which the divine presence was other, or *allos*" (78).

2. The view that sees Milton's poetry as a kind of "self-consuming artifact" is as-sociated especially with the approach of Stanley Fish in *Self-Consuming Artifacts: The Experience of Seventeenth Century Literature* (Berkeley: University of California Press, 1972), as well as in *Surprised by Sin* (New York: Macmillan, 1967), and in "Discovery as Form in Paradise Lost," in *New Essays on "Paradise Lost,"* ed. Thomas Kranidas (Berkeley: University of California Press, 1971), 1–15.

experience of the poem, where truth could be encountered in spiritual immediacy. In this way, the direct address of the Word to each individual conscience, which became paramount in the Reformation, might find a channel in prophetic poetry. This peculiar (and proto-Symbolist) figurative mode had far-reaching consequences for Milton's style and for the structural dynamics of his poem.

A close reading of a not atypical passage will serve to isolate characteristic stylistic effects of Milton's image-suspicious poetics. The concluding lines of Book II, relating Satan's emergence from Chaos into sight of the created world, illustrate the aptitude of Milton's style for shedding an emotional aura rather than achieving sharp imagistic definition:

> But now at last the sacred influence
> Of light appears, and from the walls of Heav'n
> Shoots far into the bosom of dim Night
> A glimmering dawn; here Nature first begins
> Her fardest verge, and Chaos to retire
> As from her outmost works a brok'n foe
> With tumult less and with less hostile din,
> That Satan with less toil, and now with ease
> Wafts on the calmer wave by dubious light
> And like a weather-beaten Vessel holds
> Gladly the Port, though Shrouds and Tackle torn;
> Or on the emptier waste, resembling Air,
> Weighs his spread wings, at leisure to behold
> Far off th' Empyreal Heav'n, extended wide
> In circuit, undetermin'd square or round,
> With Opal Tow'rs and Battlements adorned
> Of living Sapphire, once his native Seat;
> And fast by hanging in a golden Chain
> This pendent world, in bigness as a Star
> Of smallest Magnitude close by the Moon.
> Thither full fraught with mischievous revenge,
> Accurst, and in a cursed hour he hies.
> (*Paradise Lost* II.1034–55)

Beginning with the phrase "the sacred influence / Of light appears," Milton prefers a generally felt, rather than a specifically seen, "influence" as grammatical subject, even though what actually "appears" must be the light itself, which in a more exact statement would assume the nominative (rather than a genitive) function. This slight displacement of predication toward the impalpable gives priority to emotional radiance over image, as does also a phrase like "living Sapphire," where whatever may be living about the sapphire cannot be directly seen but only sensed. Both "sacred" and "living" are highly radiant adjectives, charged with the wonder and warmth of the divine, within the poem's Christian-symbolic idiom.

This iridescence at the linguistic level overlays a represented world (liminally Chaos) which is left "dim" and "glimmering." Heaven itself is not clearly seen but is conceptualized instead in explicitly indeterminate terms as "undetermined square or round," thereby thematizing the unfocused, in fact, unrealizable, quality of what is described. The enriching of verbal resonances but blurring of the object represented is further promoted by recurring redundancies that multiply opaque folds in the verbal veil of the verses. Redundant expressions such as "first begins" and "fardest verge" give a stirring ring of ultimacy to the words as signifiers but do not help to delineate referential content any more than does "hanging . . . pendant."[3]

On closer examination, however, these redundancies, while contributing nothing to the narrative, turn out to be among the devices by which Milton suggests thematic issues for the reader's consideration. The word "first" in this poem, as previously heard in "first disobedience" and "first seduc'd," invests what is being described with archetypal significance, inscribing it within Milton's story of all things, the alpha and the omega. The word "fardest" bears the same weight of totality implicit in the archetype, transposing it into a spatial dimension. All nature and history are thus encompassed, and this desired universality motivates the lack of distinctness in particulars that we have observed. In like manner, the other narratively superfluous repetition, the double allusion to the fact of the earth's being suspended from heaven ("hanging . . . pendant"), upgrades this structural element to a moral and theological theme: such dependency, by being doubly stated, is confirmed as the all-important characteristic of the sublunary world. As the chain from heaven to earth tautens into a tautology, this dependency becomes the necessary general character of the terrestrial.

To similar effect, when we are told that the earth is "in bigness like a Star," but then are immediately checked in our imagining this bigness

---

3. Observations on the characteristic "indistinctness and inconsistency" of Milton's descriptions, to borrow a phrase from T. B. Macaulay's famous *Essay on Milton* (1825), are commonplace throughout the critical tradition. Cf. especially T. S. Eliot's classic remarks, in "Milton I," in *On Poetry and Poets* (New York: Farrar, 1957), on Milton's style and imagery, including the statement that "Milton never saw anything."

by the sequel "Of smallest Magnitude," this description in contradictory terms of bigness and smallness, thereby thwarting our smooth reception of the image, actually facilitates our grasp of the meaning standing behind, or perhaps getting in front and in the way of, the image: it impresses on us the utter relativity of all earthly greatness, the bigness we have conceived being undercut one line lower.

The other similes in the passage similarly work not to specify and resolve descriptions but rather to set up patterns of thematic coherence at a remove from the story line. These similes, like those in Book I, suffer from syntactic dislocations that impede their smooth integration into the narrative, for instance, the uncertain connection of the "That Satan" clause with what precedes it and the conflation of tenor and vehicle in "like a weather-beaten Vessel holds / Gladly the Port, though Shrouds and Tackle torn." These descriptive imprecisions work like the simile clusters in Book I that digress from the actual situation of the fallen angels who welter on the abyss of fire, defeating its accurate depiction but indirectly suggesting its thematic significance for a reader. The Leviathan figure for Satan, for example, leads to a story about a navigator by night mistakenly anchoring in the "scaly rind," which is irrelevant to picturing Satan supine on the fiery lake, although it is proleptically ominous with regard to the central threat represented in the poem.

Something else that undermines, or at least ironizes, the similes in our passage as aids to the realization of the narrative is that they are for the most part disanalogies to the situation and action represented. Chaos's retiring is compared to an army retreating, but "with tumult less and with less hostile din." Likewise, the qualification of "the emptier waste" in which Satan spreads his wings as "resembling Air" serves more to stress that there is only a semblance of air than to provide any concrete vehicle for visualization: besides, a resemblance to air is too vague to be imagined, so we are left rather with a concept of what the empty waste is not.

The information-bearing value of Milton's images is often nil, for they do not articulate an objective state of affairs by offering a true and accurate representation. Instead, they communicate tone and other such musical values, stirring emotion, which may lead the reader to inward apprehension of an unarticulated and inarticulable truth. Exactly homologous to the reader's immediate relation to truth, in this account, is the prophetic poet's relation to his Heav'nly Muse, from whom he claims to receive the words of his poem as by a kind of mental automatic writing. She is invoked as

> . . . my Celestial Patroness, who deigns
> Her nightly visitation unimplored,
> And dictates to me slumb'ring, or inspires
> Easy my unpremeditated Verse . . .
>
> (IX.21–24)

In this description of his inspiration, Milton is being dictated to; he does not see anything. He is not like Dante—a foil to which we will recur frequently in examining Milton's representations of transcendence—a traveler through fully objectified worlds beyond the grave. His poem is the record of his being visited rather than of his visiting, and so it is not all his but also "hers who brings it nightly to my *Ear*" (IX.46–47; emphasis mine). For Milton to "see and tell" of things invisible to mortal sight seems to be all one thing, bypassing the mediation of the visual object, and in this sense his prophecy is blind.

Milton would undoubtedly have taken satisfaction in thinking that this came close to what the Hebrew prophets meant by such phrases as "The word of the Lord came upon me" and "Then I was in the spirit. . . ." Whatever truth is communicated does not inhere in the images as if in some sort of "real presences." Truth lies rather in the nonobjectifiable connection with the divine. Of course, Milton does not avoid images. His poetry is as rich in them as any. But they do not embody its truth, not even the truth that the poem would communicate about the ways of God to men. The imagery is in this relative sense irrelevant.[4]

Nevertheless, and perhaps all the more for this reason, Milton's images work upon his readers' feelings, instilling in them a sense of grandeur, arousing emotion, bringing about the heightened state of sensitivity in which one is susceptible to immediately confronting the truth about things by the light of Christian revelation and understanding with sudden moral insight the reality of one's own life story in its identity with the universal human story. Thus the images have a sacred function: they are used paraenetically, as if in preaching, to exhort and edify. But they are emphatically not sacramental, in the way that images in the *Divine Comedy*

---

4. Eliot's reading of Milton's imagery as symptomatic of a "dissociation of sensibility" is given an interesting postmodern twist by Herman Rapaport in *Milton and the Post-Modern* (Lincoln: University of Nebraska Press, 1983). Rapaport argues that "Milton's desire was to defetishize the image, to empty words of their corporeality, their *parousia*, which to Milton was but an illusion to begin with" (243). Instead of the incarnate poetic word, in which signified and signifier become one, Milton proffers "a word divested of the divine, differed and deferred from the signified" (16).

are. The *Inferno*'s images are manifest embodiments that enable us to see God's judgment, the absolute and final truth about each individual, in every visible detail of form and gesture. For Dante, the ways of God, the divine punishments and rewards in which human lives attain their absolute significance, are fully manifest in symbolic representation.[5] For Milton, in contrast, representation is radically alien from God, though like everything in creation, including evil, it is potentially an instrument for achieving God's purposes.

This theologically motivated dissociation of truth from its representation stands behind many of the quite unorthodox and perplexing features of Milton's style. In numerous cases elaborate descriptions are undercut and whisked away, detailed development notwithstanding, as mere fictions. Orpheus's mother, for instance, invoked in the proem of Book VII to save her son, turns out in the very last words of the verse paragraph to be an "empty dream," and simultaneously in her train vanish not only the Thracian bard himself but the whole "wild rout" of Bacchus and his revelers, who until that moment were vividly seen wildly rioting in the woods of Rhodope. Or again, Mulciber's picturesque fall like a shooting star from the "Crystal Battlements" of Heav'n is drawn out "from Morn / To Noon . . . from Noon to dewy Eve, / A Summer's day; and with the setting Sun . . ." (I.742–44), only to be cast off as a flight of fancy in the ensuing line, with the jolt of an enjambment: "Thus they relate, / Erring." Such illusory displays, as they suddenly turn out to be, are in this way demoted from the status of primary figurations of the poem's central myth or truth.[6] They are not accorded this highest degree of poetic reality.

The fully elaborated objectifications of the poem swing loose from its divine meaning and message. They are not allowed to incarnate the poem's true significance. The relation to truth in *Paradise Lost* remains one of sheer immediacy—of the blind poet to his directly dictating Muse, or of the reader to apprehensions stimulated by the poem through its powerful music and emotion, but not symbolically crystallized in the

---

5. A classic discussion of Dante's figurative technique for representing the eternal world in images of temporal phenomena can be found in Erich Auerbach, "Figura," in *Scenes from the Drama of European Literature: Six Essays* (Gloucester, MA: Meridian, 1969), 12–67.

6. Isabel MacCaffrey, in *Paradise Lost as "Myth"* (Cambridge: Harvard University Press, 1959), treats Milton's poem as "true myth," explaining that myth "doesn't stand for anything else; it is what everything else stands for" (55). See also Frank Kermode on the poem's "basic myth" as symbolizing contemporary and universal human experience, in Frank Kermode, ed., *The Living Milton: Essays by Various Hands* (London: Routledge, 1960).

abundant materializations of the poem. The objectively descriptive imagery of the poem drifts off as not belonging to its essential statement, as having merely facilitated the experience without permanently embodying the poem's intrinsic meanings.

The problem with Milton's style (and with the figurative mode it embodies) is not that it fails to achieve concreteness or externality. There is much more abstract theology in Dante's *Divina Commedia* than in Milton's *Paradise Lost*. The problem is that the really quite impressive realization at the visual surface is not anchored to truth: the poem's material realizations in objective images do not (and are not meant to) adequately represent its deeper meanings. The relation of sacramentality, whereby the divine manifests itself materially in the world, has been broken.[7] Whereas Dante's imagery, for the most part and in principle, asserts its veracity as unequivocal representation of truth, Milton's imagery tends to call attention to itself *qua* imagery, that is, to its status as untruth, as mere poetic invention. As soon as he departs from the express word of Scripture and its postulated truth, Milton's representations of the Garden of Eden are merely hypothetical and are even tagged as such:

> . . . Hesperian fables true,
> *If* true, here only . . .
> (IV.250–51; italics added)

Milton's lack of a figurative code for representing the true world in images results in the structures of doubling and parodic imitation that pervade *Paradise Lost*. It is no longer possible to assign univocal meanings to imagery, as is often at least apparently the case in Dante's world.[8] Thus "heaven resembles hell" (II.268), and the Father's relationship with his "Only begotten Son" (II.80) is mirrored by Satan and his "own begotten" (II.782) perfect image, Sin, as well as by the calamitous couple Adam and Eve, who are equally parthenogenetic, the woman being created out of a rib taken from the side of the man. The poet himself, whose song "with no middle flight intends to soar" (I.15), cannot escape compari-

---

7. Regina Schwartz, in *Sacramental Poetics at the Dawn of Secularism: When God Left the World* (Stanford: Stanford University Press, 2008), probes Milton in just these terms of a loss of sacramentality in language.

8. Dante is used here as a foil to bring out an aspect of Milton's imagery that was already found in the first chapter to be inaugurated in some ways by Dante himself, specifically with his poetics of ineffability in the *Paradiso*. The contrast with Milton is thus only relative and can be made also *within* Dante's own oeuvre itself by contrasting the *Paradiso* with its predecessor canticles.

son to Satan, who also "soars" (II.634), as well as association with Jove usurping, along with his Olympians, in the "middle air" (I.514–16). Similarly uncontrollable proliferation of parodies riddles the imagery of prospect as it travels from God to Adam to Satan—and thence to the poet's own implicit prospect over all the scenes narrated in the poem. Such imagery takes on a series of contradictory connotations with no clear criteria of distinction between good and evil gazing. And the same must be said for the language of dominion and monarchy which invests by turns Adam, Satan, and the Almighty. In all these instances, figuration has become equivocation: it takes place in a world that lacks objectivity, one in which the truth of things is dissociated from their visual image or apparent form.

Often lexical links such as the "link of nature" language used to describe both Adam's attachment to Eve after her fall and Sin's desire for her father, whom she pursues by building a bridge across Chaos, point up parody and ambiguity at the linguistic surface. But even at the level of the poem's narrative and conceptual foundations, the pervasive ironies that riddle the structure of *Paradise Lost* can be understood as consequences of the ineradicable equivocity of Milton's figurative mode. They have often been interpreted as undermining Milton's religious orthodoxy. The fact that God seems to be represented as a self-serving tyrant, one made gratuitously ogrelike and a power monger in Book III, just as if the Devil spoke truth about him in Books I and II,[9] may be understood as deriving from this intrinsic equivocity. Like the absolutely good Person, God himself, so also the absolutely good place a priori, the Garden, assumes finally an ambiguous valence with the suggestion at the poem's end that perhaps only once they are expelled from Paradise can Adam and Eve be "happier far" in the "Paradise within." Here, as everywhere in Milton, the inward meaning tends to ironize and to undermine all outward manifestations and their apparent meanings.

The fact that representation is incurably equivocal is effectively pointed up by the exact equivalence of the celestial and the infernal courts in the scenes representing respectively Satan's and the Son's volunteering for tasks that daunt all the others. Just as in hell "all sat mute, / Pondering the danger with deep thoughts" (II.420–21), so "all the Heav'nly Quire stood mute . . . [none] durst upon his own head draw the deadly forfeiture . . ." (III.217–21). The implication of such closely coinciding imagery

---

9. These themes are elaborated and exploited especially by William Empson, *Milton's God* (London: Chattro, 1965).

seems almost inescapably to be that both courts are full of self-servers and that God, like Satan, exploits the situation for self-glorification.

Parallels and parodies that seem to vitiate the poem's ostensible program crop up incessantly even where they could be easily avoided. It seems perverse that, just after Eve's satanically inspired dream, which entices her to covet the forbidden fruit so as to become God-like, Raphael should turn up talking about food and suggesting that it may constitute a way of participating with angels and transcending corporeality:

> . . . time may come when men
> With Angels may participate, and find
> No inconvenient Diet, nor too light Fare:
> And from these corporal nutriments perhaps
> Your bodies may at last turn all to spirit,
> Improv'd by tract of time, and wing'd ascend
> Ethereal, as we, or may at choice
> Here or in Heav'nly Paradises dwell; . . .
>
> (V.493–500)

The devilish voice in the dream, extolling the "Fruit Divine . . . able to make Gods of Men," had coaxed:

> Taste this, and be henceforth among the Gods
> Thyself a Goddess, not to Earth confined,
> But sometimes in the Air, as wee, sometimes
> Ascend to Heav'n, by merit thine, and see
> What life the Gods live there, and such live thou.
>
> (V.77–81)

Satan's false promise of being able to fly to heaven is unmistakably reprised in Raphael's divinely commissioned words, with verbatim echoes describing how to "ascend" (in metrically emphatic positions) to ethereal heaven by this divine delectation: the two passages display the very same pattern of inference and persuasion.

A related consequence of the dissociation of meaning and image is uncontrolled fertility in both images and meanings, none of which, however, is definitive. The visible heavens seem to manifest an excess of creativity—beyond the measure of the useful—and this bothers Eve. When she asks Adam the reason, he produces an excess of explanations, which nonetheless do not adequately explain why there should be so many stars shining at night, as is proved by his later posing to Raphael the same question of:

> How Nature wise and frugal could commit
> Such disproportions, with superfluous hand . . .
>   (VIII.26–27)

The unchecked fecundity of creation is similarly a problem arousing anxiety when Eve worries that the garden is getting out of control. That is why she suggests to Adam that they separate, since they are losing time from work because of amorous dalliance made irresistible by their close proximity. And again after the Fall, the fear of her own fertility prompts Eve to propose a suicide pact with Adam. All of these anxieties are erroneous but inevitable in a world whose true meaning cannot be made manifest. Such anxieties are not allayed by rational demonstrations such as Dante receives in such abundance from his guides Virgil and Beatrice, whose discourses on love and the generation of the soul, free will, predestination and the influence of heavenly bodies on human character, moon spots, angelic hierarchy, faith, and everything else that raises doubts in Dante's mind, end by satisfying his intellect within its inherent limitations. The solution for Milton's creatures can only lie in practical virtue and trust, or in other words in

> . . . what thou canst attain, which best may serve
> To glorify thy Maker, and infer
> Thee also happier . . ."
>   (VII.115–17)

In the injunctions to know only what is useful (cf., for example, VII.112–120; VIII.191–97), Adam and Eve are denied all knowledge of what is true per se. What it is right for them to believe depends on a morality of obedience rather than on how things actually are and can be seen to be. Small wonder, then, that Milton should be unable to represent truly the things that are above (or are to come), since

> God to remove his ways from human sense,
> Plac'd Heav'n from Earth so far, that earthly sight,
> If it presume, might err in things too high,
> And no advantage gain.
>   (VIII.119–22)

From a Catholic and Dantean perspective, the basic problem is loss of the interpretative key that enables human beings to know by means of their senses the true meanings of things. For Dante this key was provided by the Incarnation. The whole of the perceptible world pointed to a true Being revealed through God's entering the world, taking on body and becoming man. This sacramental value of Creation no longer has quite the same warrant for Milton, given his Protestant sense of the total depravity of the world after the Fall. Theologically Milton hedges even on the doctrine of the Incarnation. This is entailed by his Arianism, which is all but explicitly avowed in *The Christian Doctrine,* and it is evinced by the disparities, or even clashes, between the Father and Son, in Book III of *Paradise Lost.* In Milton's poetry, the incarnation of the Word transmogrifies it from revelation to equivocation. Everything divine, when reflected in the created universe, proves to be susceptible to satanic perversion.

These and a whole interweave of other ambiguities and equivocations can be understood as deriving from lack of a symbolic mode for expressing truth objectively. Because there is no objective origin in extraverbal vision—or in a transcendental signified which can stand as the unifying sense of the variety of poetic signifiers—Milton's figuration tends to disaggregation and to inadvertent, or in any case subversive, parody. The figurative becomes equivocal. Milton does claim continuity with the Christian prophetic tradition, but in his reenactment of the office of the prophetic poet, prophecy has become blind. What the poet sees and makes seen is a powerfully moving stimulus to that moral fervor in which alone it is possible to apprehend the truth. Yet that truth is never made visibly objective. It is to be encountered—even by the reader of *Paradise Lost*—only in the blinding immediacy of inspiration in the Spirit. This "Protestant principle," which effectively governs the poetics of Milton's prophetic work, by extension from his Reformed way of reading Scripture,[10] is clinched near the conclusion of the poem by the

<hr/>

10. See Hugh Reid MacCullum, "Milton and Figurative Interpretation of the Bible," *University of Toronto Quarterly* 31.4 (1962): 396–415, for Milton's adherence to Protestant models of exegesis. Northrop Frye, ed., *"Paradise Lost" and Selected Poetry and Prose* (New York: Holt, 1951), develops the distinguishably Protestant aspects of Milton, as does also Thomas Altizer in chapter 7, "Milton and the English Revolution," of *History as Apocalypse* (Albany: State University of New York Press, 1985). More recently, the detailed intellectual background for Milton's peculiar poetics and their tendency toward indicating the unsayable has been canvassed in detail by Noam Reisner in terms of "the crisis of mimesis in relation to apophatic discourse which Milton inherits from the humanist-Protestant traditions and attempts to resolve creatively *in* his poetry and

Archangel Michael's reference to

> . . . the truth
> With superstitions and traditions taint
> Left only in those written Records pure,
> Though not but by the Spirit understood.
>
> (XII.512–14)

II. Milton's Early Poems and Reformed Religion

The theologically motivated figurative mode that was to come to maturity in *Paradise Lost* can be discerned, in retrospect, as emergent in Milton's early poems. We have seen that Milton's conception of poetic inspiration as direct action exerted on the poet's faculties by the "Heav'nly Muse," his "Celestial Patroness," who dictates to him unpremeditated verses while he sleeps, with no mediation through independently real visual objects, shows up lucidly against the backdrop of certain orientations of Protestant religion, specifically its stress on the immediate relation between the individual believer and the deity itself, bypassing church hierarchy and the sacramental system. Milton's early poems in the prophetic mode record his development toward a style of prophecy consonant with these accents of Reformed theology. Indeed certain of his early efforts register the impulse toward immediacy in the relation with divinity to such a degree as to sometimes threaten to cancel out altogether expression in poetry, with its projection of a verisimilar world of manifest forms. The palpable embodiment in images and in an externalized field of figures that is so essential to prophetic poetry as we find it in Dante—to revert once more to this crucial touchstone—already runs the risk in the early poems of losing its ability to mediate the divine. Such objectively significant imagery, which was typically used in Catholic ceremony and sacramental rite, was no longer needed or tolerated in Reformed religion.

Particularly revealing of Milton's impatience with embodiment of religious truth in poetic imagery is his highly conflicted approach to—and at the same time withdrawal from—the theme of the Incarnation. Milton

---

theological thinking" (Reisner, *Milton and the Ineffable*, 11). Dante's anticipations of "the Protestant principle" are suggestively explored by John Took in chapter VII ("Dante and the Protestant Principle") of *Conversations with Kenelm: Essays on the Theology of the Commedia* (London: Ubiquity Press [University College London Arts and Humanities Publications], 2013), 155–70.

would come to reject the fully Catholic doctrine of the Incarnation and embrace Arianism only later,[11] but at this point already the theological tendency and its correlative poetics are clearly detectable.

The inaugural poem of Milton's career as prophetic poet, "On the Morning of Christ's Nativity,"[12] ostensibly pivots on this theological crux of Christian revelation, yet it betrays an aversion to its own central theme, the incarnation of a divine being, God the Son, as a human being—what the Fourth Gospel declares in the phrase: "the Word became flesh and dwelt among us." This ambivalence is seen first in the way that Nature, in the poem, recoils from a material incarnation of divinity, shrinking in shame at the approach of her Maker, taking advantage of the wintry season to "hide her guilty front with innocent Snow" (II.39). Like Nature hiding her outward, sensuous form, Milton writes shy of any material representation adequate to his divine theme, invoking rather a musical modality of pure immediacy, which induces a state of rapture that knows no external visual representation. Indeed the heavenly music that accompanies the birth threatens to short-circuit the whole history of redemption in which Christ is embodied in his Church and its work: "For if such holy song / Enwrap our fancy long, / Time will run back and fetch the Age of Gold . . ." (XIV.133–35). Time may run backward or forward—it hardly matters—to the unfallen state of concord with God or "perfect diapason," as in "At a Solemn Music," where again music represents the modality of the immediate apprehension of the divine.

More than celebrating the Incarnation, the Nativity Hymn grasps after Apocalypse. This is evident, for example, in the marshal imagery of "helmed Cherubim / And sworded Seraphim" (XI.112–13), which upstages and outshines Luke's pastoral scene of the angels appearing to the shepherds. It also registers in the persistence of allusions such as those to the trumpets clanging on Mount Sinai "while the red fire and smouldering clouds out brake" (XVII.159). This apocalyptic impetus forces the

---

11. The issue of Milton's Arianism is thoroughly explored by C. A. Patrides, W. B. Hunter, and J. H. Adanson, *"Bright Essence": Studies in Milton's Theology* (Salt Lake City: University of Utah Press, 1973).

12. Milton writes about the genesis of this poem in his verse letter in Latin to Charles Diodati known as the "Sixth Elegy." Cf. Northrop Frye's observations on Milton's discovery of himself as a "priest of poetry": "The poet's images are derived from human life, but the major poet must also use those human symbols to convey to man some inkling of the eternal worlds beyond human knowledge, 'singing now the holy counsels of the gods above, and now the deep regions where the fierce dog (Cerberus) barks,' to quote again from the *Sixth Elegy*" (Frye, *"Paradise Lost" and Selected Poetry and Prose*, v).

narrator to try to apply brakes—"But wisest Fate says No, / This must not yet be so, / The Babe lies yet in smiling Infancy" (XVI.149–51)—so as to give time to the baby Jesus to grow up, as well as time to the Church for its one and two-thirds millennia (and however much longer) of history. Despite the effort to defer it, however, still the clamor of apocalypse encroaches by the end even of this very stanza: "Yet first to those chained in sleep / The wakeful trump of doom must thunder through the deep" (XVI.155–56).

Divinity is essentially to be heard and not seen because it belongs to an other world, one which audible sounds can announce, rather than to any world that can actually be seen and concretely represented in the flesh. "At a Solemn Music" presences the vision of God enthroned in heaven, saluted by "divine sounds" of "Saintly shout and solemn Jubilee," as an essentially musical experience, invoking Voice and Verse, "pledges of Heaven's joy," in order that they "to our high-rais'd fantasy present / That undisturbed Song of pure concent" (5–6). Similarly, "Il Penseroso" dissolves its richly symbolic and almost sacerdotal religious imagination, figuring a cathedral service, into music as the mode in which transcendence is "seen" through the ear:

> There let the pealing Organ blow
> To the full voic'd Choir below
> In Service high and Anthems clear,
> As may with sweetness, through mine ear,
> Dissolve me into ecstasies,
> And bring all Heav'n before mine eyes.
>
> (162–67)

The resort to music in these poems, as in the Hymn on the Nativity itself, gestures toward an ultimate revelation and unveiling beyond images.

Only by a deflection from the Incarnation (that is, the union and organic integration of the divine with the human) to the peripheral theme of the rout of the pagan idols, drawn out over seven full stanzas, is the Nativity Ode able to create the imaginative space necessary for poetry as opposed to apocalypse. It thus allows for elegiac and pastoral excursuses, as in

> The lonely mountains o'er
> And the resounding shore,
>   A voice of weeping heard, and loud lament;

From haunted spring and dale
Edged with poplar pale,
    The parting Genius is with sighing sent;
With flower-inwoven tresses torn
The Nymphs in twilight shade of tangled thickets mourn.
                             (XX.181–89)

This lament of the departing local spirits is not part of the gospel tradition at all (although it may be suggested by Jeremiah's voice of lamenta-
tion and weeping of Rachel for her children, which is cited by Matthew
2:18 as a prophecy of the slaughter of the innocents). Nevertheless, this
motif opens an elegiac vein that runs luxuriously throughout a leisurely
and picturesque poetic dilation: "Nor is Osiris seen / In Memphian grove
or green, / Trampling the enshowered grass with lowings loud . . ."
(XXIV.213–15). Only thus is the poem saved from foreclosing, by a pre-
mature apocalyptic event, the salvation history that begins a new phase
with the Incarnation.

A similar pressure of immediacy, one that in the Nativity Ode tends
to press poetry into apocalypse and is altogether impatient of the veils,
deferrals, and endless mediations that characterize a tradition of poetry as
prophetic revelation by means of allegory, can be felt especially strongly
in the diptych made up of "L'Allegro" and "Il Penseroso," where Milton
conceives the ambition to "attain / To something like Prophetic strain"
(173–74). There is a scheme of specular correspondences between the two
poems whereby each successive motif—from shepherds to Shakespeare—
in the one poem is loosely matched in the other by some comparable
theme but is, at the same time, also given a different twist and emphasis. The "beauty" in "L'Allegro"—potentially Milton's Beatrice—who in
the tower "lies / The cynosure of neighboring eyes" (79–80) turns out
in the correlative tower image of "Il Penseroso" to be none other than
Milton himself—"Or let my lamp at midnight hour / Be seen in some
high lonely tower": he is alone and is contemplating the constellations by
"immortal mind" (85 ff.). Here again, then, there is no external object for
Milton's prophetic faculty, no feminine Other who ignites his desire, but
only his own unmediated inspiration. Prophetic/poetic power is connected
with the absence of any object standing behind the image, and that perhaps explains why Orpheus loses his "half-regained Eurydice" (105) in
the outward-oriented activity and poetry of "L'Allegro" but recovers her
("made Hell grant what love did seek"—108) in the inward contemplation of "Il Penseroso." In *Paradise Lost*, Milton would fully realize what

he already seems to have anticipated here in his "minor" poems: prophetic sight accrues with loss of the view of Nature's book (III, proem).

By the time he wrote *Paradise Lost,* Milton had learned how to manage the compulsion toward immediacy in the apprehension of the divine so as to allow room for poetry and its mediation, its unfolding in rhetoric and images, of ecstatic experience. He had learned methods of indirection, whereby the divine, although not able to be made symbolically concrete, can nevertheless be suggested to the individual reader's experience through music and imagery.

The loosening up of symbolic as well as of syntactic structure that we observed in *Paradise Lost* affords Milton the opportunity to employ the persuasive and affecting resources of poetry—rather than apodictic statement and sacramental image of truth, such as we find in Dante—to the end of provoking in the reader an apprehension of the divine. This experience of immediacy, of transcendence, of accession of imaginative power in the Spirit, is Milton's substitute for an objective language of truth. Thus debate as to whether the symbolism in the Garden (for instance, of the "four main streams" that flow from Paradise's fountain and ramify into "mazy error") is Neoplatonic or typological, as found, for example, in Madsen,[13] misses the fundamental point that either type of symbolism is there, in any case, primarily just for "effect." Such debate is itself somewhat erroneous because these are not, for Milton, modes of figuring the true and real but are at most techniques for creating resonances or a sense of foreboding—with the proviso that the calculated effect may be as momentous as religious conversion and, consequently, salvation.

---

13. John Madsen, *From Shadowy Types to Truth: Studies in Milton's Symbolism* (New Haven: Yale University Press, 1968).

the logic of infinity in european romanticism

blake or leopardi?

I. Blake and the Logic of the Infinite

Even as elastic a term as *Romanticism,* while not necessarily in need of a univocal definition, has an intuitive sense and suggests paradigmatic qualities shared by typical exemplars. According to Northrop Frye, "the central theme of Romanticism is that of the attaining of an expanded consciousness,"[1] while for Thomas McFarland, among a number of leading motifs of the Romantic "sensibility"—solitude, imagination, organicism, medievalism, subjectivity—"the most constant of all defining factors is nature."[2] Not directly competing with these authors' approaches to Romanticism through myth and pastoral respectively, I wish to propose a different sort of dominant family resemblance trait. From the point of view of logic, or of the basic principles and schema that condition thinking, a crucial change comes about in the Romantic period: a shift from

---

1. Northrop Frye, *A Study of English Romanticism* (Chicago: University of Chicago Press, 1968), 42.

2. Thomas McFarland, "Romantic Imagination, Nature, and the Pastoral Ideal," in *Coleridge's Imagination: Essays in Memory of Pete Laver,* eds. R. Gravil, L. Newlyn, and N. Roe (London: Cambridge University Press, 1985), 8.

thinking in terms of the finite to thinking in terms of the infinite. Earlier, in the eighteenth century, man was more likely to mind only the finite, operating within well-defined limits. As Pope puts it in his *Essay on Man*,

> Know thy own point: this kind, this due degree
> Of blindness, weakness, Heaven bestows on thee.
>
> (Epistle I.vv.283–84)

And later, in the nineteenth century, another epochal shift would put the emphasis back on the finite: thus Kierkegaard conceived of his Knight of Faith as making the movement of infinity "but so that he keeps getting finitude out of it,"[3] and Nietzsche would pronounce God (and metaphysics) dead in order to affirm the finite as such.[4] These were understandable reactions to radical Romanticism, which made dizzying leaps to heady infinity that could not be sustained without some more solid grounding in the finite. Just during the historical span of European culture which has come to be recognized as the Romantic era, roughly 1775 to 1825, a window was opened upon infinity. In the mind-boggling words of Blake: "If the doors of our perception were cleansed everything would appear to man as it is, infinite" (*The Marriage of Heaven and Hell*, 1793). For a historical moment, reality was not within confines, and every characteristic production of the age gestured toward the infinite.

What was new was not simply a preoccupation with the concept of infinity. Instead, the way anything at all was viewed became conditioned by infinitely open-ended (but also, in some cases, infinitely totalizing) structures. Perception itself, far from being a mere datum, a "sense-impression," a given once and for all, became a never-ending quest, its object often intrinsically incomplete. All this I characterize as a matter of logic, not in order to throw down the gauntlet to philosophers who maintain that there are unchanging laws of thought, nor to suggest that the biology of the human mind would have evolved appreciably in a century, but simply to indicate that structures of infinity have become incorporated into the basic conceptual paradigm that underlies and regulates

---

3. Søren Kierkegaard, *Fear and Trembling*, trans. Alastair Hannay (New York: Penguin, 1985).

4. Cf., however, "Our New Infinite" and "Towards New Seas," *The Gay Science*, trans. Kaufman (New York: Random House, 1974), aphorisms 374, 371. Friedrich Nietzsche is in some ways a super-Romantic as well as an arch-critic of Romanticism through his constant self-overcoming. He, too, strives after the infinite—a new infinite of unlimited interpretations of "the unknown."

cultural production and exchange at this time. What counts as being real, and the sorts of activity considered as possible ways of knowing, are determined accordingly. The causes of the election or assimilation of such a paradigm might verisimilarly be found in the industrial revolution and urbanization, with the resultant desire to break free of the particularly stifling forms of confinement and bondage that were produced by these historical developments. But regardless of its causes and genealogical derivation, this new logic remains fundamental and peremptory in informing the thinking of the Romantics.

For the Age of Reason, reared on a classical foundation, any attempt to reason about things necessarily began with the procedure of defining—or we might say, more explicitly, "finitizing"—the objects of inquiry. Only what was determinate and encompassable was admitted as a reality worth reasoning about. It was believed that reason could stand outside of time and perform this work of defining "before" the actual experience or examination of the object began. In this way, one always began with a definite, a defined, a finite object. But if this act of defining is itself taken as part of the process of perceiving an object, then what is *first* perceived is something as yet *un*defined; the indefinite becomes prior to any finite object, and reality as such (as yet uninterpreted) becomes the infinite. This is how it was for the Romantics. For them, typically the only reality that counted was one that could *not* be fully grasped, one that was more glimpsed and guessed at, dreamed and desired, than demonstrably present or possessed.[5]

The historicizing of reason which makes possible the turn from an eighteenth-century worldview, in which the world could still be taxonomized, was worked out on a philosophical plane most thoroughly by Hegel. He took the categories that Kant had set up as "pure reason" and dragged them into history, showing them to be part of an evolving phenomenology of the mind. This maneuver seems to immerse man in the infinite rather than allowing him sovereignly to attain or possess knowledge of it. Indeed, myriad are the works representing the "knower" or world explorer as lost in a sea of mystery. Accordingly, the sea voyager becomes a stock topos of Romantic literature. It is uncanny how often Romantic form in general and would-be Romantic masterpieces in particular turn out to be incomplete. However, there was also a powerful

---

5. This has rendered Romanticism particularly prone to revivals in our postmodern context. On current efforts to "re-inherit" Romantic thought in contemporary continental philosophy, see *Philosophical Romanticism*, ed. Nikolas Kompridis (New York: Routledge, 2006).

conquering impulse among the Romantics, a conviction that no limit was unsurpassable, no imaginable possibility beyond the reach of actual achievement. In his later philosophy, particularly in the *Logic* and the *Encyclopedia,* Hegel theorized the infinite as a completed whole, and thus as something that *could* actually be realized.

The key movement in this later dialectical logic of infinity, which abstracts from the temporal element of the more commonly known thesis-antithesis-synthesis pattern famously applied to historical conflict, is the negation of the negation. All limits can be suspended, since they are merely negative: they presuppose something prior as positively given even in order to register at all. Negation is not necessarily the full stop of contradiction: simple difference is itself already a form of negation. But negation in this sense is internal to what is negated. It can be expounded in terms of what can be called the doctrine of internal relations. That is: all relations of a thing, consisting in its difference from everything else, every "other" or negation of it, are considered to be essential to the identity of the thing. Another way of putting this is to say that all relations are intrinsic. Any given thing comes to represent the Whole inasmuch as it is what it is only by virtue of *not* being, that is, of being different from, everything that it is not. Thus all the rest of reality is constitutive of its intrinsic nature. So the thing in this sense becomes identical with the Whole—as seen from a particular angle. The Whole can be grasped or understood in any particular through that particular's internal relatedness to all other particulars. Finally, by virtue of this universal relatedness, the particular becomes a "concrete universal."

This notion of infinity was elaborated by Hegel in deliberate contradistinction to the infinite as unlimited extension or unending duration—something that goes on without ever stopping—which became for him the "bad infinite" ("die schlechte Unendlichkeit"). What was bad about it, evidently, was that it could not be grasped: it eluded and frustrated every sort of comprehension. At least, this would be a frequent experience for the Romantic poets. Hegel saw it as illusory and incoherent, though we may suspect that his underlying motivations were not so different from theirs. The idea of the infinite as the completed whole, or as the concrete universal—the particular that becomes a symbol of every other particular in the universe—was intuited as powerfully as it ever would be by Blake in "Auguries of Innocence":

To see the World in a Grain of Sand
And a Heaven in a Wild Flower,

Hold Infinity in the palm of your Hand
And Eternity in an hour.

Perhaps no document besides Blake's "There is NO Natural Religion" [b] gives so explicit and succinct an exposition of the logic of infinity that becomes the most original and revolutionary conceptual paradigm of the Romantics. It will be worth examining point by point this declaration of philosophical principles in order to understand the inherent tendencies and commitments that the Romantic logic of infinity entails. The philosophical pedigree of this quintessentially Romantic mode of conceptualizing, and its inevitable ideological alignments, will turn out to be important for assessing even a poet as equivocally "Romantic" as Giacomo Leopardi. In "There is NO Natural Religion," Blake articulates intuitively and poetically, and for his own programmatic purposes, some of the impulses that were worked out with philosophical rigor and speculative power and precision in the tradition of German idealism.

> *I. Man's perceptions are not bounded by organs of perception. he perceives more than sense (tho' ever so acute) can discover.*

This is tantamount to asserting the primacy of feeling and/or intuition over sense-perception. There is an infinite subjective dimension to every perception. The sense datum is not just what it is, a "given" for the external organs of sense; rather, it is always already mediated by a human individual's inner world.

> *II. Reason or the ratio of all we have already known. is not the same that it shall be when we know more.*

This is Blake's assertion that reason is dialectical, that it is not a fixed foundation on which knowledge can be built but rather changes through its participation in the process of knowing. The categories of thought (the various 'ratios') that make experience comprehensible are not known prior to experience (a priori), as Kant maintained, but rather come to light themselves together with it.

> *III. [lacking]*

> *IV. The bounded is loathed by its possessor. The same dull round even of a univer[s]e would soon become a mill with complicated wheels.*

Here, Blake sets rolling the dynamic of desire which will be for the Romantics, and especially for Leopardi, one—and often *the*—crucial dimension of the infinite. Whatever is bounded and not infinite quickly becomes repugnant to human desire, which is conceived of as naturally open upon infinity rather than as directed to any definite object of finite fulfillment. And yet, not just more, but *all,* is demanded by this infinite desire:

> V. *If the many become the same as the few when possess'd, More! More!*
> *is the cry of a mistaken soul, less than All cannot satisfy Man.*

The notion that All is necessary to satisfy our desire is not found only in abstruse reaches of Idealist philosophy; it is a common Romantic apprehension:

> Yourself—your soul—in pity give me all,
>   Withhold no atom's atom or I die . . .
>   (Keats, "I Cry Your Mercy")

Such an exclamation expresses the logic of infinite desire. It can be satisfied only by an infinite object, a need to which Hegel tried to answer by means of the concept of the completed whole ("das vollendete Ganze") in place of the bad infinite. With this conception, Hegel refused to accept a perpetual state of unfulfillment, which aims always at something more, but opted rather to live the infinity of desire as itself a form of perfect fulfillment.

A "bad" infinite is always only potential: its basic representation is the endless series of integers, to which one can always add, $n + 1$, ad infinitum—unlike the actual infinite, which *exists* and is not merely a constructible idea. The actual infinite, for its discoverer in modern mathematics, Georg Cantor, was, in effect, God. Cantor understood mathematical set theory to be a proof of God's existence.[6] More recently, Alain Badiou has given an avowedly atheistic interpretation of the actual infinite as inherently multiple.[7] The Romantics are situated in the history of

---

6. Georg Cantor, *Grundlagen einer allgemeinen Mannigfaltigkeitslehre (Foundation of a General Theory of Aggregates,* 1883). For Cantor's correspondence with the Vatican on this subject, see "On the Theory of the Transfinite: Correspondence of Georg Cantor and J. B. Cardinal Frenzelin (1885–86) with an Afterword by Lyndon H. LaRouche, Jr.," *Fidelio* 3/3 (Fall 1994): 97–110.

7. Alain Badiou, *L'être et l'évévement* (Paris: Seuil, 1988).

infinity, with special attention to its theological implications, by Markus Enders,[8] as renovating the idea of the bad infinite. However, Blake still agrees with Hegel that desire must be capable of fulfillment—infinitely, and this entails that infinity must actually exist. As Blake explicitly states:

> VI. *If any could desire what he is incapable of possessing, despair must be his eternal lot.*

Precisely this proposition could hardly be more acutely actualized or more authentically expressed than it was by Giacomo Leopardi. To him fell the lot of living out the drama of infinite *un*fulfillment. Leopardi builds his pessimistic view of the human predicament on exactly this premise. But, for Blake, the conclusion is just the opposite:

> VII. *The desire of Man being Infinite the possession is Infinite & himself Infinite.*

This seems to be an outright inference from wish to reality. Is it just wishful thinking? Desire itself was for Blake a truer, more accurate index of reality than either reason or sense. The latter faculties attempted to place limits upon which among man's infinite dreams and fancies could actually be realized in the world, but for Blake the fact of a thing's being desired or imagined was existence itself. It could not be more real than what it was felt or fancied to be, since intellectual or mental or imaginative existence was the only, or at least the truest, reality. This priority was written into Blake's very way of having a world:

> My Houses are Thoughts; My Inhabitants; Affections . . .
> (*Jerusalem*, chapter 2, verse 32)

Indeed the tendency in Blake and in Romanticism in general was to view all reality as a projection from human consciousness. Frye describes Romanticism as "the first major phase in an imaginative revolution which has carried on until our own day," and he cites a "recovery of projection" and the view of God as "an aspect of our own identity" as fundamental to the "new mythological construction."[9] As Blake declares in *The Marriage of Heaven and Hell*:

---

8. Markus Enders, *Zum Begriff der Unendlichkeit im abendländischen Denken: Unendlichkeit Gottes und Unendlichkeit der Welt* (Hamburg: Boethiana, 2006).

9. Frye, *A Study of English Romanticism*, 13–15.

> Thus men forgot that All deities reside in the human breast
>
> (plate II)

Morris Pecham, making even more astounding claims than Frye for Romanticism at the end of eighteenth century as the greatest shift in consciousness since the beginning of cities in the fourth millennium BC, defines the transformation in terms of mind having no access to what is not mind but rather moving always within some mental modality, never confronting anything else.[10]

This equating of the mental (Blake's preferred term, as in "I have Mental Joy & Mental Health / And Mental Friends & Mental Wealth," "I rose up at the dawn of day") with the real links Romanticism to a kind of philosophical idealism. In Blake, of course, the connection is made more by poetic intuition and religious belief than by reasoned demonstration. He wages a characteristically enthusiastic polemic against the scientific materialism of his England, discerning another visionary and much more compelling reality beneath or above it:

> The atoms of Democritus
> And Newton's particles of light
> Are sands upon the Red Sea shore
> Where Israel's tents to shine so bright.

In this regard Blake, who is otherwise so eccentrically individual, was not at all alone. He expressed the sentiments of a new age of culture. The idealist influences on Romantic thought are made more patent by Novalis's enthusiastic embrace of Fichte's philosophy of absolute self-reflection and by Coleridge's appropriation of Kant's transcendental philosophy. However, Blake's idealism, too, has clear affinities, not only with empirical idealism in the style of Bishop Berkeley's philosophy of ideas as the only fundamental reality, but also with the speculative thinking of the infinite that, just a little later, would be pursued on the continent by the German idealists, especially Hegel.

Nevertheless, Blake's imaginative and visionary idealism is vehemently opposed to any type of absolute idealism of the human "I." For Blake, rational, scientific culture, with its apparatus of subject and object, inevitably brings with it a reduction to the navel-gazing self or ego. The next plank of his manifesto against Natural Religion declares:

---

10. *Romanticism and Culture: A Tribute to Morse Peckham and a Bibliography of His Work*, ed. H. W. Matalene (Columbia, SC: Camden House, 1984).

Application. He who sees the Infinite in all things sees God. He who sees the Ratio only sees himself only."

And from this theocentric vision follows Blake's "Conclusion" high-lighting poetic and prophetic perception as necessary to avoid the self-enclosure of the secular and scientific worldview that he perceives from his vantage point in the eighteenth century already in all its menacing oppressiveness:

> Conclusion. If it were not for the Poetic or Prophetic character the Philo-sophic & Experimental would soon be at the ratio of all things, & stand still unable to do other than repeat the same dull round over again.
> Therefore God becomes as we are, that we may be as he is.

Blake's idealism is a prophetic and poetic idealism that abhors the rationalization that was one of the driving impulses of German idealism. Of course, the reason ("Vernunft") of Hegel and Hölderlin and Schelling is itself a higher faculty capable of intuitively perceiving the unity of things rather than the dissecting, analytic faculty abominated by Blake as "ratio." The latter is closer to what the German idealists call "Ver-stand" (usually translated as "understanding"). Elaborated rather by the higher faculty of unitive vision, which discerns "what holds the world together in its inner core" ("was die Welt / Im Innersten zusammen halt"), as Goethe's Faust puts it,[11] Blake's intellectual idealism shares a common source with German idealism in Jacob Boehme. It annexes, moreover, a type of Platonic idealism in affirming the permanent archetypal forms of "Vision or Imagination" that are constantly (re)created by artists as "What Eternally Exists, Really and Unchangeably" ("A Vision of the Last Judgment").[12]

This natural proclivity of Romanticism for idealist philosophical underpinnings will help us to understand why Leopardi, a committed materialist, was such an anomalous sort of Romantic. It will also help us to explain why Romanticism was in general so much less successful in Southern Europe, where idealism of volition and feeling never carried complete conviction or developed with untrammeled vigor. (Idealism, of

---

11. Johann Wolfgang von Goethe, *Faust Eine Tragödie* (Stuttgart: Reclam. 1971) part I, line 383.

12. On "Blakes platonischer Idealismus," see further Bernadette Malinowski, "*Das Heilige sei mein Wort*": *Paradigmen prophetischer Dichtung von Klopstock bis Whitman* (Würzburg: Königshausen und Neumann, 2002), 312–17.

course, is meant here in an epistemological, not a moral, sense.) In Mediterranean regions, discovering myth as projection was not the revealing of an infinite inner world but rather the exposure of the emptiness of the very ideas that had been cherished as explaining the fundamental nature of things. Only in Northern Europe could the world be interpreted as a representation of the will—most consistently and provocatively by Arthur Schopenhauer in *The World as Will and Representation* (*Die Welt als Wille und Vorstellung*, 1844), and he was followed in this by Nietzsche. Wherever classical culture dominated over gothic, the intellectualist bias of the Greeks prevented the substitution of affective and conative dimensions—which are much more palpably amenable to the logic of the infinite—for the cognitive as primary reality. Unlike emotion and volition, rationality, taken in isolation and according to Leopardi's way of construing it, has no inherent or substantial content: reason can only supply the form, pictorially the outline, of its world of objects. And this is precisely the antithesis of the infinite. Hence the difficult adaptation of Romanticism to Leopardi's cultural environment and epistemological framework.[13]

II. Leopardi and the Logic of the Infinite

The logic of infinite—and therefore unfulfillable—desire lies at the very heart of Leopardi's poetic vision: such a logic determines the valences of his poetry's obsessive themes of youth, illusion, and love. All of Leopardi's personae are indelibly marked by it. Consalvo's "infinite affection" ("infinito affetto") typifies the nature of precisely "romantic" love in Leopardi, the envisaged end of which can be nothing less than "infinite Happiness" ("infinita / Felicità," "Amore e Morte," vv.38–39). And not only love but beauty or anything whatever that is desirable necessarily takes on the dimensions of infinity. Thus life can be felt as happy and worth living only by the very young, for whom it is still an unlimited unknown lying before them, or else by those who live through them vicariously. Leopardi often speaks in his poems from the point of view of his own past youth:

---

13. For reflections on some of the anomalies of Italian Romanticism as it emerges from its Enlightenment heritage and a contestation of its almost universally assumed marginality, see Joseph Luzzi, *Romantic Europe and the Ghost of Italy* (New Haven: Yale University Press, 2008).

E che pensieri immensi,
Che dolci sogni mi spirò la vista
Di quel lontano mar, quei monti azzurri,
Che di qua scopro, e che varcare un giorno
Io mi pensava, arcani mondi, arcana
Felicità fingendo al viver mio![14]
   ("Le Ricordanze," vv.19–24)

But what vast thoughts and what sweet visions then
That distant sea called forth, and those blue mountains
Discerned from far away!—which then I thought
To cross some day, inventing for myself
An unknown world, and unknown happiness
To suit my life to come . . .

The fundamental condition of the dear time of youth ("il caro tempo giovanil"), or more accurately of preadolescence, which is "the only good time," is limitless hope: the faraway sea and azure mountains are looked upon as horizons marking the thresholds beyond which inexhaustible worlds will be gained in the future. Similarly, the vague hope of a future ("quel vago avvenir che in menti avevi," v.12) inspires Sylvia's "perpetual song" ("perpetuo canto," v.9). Yet further permutations, according to which only time unbegun can be contemplated eagerly, include the affirmations that the very early part of the day, just after awaking, before daily experience, is the only good part ("Cantico del gallo silvestre") and that only future times can be thought of with pleasure ("Dialogo di un venditore d'almanacchi e di un passegere").[15] Leopardi believed that whatever was actual rather than only anticipated became too sharply defined; it lost its appearance of infinity and so could no longer delight or attract. The playful little lad or "garzoncello" in "Il sabato del villaggio" has reason to be cheerful on the day that *precedes* his beginning the festival of life ("Giorno . . . che precorre alla festa di tua vita," vv.46–47), when *all* still awaits him: better that it not begin, not enter into the dimension of expiring time that renders hopes and dreams finite, which is as much as to say, for Leopardi, totally frustrating and futile.

---

14. Leopardi's poems are quoted from the edition of G. Getto and E. Sanguinetti, *Canti* (Milan: Mursia, 1977–82). Verse translations, unless otherwise indicated, are from John Heath-Stubbs, *Poems from Giacomo Leopardi* (London: John Lehman, 1946).

15. *Operette morali*, ed. Saverio Orlando (Milano: Rizzoli, 1976). Translations from the *Operette morali* follow the bilingual edition of Giovanni Cecchetti (Berkeley: University of California Press, 1982). Other translations are my own.

Leopardi produced an explicit theoretical formulation of what he took to be the fact that human desire is dominated by the logic of the infinite (or that only what is infinite can be desired) in his "teoria del piacere" ("theory of pleasure"):

> La somma della teoria del piacere e si può dir anche, della natura dell'animo nostro e di qualunque vivente, è questa. Il vivente si ama senza limite nessuno, e non cessa mai di amarsi. Dunque non cessa mai di desiderarsi il bene, e si desidera il bene senza limiti. Questo bene in sostanza non è altro che il piacere. Qualunque piacere, ancorché grande, ancorché reale, ha limiti. Dunque nessun piacere possibile è proporzionato ed uguale alla misura dell'amore che il vivente porta a se stesso. Quindi nessun piacere può soddisfare il vivente. . . . Dunque ogni vivente, per ciò stesso che vive (e quindi si ama, e quindi desidera assolutamente la felicità, vale a dire una felicità senza limiti, e questa è impossibile, e quindi il desiderio suo non può esser soddisfatto), per ciò stesso, dico, che vive, non può essere attualmente felice.[16]

> The sum of the theory of pleasure and one could also say, of the nature of our soul and of whatever lives, is this. The living creature loves itself without any limit, and never ceases to love itself. Therefore it never ceases to desire the good for itself, and it desires its own good without limits. This good is substantially nothing other than pleasure. Any pleasure, though it be great, though it be real, has a limit. Therefore no possible pleasure is proportionate and equal to the measure of love that the living creature bears to itself. Thus no pleasure is able to satisfy the living being. . . . Therefore every living being, by the very fact that it lives (and thus loves itself, and thus desires happiness absolutely, which is to say a happiness without limits, which is impossible, and thus its desire cannot be satisfied), by the very fact, I say, that it lives, cannot be actually happy.

In this insistence on the infinity of human desire, Leopardi is fully comparable with his contemporaries. Percy Bysshe Shelley, for example, writes of his Alastor that "so long as it is possible for his desires to point towards objects thus infinite and unmeasured, he is joyous, and tranquil, and self-possessed" (*Alastor,* Preface).[17] Where Leopardi differs

---

16. *Zibaldone*, 646–48. Quoted in Luigi Blasucci, "La Posizione Ideologica delle *Operette morali*," in *Critica e storia letteraria, studi offerti a Mario Fubini* (Padova: Liviana, 1970).

17. *Shelley's Poetry and Prose*, eds. Donald Reiman and Neil Freistat (New York: Norton Critical Edition, 2002).

from other Romantics is in never believing that this feeling for infinity could in any way coincide with reality. For Blake, desire became a primary dimension of reality, a world in itself, in fact "infinite worlds of delight" expanding in the human imagination, which was the "real and eternal world," as he declares at the outset of *Jerusalem*; and for others, some kind of idealism of the spirit made viable a superior order of reality, where the infinite and the eternal were realized at least in moments of transcendent vision. Even the usually anti-metaphysical Shelley is representative in his affirmation that "a poet participates in the eternal, the infinite, and the one."[18] For Leopardi, however, as fundamental as the infinite was to every human desire, it remained unambiguously unreal, indeed a total illusion. The history of the human race ("storia del genere umano") is fundamentally conditioned from its inception by the inability of God Himself (Jove) to satisfy men's infinite desire—"Neither could he share his own infinity with mortal creatures, nor make matter infinite, nor infinite the perfection of things and the happiness of humans" ("Né anche poteva communicare la propria infinità colle creature mortali, né fare la materia infinita, ne infinita la perfezione delle cose e la felicità degli uomini").[19] From this premise Leopardi infers that, in order to stem the rising tide of suicides, the god resolved to create illusions of the infinite in such shapes and forms as echoes, dreams, and ideals. Such unreal existences have something vague and indefinite about them and can be objects of infinite passion, so as to satisfy at least men's imaginations:

E risolutosi di moltiplicare le apparenze di quell'infinito che gli uomini sommamente desideravano (dappoi che egli non gli poteva compiacere della sostanza), e volendo favorire e pascere le coloro imaginazioni. (68–69)

And resolved to multiply the appearances of that infinite that men most highly desired (since he could not gratify them with the substance of it), and wanting to favor and feed their imaginations.

Thus the infinite belongs unequivocally to the illusory, and illusions are humanly attractive and comforting just insofar as they wear the aspect of infinity, which alone can answer to the longings of human desire.

---

18. *English Essays: Sidney to Macaulay; Shelley, A Defence of Poetry* (Cambridge: The Harvard Classics, 1909–14), par. 4.

19. "Storia del Genere Umano" is the first composition in *Operette morali*.

At an early stage in his career, Leopardi took a positive view of the value of illusion. His *Discourse on Romantic Poetry* (*Discorso di un Italiano intorno alla poesia romantica,* 1818) maintains that poetry's function is to deceive the fancy, now that in the scientific age it can no longer deceive the intellect, as it presumably did in the guise of myth in ancient times. He accuses the Romantics (whom he is acquainted with, very inadequately, through articles in Milanese journals) of denying poetry the privilege of deceiving and of insisting instead that it conform to reason and truth. He attributes to the Romantics the following prescription: "poetry no longer being able to deceive men, it must no longer pretend or lie, but must always follow after reason and the truth" ("la poesia non potendo più ingannare gli uomini, non deve più fingere né mentire, ma bisogna che sempre vada dietro alla ragione e alla verità").[20] Leopardi would not accept the Romantic interest in themes drawn from contemporary life—often urban and industrial—nor their departure from classical models. He maintained that poetry was eternal and immutable and should always imitate nature, specifically the nature that the Greeks had imitated, since only they were ingenuous enough to imitate nature "naturally." At this stage in his career, Leopardi made a clear choice for the fictive rather than the real, and in so doing he refused the Romantic renewal. The Romantics were interested not in Arcady but in real life, the contemporary scene—or else in a visionary reality that was revealing in a prophetic sense of the deeper meaning of the times. Young Leopardi would have none of this. He contemptuously charges the Romantics with maintaining that the poet must adapt himself "to our customs and opinions and to the truths that are known presently" ("ai costumi e alle opinioni nostre e alle verità conosciute presentemente," 777).

A little later, however, Leopardi reversed these positions and became the great poet of the pathetic—his vehement condemnation of the pathetic manner of the Romantics notwithstanding. Rather than by the naive imitation of nature, in the classical mode of the Greeks, he thenceforth made poetry by introspective reflection lamenting the loss of illusion through the ineluctable encroachment of truth. In this new approach, instead of insisting that the poet's task is to felicitously deceive the fancy, he makes his poetry out of the crushing pathos of the demise of just such a beautiful illusion of natural harmony and innocence. Leopardi transforms

---

20. *Opere,* ed. G. Getto (Milano: Mursia, 1966), 915. Also highly illuminating on this subject is Bruno Biral, *La posizione storica di Giacomo Leopardi* (Turin: Einaudi, 1974).

Enlightenment disillusion brought about through implacable philosophical reflection and its inevitable consequence of disenchantment into a fertile resource for poetic inspiration. This can even be understood psychoanalytically in terms of the processes of mourning and melancholia and their being channeled into artistic expression.[21]

Leopardi recounts his conversion, the "total mutation in me, and passage from the ancient to the modern" ("mutazione totale in me, e il passaggio dallo stato antico al moderno"), which took place in 1819, in a *Zibaldone* entry from July 2, 1820. Nevertheless, what remains constant for him before and after this transformation is the absolute incompatibility of truth and illusion. Whether he is fulminating against the Romantics for contaminating sweet illusion with the poison of truth, or making poetry out of truth's pathetic destruction of illusion, the two together, in his thought, make a sign of contradiction over human life. This is his theme from the beginning to the end of the *Canti*: the complete and total antagonism between "il vero," the true, and anything lovely, hopeful, comforting, pleasant, or even just tolerable. All such amenable perceptions are illusions that cannot withstand the light of day or of truth. This is succinctly and poignantly expressed at the core of Leopardi's poetry in words addressed to Silvia (representing for him youth, beauty, and life itself):

> All'apparir del vero
> Tu, misera, cadesti . . .
>   (vv.60–61).[22]

> For when the truth appeared,
> Poor thing, you fell away; . . .

For Leopardi, there can be no dialectical mediation between the "sweet deceits" ("dolci inganni") of Nature and the "unpropitious truth" ("infausta verità") of Fate ("Il risorgimento"). The *Operette morali* mount a relentless series of attacks on the anthropocentric illusions of mankind in the name of the truths that nature is indifferent to men and

---

21. Fabio Camilletti, *Leopardi's Nymphs: Grace, Melancholy, and the Uncanny* (Oxford: Legenda, 2013).

22. It is incredibly ironic that Leopardi should at this moment precisely speak of the *appearance* ("apparir") of truth. Does his rhetoric undercut his overt intention, or does he show himself to be conscious after all (or before all, even before Nietzsche) that truth itself is an illusion?

the universe not at all designed with a view to their happiness. "Aspasia" and the cycle of love poems together comprise another, later, concerted effort to represent the triumph of truth over illusion, which is never absent from Leopardi's thought; hence they have been aptly described as a kind of "canto di disinganno" ("song of disillusion").[23]

This absolute dichotomy between illusion and truth, poetry and reality, distinguishes Leopardi from other Romantics. Integral to the Romantic revolution was a new conception of the poet's art as one of creating and shaping, as well as interpreting, reality itself and even higher reality. Poetry claimed for itself the status of a higher truth. It would no longer settle for being a mere adornment to other more basic or powerful kinds of knowledge, a rhetorical ornament to be exploited for society's entertainments or indoctrinations. Poets became for Shelley the "unacknowledged legislators of the world" ("Defence of Poetry"), while Wordsworth and Coleridge were convinced that the imagination at least "half creates" the world that humans perceive. This redefinition of the poet's role can be seen as an inevitable consequence of the dialectical sort of logic which, subsequent to Kant's *Critique of Judgment,* dethroned pure, analytic reason and placed it on a level with imagination and will and emotion to vie for authority—or, more commonly, in an outright subservient position: "Reason is to imagination as the instrument to the agent" (Shelley, "Defence").[24] The truth for the Romantics was at least as likely to lie in what one felt instinctively or emotionally as in what one conceived rationally or perceived by the physical senses. This much was contained from the beginning in Goethe's famous dictum, "Gefühl ist alles—Feeling is all." Faust brings forth this declaration in answer to Gretchen's question concerning his religious skepticism and concludes that names and concepts are but empty sound and smoke ("Name ist Schall und Rauch," *Faust* I, lines 3457–58). But precisely in this regard, Leopardi is an anomaly, for he would never relinquish reason as the only adequate organ for the discovery of truth and for the unveiling of the real: for him, poetry, with its wooing of the imagination and arousal of emotion, was nothing but a lie and an illusion.[25]

---

23. Leo Spitzer, "L'Aspasia di Leopardi," *Cultura Neolatina* (fasc. 2–3, col. XXIII, 1963).

24. Text available online at www.gutenberg.org.

25. Exceptions to this "never" can be found in a few *Zibaldone* references to analogical and imaginative capacities of children and poets to apprehend truths and causes intuitively. Within Leopardi's thought, such stock notions of aesthetic theory are "uncharacteristic and undeveloped," as is pointed out by Nicholas Perella, *Night and the Sublime in Giacomo Leopardi* (Berkeley: University of California Press, 1970), 114–15.

Whereas for Keats, Beauty and Truth were one, for Leopardi they were absolutely irreconcilable. Beauty could subsist only where Truth was not, for Truth automatically extinguished every amenable illusion. It is interesting that something of this antagonism between Truth and Beauty is registered even by Keats, who defined the supreme poetic gift as the negative capability of "being in uncertainties, mysteries, doubts, without any irritable reaching after fact & reason" (Letter to George and Thomas Keats, 21, 27 December, 1817).[26] And this disjunction between what is true and poetic experience is the presupposition also of Coleridge's famous formulation: "that willing suspension of disbelief for the moment, which constitutes poetic faith." A poem, says Coleridge, "proposes for its immediate object pleasure, not truth" (*Biographia Literaria,* chapter XIV).[27] Nevertheless, Coleridge understands imagination as a repetition of the power that creates the real world: "The primary imagination I hold to be the living power and prime agent of all human perception, and as a repetition in the finite mind of the eternal act of creation of the infinite I AM. The secondary I consider as an echo of the former . . . differing only in degree . . ." (*Biographia Literaria,* chapter XIII). And for Wordsworth, "Poetry is the first and last of all knowledge." He does not hesitate to claim that poetry is self-evident truth: "Aristotle, I have been told, has said that poetry is the most philosophic of all writing; it is so: its object is truth, not individual and local, but general, and operative; not standing upon external testimony, but carried alive into the heart by passion; truth which is its own testimony . . ." (preface to 2nd ed. of *Lyrical Ballads*).[28]

These positions on the relation of poetry and knowledge, beauty, and truth, far from being always self-consistent, are remarkable mainly for their fluidity, but this is just what makes them so different from Leopardi's. There is in them exactly that dialectic between truth and appearance that Leopardi never countenanced. The Italian poet and thinker never accepted that illusion is in a dialectical relation with the true and real, the mind's phantoms sometimes becoming more real than external objects—as is so typical in Romantic literature. For the German and English Romantics, empirical reality had been relativized, turned into mere appearance—programmatically by the philosophy of Kant. Illusions, real to the mind or experienced as real, had the same general onto-

26. *Keats's Poetry and Prose,* ed. Jeffrey N. Cox (New York: Norton Critical Edition, 2008).

27. Text available online at www.gutenberg.org.

28. Text available online at www.gutenberg.org.

logical status—namely, phenomenal—as the outer sensible world. Indeed most often an interior, an individual, a passionate dimension of existence asserted itself as the true, real, and important one. Moreover, as the empirical objects in which the world consisted for Enlightenment reason turned to appearance, another reality was "sensed" to stand behind them (in Kant's system, the "things-in-themselves," *Dinge an sich*). This other reality could not be grasped conceptually in the way that things in the orderly world of the age of reason presumably could be. It was beyond rational comprehension and in its essence infinite. However Leopardi's epistemological assumptions, in spite of all this, remained substantially those of the eighteenth century: French rationalism on an empirical basis derived from Locke through Gravina.[29] That appearance and reality should somehow be interdependent and interpenetrating was anathema to philosophies bent precisely on separating the one from the other clearly and distinctly. Nevertheless, this refusal to surrender critical rationality could be viewed not as retrograde but as a rejection in advance of dialectical reason and a leap forward *almost* to Nietzsche, minus the latter's radical skepticism with regard to truth.[30]

Leopardi never abandoned his tenacious adherence to Enlightenment reason. In the culminating poem of his last period, "La Ginestra," he castigates his own "proud and foolish century" ("secol superbo e sciocco"), for having turned its back on the "light" that had shined because it could not bear to face the harsh truth that nature had ordained:

Così ti spiaque il vero
Dell'aspra sorte e del depresso loco
Che natura ci diè. Per questo il tergo
Vigliaccamente rivolgesti al lume
Che il fè palese; . . .
    ("La Ginestra," vv.78–82)

And thus
The truth displeased you, telling

---

29. Ettore Mazzale, "Osservazioni sul *Discorso di un italiano*," in *Leopardi e il Settecento: Atti del I Convegno internazionale di studi leopardiani* (Florence: Olschki, 1964).

30. Massimo Lollini, *Il vuoto della forma: Scrittura, testimonianza e verità* (Genova: Marietti, 2001), and Nicholas Rennie, *Speculating on the Moment: The Poetics of Time and Recurrence in Goethe, Leopardi, and Nietzsche* (Göttingen: Wallstein, 2005), are both attentive in their different ways to these intriguing connections between Leopardi and Nietzsche.

Of that low station and harsh destiny
Nature has given us. So, like a coward
You turned your back upon the light, which showed
This truth to you . . .

Romantic feeling for the infinite unhappily married to Enlightenment rationality was Leopardi's prescription for pessimism. He accepted as fact that human desire was ineradicably determined by the logic of infinity, yet he never confounded this *feeling* with reality, which could be known with certainty, according to him, in all its miserable paltriness and caducity, by the powers of reason.

Thus Leopardi left no possibility of escape from the "infinite vanity of all," ("l'infinita vanità del tutto," 'A Se Stesso'). And he seemed to relish the most unrelieved, unbearable formulations of his dismal conviction. In one letter to his friend Pietro Giordano (6 March, 1820), he turned the idea three different ways just to show how it was always exactly the same:

la certezza della nullità delle cose
(the certainty of the nullity of things)

quella verità universale che tutto è nulla
(that universal truth that all is nothing)

non c'è altro vero che il nulla
(there is no other truth than the nothing)

All this he puts down to "the barbaric instruction of reason" ("il barbaro insegnamento della ragione").

We cannot but note the unequivocal tone and unqualified form of these declarations and identify them as the handiwork of dogmatic rather than dialectical reason (here we recall the aggressively mechanical style of the syllogisms binding together the necessary links in man's unhappiness which formed the "teoria del piacere"). This form is intrinsic to the meaning of such utterances. To give reasons for them would be to weaken and belie their nature as axiomatic, self-evident, unqualified truths.

Tutto è male. Cioè tutto quello che è, è male; che ciascuna cosa esista è un male; ciascuna cosa esiste per fin di male; l'esistenza è un male e ordinato al male; il fine dell'universo è il male; l'ordine e lo stato, le leggi, l'andamento naturale dell'universo non sono altro che male.

All is bad. That is, all that which is, is bad; that each thing exists is an ill; each thing exists for the purpose of ill; existence is an ill and is ordered for ill; the end of the universe is the ill; the order and the state, the laws, the natural going on of the universe are nothing but bad.

The same absolute and objective mode characterizes the poet's declarations in verse that unhappiness is the inevitable lot, by a universal law of nature, of every creature born, without exception:

Però, se nominar lice talvolta
Con propria nome il ver, non altro in somma
Fuor che infelice, in qualsivoglia tempo,
E non pur né civili ordini e modi,
Ma della vita in tutte l'altre parti,
Per essenza insanabile, e per legge
Universal, che terra e cielo abbraccia,
Ogni nato sarà.
("Palinodia al Marchese Gino Capponi," vv. 190–97)

However, if it is sometimes permissible to name
the truth with its own name, nothing other than
unhappy, finally, in whatever time,
and not only by virtue of civil orders and customs,
but of life in all its facets,
by incurable essence, and by universal
law, which embraces heaven and earth,
will be every creature born.

Given that desire, will, and emotion are inexorably subject to the logic of infinity, which yet totally fails to coincide with a reality that is known with certainty (Leopardi's "certezze") by reason, human beings are doomed to be unhappy. Most distressingly, they know rationally that infinity itself, which they cannot help desiring, is an illusion. Such happiness as may be possible could be based only on ignorance—hence happier the beasts, and hence most miserable of all the most intelligent and sensitive of humans (cf. "Dialogo della Natura e di un' Anima," "Tasso," etc.).

The logic of an infinity felt as necessary and yet known to be impossible for humans to attain is the key to understanding Leopardi's obsessive utterances about the nothingness or "nullità" of everything. It is not obvious how Leopardi can insist that all is nothing. Is that not being absurdly (and uninterestingly) pessimistic? There is *something*, after all—even if only this very denial itself. That much is evident. Yet what Leopardi says is true and of the utmost significance, if we consider that all that exists in the finite world *is* as nothing when measured against the infinite. As Pascal had perceived: "The finite annihilates itself in the presence of the infinite and becomes pure nothing" ("Le fini s'annéantie en présence de l'infini, et devient un pur néant").[31] Leopardi states the same principle in his *Zibaldone* (4174), only for him, unlike Pascal, the true Infinite is not God but is, instead, Nothing: "all that exists is infinitely small in comparison with the true infinite, so to speak, of the non-existent, of the nothing" ("il tutto esistente e infinitamente piccolo a paragone della infinità vera, per dir così, del non esistente, del nulla"). What would be something, what would be real, if reality were commensurable to human need and desire, is only the infinite. To this extent, Leopardi is thinking on the basis of the paradigm that we have described as the logic of infinity: it is integral to his thought, so much so that it is not even adduced as a premise but is simply assumed. It functions for him, in effect, as a kind of underlying logical necessity.

This same type of logic also explains the definitive form of Leopardi's pessimism, his so-called materialistic pessimism.[32] Again, it is puzzling to us why the pains and problems that confront man as a material creature should be taken as so absolutely negative and defeating of every good thing in life. Is it true, as the "Dialogo della Natura e di un Islandese" insists, that no happiness, no positive experience of life whatsoever, is possible just because there are some pains, some nuisances, and some calamities to be endured at the hand of nature? This seems to be an unduly pessimistic way of adding up the sums of good and ill—only the ill counts. Yet now we are in a position to understand why for Leopardi the good is not good at all unless it is infinitely good. Indeed, from the perspective of the logic of infinity, the fact that any external ills can impinge on consciousness is itself devastating, for it makes the illusion of consciousness's infinity untenable. If something other than consciousness can stand over against it and even hurt it, consciousness is not absolute: it is placed in the midst of and is subjected to a world of contingencies. Evidently, the state that Leopardi would consider happy, in true Romantic fashion, is one where everything would be incorporated by the subject's consciousness, which would thus become the infinite.

---

31. Pascal's *Pensées* are quoted by Giuseppe Ungaretti, "Secondo Discorso su Leopardi," *Paragone* 10 (Firenze: Sansoni, 1950), 26.

32. Cf. Sebastiano Timpanaro, "Alcune Osservazioni sul Pensiero del Leopardi," *Classicismo e illuminismo nell'Ottocento* (Pisa: Nistri-Lischi, 1965), 133–228.

All this is so Romantic as to make us feel that Leopardi, rather than being a marginal Romantic, is the one who followed certain of its premises most unswervingly and without compromises to their radical conclusions. The whole crisis of modernity is contained in embryo in Leopardi's taking for granted that man no longer fits into the universe, that it ought rather to be *for him*. In "Storia del genere umano," man's role and the source of his happiness, it is assumed, originally is and should and can only be the contemplation of the natural world that surrounds him, with the correlative implication that this is the purpose nature should serve, namely, mankind's amusement. Men have at first "little less than a feeling of happiness" ("poco meno che opinione di felicità") because they are pleased "insatiably to look at and contemplate heaven and earth" ("insaziabilmente di riguardare e di considerare il cielo e la terra").

This is crucially different from the medieval idea of *contemplatio Dei*, according to which the human being is not the center of the universe of contemplation but rather is called toward a center above and beyond—namely, God—out of the distance and alienation of the world. Nevertheless, even the medieval notion underscores the dignity of man, who is valued not for any extrinsic function or service he performs but for his most intimate capacity of loving, for his very (albeit derivative) being. Contemplation was considered to be the highest calling of humanity: "Mary has chosen the better part, and it shall not be taken away from her" (Luke 10:42).

But, in the modern age, humanity's whole reason for being must be defined exclusively in terms of itself. Leopardi's parable in "Storia del genere umano" represents the inherent contradictions that man experiences in trying to do this as his subservience to the gods. Because the gods create him in order to serve their own purposes, he cannot be infinite and an end unto himself. That would be contrary to "those functions and purposes that, in accordance with divine decrees, men had to exercise and fulfill" ("quegli uffici e quelle utilità che gli uomini dovevano, secondo l'intenzione e i decreti divini, esercitare e produrre"). Indeed man would have opted out of existence altogether had not the gods reacted in order that this not happen and mar the perfection of the whole that they had created. However, the perfection in question is for the gods and emphatically not for humans, and this is a motive for complaint also in "Canto di un pastore errante per l'Asia":

Questo io conosco e sento,
Che degli eterni giri,
Che dell'esser mio frale,

Qualche bene o contento
Avrà fors' altri; a me la vita è male.
       (vv. 100–104)

Yet this I know and feel:
The everlasting round,
And my own feeble being,
May be a source of pleasure and of good
To others, but for me this life is evil.

This implicit protest against the conditions of human existence as serving a purpose extrinsic to itself is easily demythologized: the divine decrees, as is fully elaborated in the "Operette" which follow the "Storia del genere umano," turn out to be the structures of finiteness—biological needs, physical limitations, and vulnerability.

For Leopardi, any limitation per se is felt as an impediment to happiness. Whereas medieval and even Renaissance human beings founded their happiness upon the place assigned to them in the scheme of things, and classical humanity, too, in the injunction "know thyself," was enjoined to keep within its limitations, the Romantic cannot abide finitude. And no Romantic demonstrates this better than Leopardi. As such, he represents the epitome of the secular predicament of the modern poet and person in general. He found no escape—unlike other poets after him, including Dickinson, who do find ways of connecting with a theological vision of the infinite even from within the straits of this predicament. Most striking of all is the abyss that separates him from his fellow countryman, Dante. Leopardi's personal plight and dramatic poetic struggle graphically display the extreme consequences to which Dante's secular-mindedness would lead once it was uncoupled, among his modern successors, from his religious vision of faith.

the linguistic turning
of the symbol

baudelaire and his
french symbolist heirs

I. Baudelaire's Denaturalization of the Symbol

The process of symbolization begins when one thing is used to stand for something else. A stone thrown into a pit for the purpose of counting sheep or whatever other sort of object may be considered to be a primitive symbol. A link between items that have nothing to do with each other in the nature of things is thereby forged simply by virtue of the one's being made to take the place of the other. Some such model as this generally informs the notion of the symbol current in linguistics and semiotics and in a broad spectrum of empirical disciplines where phenomena of signification are studied scientifically. The aspect of the symbol that is stressed in these fields is its arbitrariness or conventionality and the fact that it is *not* the object it symbolizes but just some substitute for it in the object's absence.

The prevalence and authority of this linguistic notion of the symbol, which equates it with a sign that signifies by absence, show up in anthropological discourse, for example, in the theories of Claude Lévi-Strauss: "It is a relation of symbol to thing symbolized, or to use the vocabulary of the linguists, of signifier to signified" ("c'est une relation de symbole

à chose symbolisée, ou pour employer le vocabulaire des linguistes, de
signifiant à signifié").¹ One of the most determined and extensive of such
theorizations of the symbol taken in the linguistic sense as implying essentially absence is Lacanian psycholinguistics. Entry into the symbolic stage
is marked by loss of presence and plenitude in undifferentiated union
with the mother's body. Thus the symbolic per se symbolizes absence and
alienation, specifically in the form of castration fears vis-à-vis the symbol
of all symbols, the father's phallus. Even in as literature-oriented a version of Lacanianism as Julia Kristeva's, the symbolic order ("l'ordre symbolique") emerges as "the yawning gap between signifier and signified"
("la béance entre le signifiant et le signifié").²

For poets, and generally in aesthetic theory, the symbolic has quite
a different meaning. The symbol distinguishes itself from other types
of signs (or as against the sign altogether) by virtue of its making concretely present the thing it signifies. This function of making present has
consistently been described in the language of "participation," with the
implication that the symbol is actually a part of the larger whole it represents—*pars pro toto*. In Coleridge's famous formulation, the symbol
"always partakes of the reality which it renders intelligible; and while it
enunciates the whole, abides itself as a living part in that unity of which it
is the representative."³ Consequently, in aesthetics the idea of the symbol
has tended to imply an intrinsic affinity with what is symbolized—to the
point of *being* it, at least in part. And often this entails, further, the fundamental unity of all things—all things being reflected in the symbol as in a
microcosm or monad.⁴ In addition to the monadology of Leibniz, Hegel's
doctrine of the concrete universal and Kant's notion of an a priori intuition that is not "schematic" but rather "analogical" (*Kritik der Urteils-
kraft*, sec. 59) supply some of the German idealistic underpinnings for
this originally Romantic conception of the symbol.⁵ Another important
source can be found in magic and totemism, as is signaled by the interest

1. Claude Lévi-Strauss, "L'efficacité du symbolique," in *Anthropologie structurale*
(Paris: Plon, 1958), 218.

2. Julia Kristeva, *La révolution du langage poétique* (Paris: Seuil, 1974), 45.

3. Samuel Taylor Coleridge, *The Statesman's Manual*, quoted in Angus Fletcher, *Allegory: The Theory of a Symbolic Mode* (Ithaca: Cornell University Press, 1964), 16.

4. Cf. Robert Greer Cohn, "Symbolism," *The Journal of Aesthetics and Art Criticism* 33 (Winter 1974): 181–92.

5. Jena Romanticism, particularly that of Schelling and Schlegel, is documented
in its influence specifically on Baudelaire by Michel Brix, "Modern Beauty versus Platonist Beauty," in *Baudelaire and the Poetics of Modernity*, ed. Patricia Ward (Nashville:
Vanderbilt University Press, 2000).

of symbolist poets in the occult. This interest can be traced from Baudelaire to Yeats and beyond, for example, to James Merrill (*The Changing Light at Sandover,* 1976–80). In occult tradition and lore, the symbol participates in reality to the extent of being able effectively to transform it, typically through the manipulation of tokens, rather than remaining just an external representation devoid of any real efficacy and without power over what it represents.

That the symbol is a part of the whole it represents (which, by universal analogy, expands to include the whole universe) and that it thereby makes present what it signifies, presenting it, precisely, *in part,* means also that the symbol may be said to signify not merely by virtue of convention but, more importantly, by its "nature." What it actually *is* in itself, and not just what it may be arbitrarily used to stand for, determines what the symbol signifies. To say a "sail" was seen on the horizon in order to mean that a ship was seen (as in Coleridge's own example) is in some sense a natural mode of expression. There is something not entirely arbitrary about using a sail to represent a ship. A ship is indeed in a certain manner present in a sail: it is present in part. And a sail *is,* however partially, a ship: it is a piece of a ship.

The goal of giving access to nature beneath the level of social conventions of signification has remained fairly constantly in view throughout the history of symbolic expression in poetry: it is epitomized by the myth of Orpheus as the singer-poet whose music tames beasts and even moves the inanimate elements. His mastery over the natural world symbolizes the notion that his poetry is the very language of nature. The endeavor to return to a state in which language would signify by virtue of its being and intrinsic nature rather than by conventions socially imposed was a program already of the Romantics. Hölderlin's "Nun, nun, müssen die Worte dafür, wie Blumen, entstehen" ("Now, now, must words therefore like flowers originate," "Brot und Wein") can be taken as emblematic of the exigency of rediscovering language as a natural thing. This is the ideal of a poetic language that would be literally things, one in which the breach between sign and referent that characterizes (and curses) postlapsarian language would be repaired.[6] The symbolist tradition from Hölderlin to Rilke activates this Orphic claim for poetry in a particularly intense and self-conscious, and even at times self-ironic, mode. The notion often holds a powerful attraction still for contemporary poets, however

6. On the philosophical motivations and historical context for this endeavor, see Charles Taylor, *Sources of Self: The Making of the Modern Identity* (Cambridge: Cambridge University Press, 1987), chapters 22 and 23.

far they may be from considering it possible to realize such an ideal. The undiminished contemporary fascination with the Orpheus myth bears witness to this perennial impulse simply to speak things, or to let things themselves speak, that lies near the source of so much poetry.[7]

The art of the symbol, accordingly, at least from the Romantic period on, was supposed to make beings speak: it provided a channel that could make their natural speech audible. Baudelaire crystallized the idea that language should ideally be the natural speaking of things in a few quintessential verses of "L'invitation au voyage":

> Tout y parlerait
> À l'âme en secret
> Sa douce langue natale.[8]

> There everything would speak
> To the soul in secret
> Its sweet native language.

These lapidary lines seem to envisage a language unmediated by arbitrary conventions and by meanings imposed through practical functions of communication that are deaf to the things' own native voices. Things speaking to the soul in their own native language, and thus attuned to its own inner being, communicate by virtue of what they *are*. What speaks in the symbol or in the space to which Baudelaire voyages in the poem is everything, "tout," since by universal analogy any particular thing speaking its sweet native language, that is, the language of things, speaks for all beings and perhaps for being itself. Of course, Baudelaire is also, in decisive ways, fiercely negative on nature, loathing it as ugly and evil, yet his "*flowers* of evil" are nonetheless themselves produced by descent onto precisely this soil in order to transform it into art. It is all the more necessary, therefore, to begin from these Romantic doctrines in order to account for his transmutation—in effect, a denaturalization—of the symbol.

In the symbolic universe, all things are interconnected, and all are immanent in each individual thing. This is to say that the world is composed of correspondences: its qualities "answer to one another," as Baude-

---

7. Charles Segal, *Orpheus: The Myth of the Poet* (Baltimore: Johns Hopkins University Press, 1989).

8. Baudelaire's texts are quoted from Charles Baudelaire, *Oeuvres complètes*, ed. Claude Pichois (Paris: Gallimard, 1975–76). Translations are my own.

laire puts it in "Correspondances" ("Les parfums, les couleurs et les sons se répondent"), just like the mutually defining elements of a language. Indeed, as the linguistic metaphor of "answering" suggests, the things that make up the world, at least as it is reflected in poetry, *are* the elements of a language. Baudelaire was fond of describing all of nature as a vocabulary for the artist's use ("La nature n'est qu'un dictionnaire").[9] However, although he evokes the Romantic topos of the language of things—as again in "Élévation": "le langage des fleurs et des choses muettes" ("the language of flowers and of mute things")—Baudelaire turns out ultimately to be more interested in artistically recreating the whole order of things as a language and therefore as *not* natural. The implication is less that language should return to a state of nature and more nearly the reverse—that even nature might be subsumed into language.

Baudelaire's closed, symmetrical stanzaic forms and the interiorization of the world in the supposedly authentic dimension of "coeur" ("heart") contribute to construing reality as a language where everything is differentially defined, so that all elements are ordered by internal relations into a self-enclosed system.[10] In "L'invitation au voyage," "things" such as "les soleils mouillés" ("the misty-wet suns") and "ces ciels brouillés" ("these storm-tossed skies") are not just kindred natural phenomena. They actually create each other in relation to one another, among other ways, by the reciprocity of their rhyming and the differential play of assonances and consonances, which contribute to the splendor in which they poetically exist each as distilled out of the other and as fused together into a whole. The experience of reading a Baudelaire poem is (or at least can be) one of being rapt away to a sphere where all things and sensations are transubstantiated by appearing within the structural whole of the poem. The world is presented as essentially translated into a poetic idiom and as articulated in a harmony of purely formal, mutually defining values. Things sublated thus into a system of correspondences or relative differences have been turned essentially into language.

Romantics, and long before them medievals, had conceived of nature as a language, that is, as a system of signs, or, metaphorically, a Book. But the idea that the experience of everything as one should be a possibility

---

9. Baudelaire is actually quoting Delacroix on this, for example, in "Salon de 1846," section IV.

10. This suggests why Baudelaire's poetry has lent itself so beautifully to formalist analyses such as Roman Jakobson and Claude Lévi-Strauss's "'Les chats' de Charles Baudelaire," *L'Homme* II (janvier–avril 1962): 5–21. Henri Meschonnic's numerous writings have further developed such a linguistic approach to Baudelaire.

engendered specifically by poetic language became an aesthetic creed first for the Symbolists, and they recognized Baudelaire as having revealed this possibility. The sensuously symbolic power of his verse made it a superior, all-encompassing kind of "seeing," one to which a veritable universe accrued. Hence Baudelaire could be hailed as "voyant" ("seer") and a "vrai dieu" ("true god") by Rimbaud. Baudelaire's essential achievement and legacy to symbolism is to have convincingly created the experience of how everything (at least as sensed and felt by an individual) can be known in and as language. Feelings and perceptions themselves become an alphabet to be used according to the grammar of poetic art. Even when it is strongly evocative of a specific historical epoch and milieu, Baudelaire's poetry refers to these external phenomena only as essentially transfigured by their representation in and as poetic language: "everything for me becomes allegory" ("tout pour moi devient allégorie," "Le Cygne"). Baudelaire tended to use "allégorie" interchangeably with the term "symbole" (for example, at the end of "Un voyage à Cythère"), since both serve equally well to indicate the linguistic transfiguration of the real.[11] In this perspective, which is the soul of symbolism, language is not just *a* reality but *all* reality, and perhaps supra-reality as well.[12]

Language tends to become identical with all that it represents in Baudelaire's poetry: it is the part that concretely embodies and becomes symbolically identical with the whole. Yet this is not to be confused with a metaphysical thesis that there is nothing but language.[13] It is rather a poetic experience of everything becoming accessible to be known symbolically, that is, as identical, on the model of part and whole, with the concrete, sensuous instance of the poem itself. A symbol is the presence of

11. Michael Hamburger, in *The Truth of Poetry: Tensions in Modern Poetry from Baudelaire to the 1960s* (New York: Harcourt Brace Jovanovich, 1969), argues that Baudelaire is an allegorical poet, which is true, but it does not follow that he is "not a Symbolist" (6). Basic contributions for situating Baudelaire as a symbolist include Guy Michaud, *Message poétique du symbolisme* (Paris: Nizet, 1947), vol. I; Lloyd Austin, *L'univers poétique de Baudelaire: symbolisme et symbolique* (Paris: Mercure de France, 1956); and Henri Peyre, *Qu'est-ce que le symbolisme?* (Paris: Presses Universitaires de France, 1974).

12. I develop the wider theoretical implications and applications of this thesis concerning symbolic signification in "Symbol and Allegory," chapter 29 in *The Routledge Companion to Philosophical Hermeneutics*, eds. Jeff Malpas and Hans-Helmuth Gander (New York: Routledge, 2015), 367–77.

13. A corrective to the idea promulgated influentially by Hugo Friedrich that referentiality is simply eliminated and reality liquidated in symbolist poetry is persuasively argued by Paul de Man in "Lyric and Modernity," in *Blindness and Insight: Essays in the Rhetoric of Contemporary Criticism* (Minneapolis: University of Minnesota Press, 1971).

a unity that is not completely given as such to the senses but is present in language through the partial, or rather participatory, identity of the symbol with the symbolized. The poem as symbol is, at least in part, what it represents. This results directly from the drive toward identity at work in language as symbol. The symbol annexes to itself everything with which it comes into contact. It makes everything it touches over into itself. By virtue of its intense sensuality and almost hallucinatory inebriation, moreover, Baudelaire's language becomes the palpable presentation or incarnation of a whole—and, to this extent, a symbolic—universe.

The symbol proposes to participate in a larger reality, but for the symbolist this means, by a logic of supplementarity, that it ends up reproducing virtually, in the element of language, the reality it was supposed to symbolize. Its synthetic energy becomes the creative force that constitutes the world it symbolizes. For the symbol is invested with a force for becoming symbolically the whole that it is not literally—either by throwing things together into unity ("symballein"), or as the part of a token ("symbolon") that represents, in the absence of the missing half, the whole of which it was originally part. The drive to identity at work in language as symbol is concentrated and heightened by the harmonious language of lyric based on symmetries and correspondences, that is, on various linguistic forms of repetition of the same, for example, rhythm and rhyme. All such devices of the lyric imagination serve in the production of varieties of identity.

Identity is forged by the very symbolic nature of language, which is brought out and enhanced by the form as well as the intent and meaning of Baudelaire's verse. Identity surfaces as a totally obsessive trope in a poem like "L'invitation au voyage":

Mon enfant, ma sœur,
Songe à la douceur
D'aller là-bas vivre ensemble!
Aimer à loisir,
Aimer et mourir
Au pays qui te ressemble!
Les soleils mouillés
De ces ciels brouillés
Pour mon esprit ont les charmes
Si mystérieux
De tes traîtres yeux,
Brillant à travers leurs larmes.

Là, tout n'est qu'ordre et beauté,
Luxe, calme et volupté.

Des meubles luisants,
Polis par les ans,
Décoreraient notre chambre;
Les plus rares fleurs
Mêlant leurs odeurs
Aux vagues senteurs de l'ambre,
Les riches plafonds,
Les miroirs profonds,
La splendeur orientale,
Tout y parlerait
À l'âme en secret
Sa douce langue natale.

Là, tout n'est qu'ordre et beauté,
Luxe, calme et volupté.

Vois sur ces canaux
Dormir ces vaisseaux
Dont l'humeur est vagabonde;
C'est pour assouvir
Ton moindre désir
Qu'ils viennent du bout du monde.
—Les soleils couchants
Revêtent les champs,
Les canaux, la ville entière,
D'hyacinthe et d'or;
Le monde s'endort
Dans une chaude lumière.

Là, tout n'est qu'ordre et beauté,
Luxe, calme et volupté.

INVITATION TO THE VOYAGE

My child, my sister,
Think of the rapture

Of living together there!
Of loving at will,
Of loving till death,
In the land that is like you!
The misty sunlight
Of those cloudy skies
Has for my spirit the charms,
So mysterious,
Of your treacherous eyes,
Shining brightly through their tears.

There all is order and beauty,
Luxury, peace, and pleasure.

Gleaming furniture,
Polished by the years,
Will ornament our bedroom;
The rarest flowers
Mingling their fragrance
With the faint scent of amber,
The ornate ceilings,
The limpid mirrors,
The oriental splendor,
All would whisper there
Secretly to the soul
In its soft, native language.

There all is order and beauty,
Luxury, peace, and pleasure.

See on the canals
Those vessels sleeping.
Their mood is adventurous;
It's to satisfy
Your slightest desire
That they come from the ends of the earth.
—The setting suns
Adorn the fields,
The canals, the whole city,
With hyacinth and gold;

The world falls asleep
In a warm glow of light.

There all is order and beauty,
Luxury, peace, and pleasure.[14]

The *incipit*—"Mon enfant, ma sœur" ("My child, my sister")—creates identity immediately by its grammar of apposition. This identification already suggests some sort of collapse of natural boundaries of difference, a promiscuous mix of distinct kinds of kinship. All intimate relations seem to be embraced together in one, in an incestuous intimacy disregarding essential differences between progeny and sibling and, implicitly, lover. The country to which the voyage is directed is itself, at least partially or approximately, equated with the beloved in the phrase "In the land that is like you" ("Au pays qui te ressemble"). The skyscapes and weather are for the poet-speaker but the reflection of the beloved's eyes and stormy emotions. Even love and death collapse together into identity by conjunction: "Aimer à loisir, / Aimer et mourir" ("To love at leisure, / To love and die"), as loving here becomes at the same time a suspension of activity and a dying. This world of indiscriminate identity is expressed finally in the last stanza of the poem in that the ships traveling from the furthest limits of the earth nevertheless move wholly within the sphere of the beloved's desire: "C'est pour assouvir / Ton moindre désir / Qu'ils viennent du bout du monde" ("It is to satisfy / Your least desire / That they come from the end of the world"). The external world here is totally at the service of—and has no determination or consistency independent of—the innerness of desire. By thematizing the principle of identity in this way, the poem sets up a lyric image of how language in fact operates in symbolist poetry, namely, by identifying itself concretely with what it represents and erasing the difference between representation and reality, the inner world and the outer.

The intrinsic relation of language and world in symbolism is grounded not only in the Neoplatonic trope of participation but also in the language of revelation or "Offenbarung." This is so particularly for Romantic theorists of the symbol like Coleridge, Goethe, and Hamann, and such religious vocabulary intimates a prophetic precedent for symbolist poetics. In biblical Logos tradition, the Word of God creates all things and, con-

---

14. Translation by William Aggeler, *The Flowers of Evil* (Fresno, CA: Academy Library Guild, 1954) in text of the complete poem but not in the following discussion.

sequently, all creatures are symbols bespeaking their Creator. Hence this paradigm, too, induces to construing language and world as communicating with, and indeed as intrinsic to, one another at the most originary level. Baudelaire explicitly alludes to the Creator Word's becoming flesh ("Et verbum caro factum est") in his preface to *Les fleurs du mal*.

Whether Neoplatonically or biblically backgrounded, whether conceived in terms of ontological participation or of creation as revelation, symbolist poetics are predicated on a peculiarly privileged relation of language and world. Indeed the absorption of all reality into language as *poiesis* may be taken to be the key premise of the entire symbolist outlook. The consequences of this fundamental premise, however, turn out to be diverse and even contradictory. On the one hand, reality puts up no more resistance: all is simply fused into unity in an exquisite and unrestricted universal harmony forged in and by language. On the other hand, the collapse of all extra-linguistic reality into language leaves language empty of real substance and consequently disoriented. Without being anchored to anything real beyond itself, language has trouble maintaining even its own unity and integrity.

The essential tension between these opposite sorts of consequences of its pan-linguisticism can, in fact, be detected in every aspect and dimension of symbolist art. Ineluctably, together with the presence of the object in and to the symbol—the object's immanence to language—comes also an emptying of all objective content. The symbol contains everything immediately within itself, but only at the price of becoming a pure ideality devoid of relation to anything beyond the purely linguistic sphere. Every supposedly external object of language collapses into merely a linguistic artifact. This makes it possible ultimately to dissolve the presumed external sources of language, including subjectivity and all its attendant postulates, into material forces and drives conceived of as working and manifest immanently in language. And it is this direction in which symbolist poetry subsequent to Baudelaire and down to our own times decisively turns.

Baudelaire used his art of the symbol in order to discover the mysterious and profound unity ("une ténébreuse et profonde unité") of all things based on revelation by the word or on correspondences in a Neoplatonic order of being. But that this is peculiarly the poet's prerogative, a secret reserved for disclosure by the master of language or the magician of words, suggests that it is a unity that exists essentially in the order of language. As the purely linguistic status of the vision proclaimed in Symbolist poetry becomes more overt, the synthesis Baudelaire's poetry celebrates shows itself to be not just a synthesis of what is supposed to be higher reality but equally, and paradoxically, an escape from and avoidance of the real: hence the "double aspect" of symbolism individuated by Paul de Man in his homonymous article.[15] It is because the poet in the solitude of his individual consciousness finds himself alienated from the world that, according to de Man, he attempts in vain to recover lost unity by means of his symbolic language and gnosis. Fredric Jameson describes the shift between what can be recognized as these two aspects of symbolism as a transition from production of the referent to its erasure and elimination, and he articulates these two phases in terms of a modernist and a postmodernist Baudelaire.[16] Hans-Jost Frey makes a similar point in discussing Baudelaire as a critic of mimetic representation and as imitating only what is immanent to his own representations.[17]

Given this double aspect of symbolism, together with the aspiration toward an ideal life of unity goes a discomfiting and even shocking avowal of the ultimate truth of dissolution and death. For it is only too clear that the ecstatic experiences so exuberantly enjoyed are dependent upon and even transpire within, in fact wholly within, language. Language is the element in which the symbol lives and dies. It is a synthetic, unifying medium, but it is also in itself purely formal, empty of substance, a kind of dead artifact destined to be identified with the dead letter of writing. Consequently, its use to synthesize unity is inevitably artificial. The pure religion of art, practiced self-consciously as a calculated linguistic craft or alchemy, is constrained to exploit the very sorts of mechanical and material means that the symbolist artist otherwise affects to despise. Thus, to the extent that it is a faith, symbolism is almost inevitably in bad faith, for it is acutely aware of its own artifices and, in effect, of the contradictoriness of striving to *synthesize* unmediated experience of the whole harmonious unity of things.

This precarious posture of symbolist poetry is held intact by Baudelaire, buoyed up on the exuberance of his discovery of an almost all-powerful verbal magic. As the historical distance from this burst of creative inspiration lengthens, it becomes more difficult for the sheer passion of

15. Paul de Man, "The Double Aspect of Symbolism," *Yale French Studies* 74 (1988): 3–16.

16. Fredric Jameson, "Baudelaire as Modernist and Postmodernist: The Dissolution of the Referent and the Artificial 'Sublime,'" in *Lyric Poetry. Beyond New Criticism* (Ithaca: Cornell University Press, 1985).

17. Hans-Jost Frey, in *Studien über das Reden der Dichter* (München: Wilhelm Fink, 1986).

poetry either to make good on or to render irrelevant the self-deceptions that go into the making of the symbol. It is language that permits the total, unified knowledge sought by symbolists, yet language is also at the same time a false, or at least a fictive, element of such knowledge. What is "merely" linguistic is also in a sense nothing. The nothingness and death with which symbolist voices are so seductively obsessed has its remote motivations in this predicament. Irrepressibly, this sense of an encroaching emptying out and annihilation of reality by language asserts itself as a dominant mood throughout French symbolist poetry, starting from Baudelaire's poetry and its being precipitated into the abyss ("le gouffre") opened up by its own infinite expanse. Unlimited by any reality that it cannot absorb, symbolic language is destined to expand to the point of its own annihilation by extenuation. In the end, extinction comes to be figured as the very perfection sought, and the goal of knowledge by poetry's symbolic gnosis is represented as being reached precisely in death.

As Walter Benjamin perceived, Baudelaire's poetry presents a challenge to conceive language in its purity. In introducing his translation of "Tableaux parisiens," he describes his attempt to translate the pure essence of language itself. Translation allows pure language "to shine upon the original more fully. It is the task of the translator to release into his own language that pure language which is under the spell of another. . . ." ("Jene reine Sprache, die in fremde gebannt ist, in der eigenen zu erlösen . . . ist die Aufgabe des Übersetzers").[18] However, while insisting on the absoluteness of language, taking inspiration from Baudelaire's *Fleurs du mal*, the last work of lyric poetry with European-wide significance ("Die 'Fleurs du mal' sind das letzte lyrische Werk gewesen, das eine europäische Wirkung getan hat"), Benjamin also encompasses the other, inseparable aspect of symbolism in analyzing Baudelaire's lyric art as a way of coping with shock, the most distinctive modern experience, as registered first in Baudelaire's poetry. Originally shocking experience can be confronted and digested by being assimilated into a total structure of meaning: this means assimilating it essentially as language, but as language scarred with the traces of trauma. Baudelaire's lyric production represents a highly conscious reworking in and as lyric language of lived stimuli that have left the psychic mechanism traumatized, and Benjamin deciphers beneath the smooth surface of the mellifluous verses the rup-

---

18. Walter Benjamin, "Die Aufgabe des Übersetzers," in *Illuminationen: Ausgewählte Schriften*, I (Frankfurt am Main: Suhrhamp, 1977), 50–62, translated as "The Task of the Translator: An Introduction to the Translation of Baudelaire's *Tableaux Parisiens*," in *Illuminations*, ed. Hannah Arendt (New York: Schocken, 1969), 227.

tures and impasses of Baudelaire's quintessential experience as inaugural of the modern. The apparent wholeness of language, into which experience was lifted by symbolic lyric, in fact shows through to another aspect of language, especially of prophetic or messianic language, as consisting essentially in ruptures and abrasions. Still on the basis of its sublation of reality into language, symbolism's language thus reveals quite a different, unsuspected face marked by materiality and fragmentation. Baudelaire's language, read profoundly, translates the breakdown that the modern age was witnessing: the aura of things that connects them with their human context and historical past by involuntary memory was disintegrating.[19]

Benjamin's reflections confirm the two aspects of symbolism and adduce a sort of historical, materialist account of their derivation. But it is also possible to interpret how the drive toward unity and presence inherent in the symbol converts into disunity and rupture with the real by its own internal logic—that is, by the very fulfillment of its own impulse to total unity and the consequent cutting asunder of the tension between reality and symbol, language and world. Not only does the grand symbolic vision of the identity of All lead to a total structure or monism of the universe: it entails equally a shattering into autonomous fragments, since each individual element is wholly self-contained, indeed is in itself all-containing. The totally relational identity characteristic of language and therefore also of a linguistic universe turns into an equally total self-sufficiency of every particle, since each is endowed with an absolute identity already in itself: it is unconditioned by any external relations, since all relations have become internal to it. In symbolism, everything has become language, but as a result language no longer mediates anything extra-linguistic. Without any real content, language becomes purely image or, as is suggested by other forms of symbolist art, purely musical incantation: it is unbounded, but it is lacking in any rule or concept such as only an external limit or object could provide, and this leads eventually to language's being threatened even in its own internal cohesion.

The breakup of language and of everything *in* language was to be overtly pursued by Baudelaire's poetic successors and has been discovered retrospectively as a subtext in Baudelaire himself by recent critics, especially those writing in Benjamin's wake.[20] It can be understood as result-

---

19. Walter Benjamin, "Über einige Motive bei Baudelaire," in *Illuminationen. Ausgewählte Schriften 1* (Frankfurt am Main: Suhrkamp, 1977).

20. In addition to de Man, Frey, and Jameson, also influential are Georges Poulet, *La poésie éclatée* (Paris: Presses Universitaires de France, 1980), and Jean Starobinski, *La mélancolie au miroir: trois lectures de Baudelaire* (Paris: Julliard, 1989).

ing ineluctably from the logic and dynamic of the symbol itself, with its absolute exigencies of identity, presence, and immediacy, achieved no longer just by means of, but actually in and as, language. For once language has totally penetrated nature, leaving no remainder, nature is turned wholly into artifice. Nature can no longer supply the paradigm of organic unity on which language models itself in Romanticism. Instead, everything becomes subject to the nature of language as an artificial synthesis with no substance in itself and therefore in a constant state of dissolution. When the universal identity forged by the symbol turns into an identity of all with language itself, the symbolic order of things is poised to collapse in upon itself, to implode in an uncontrolled proliferation of pure form. Baudelaire's transmission of the Romantic doctrine of the symbol radicalizes and in effect reverses it; this results in the symbol's no longer effecting union with all that is but rather causing an alienation from nature and the real. Although he at times embraces the idea of a harmoniously ordered universe of natural correspondences, Baudelaire also lays the groundwork for its undoing in and by the symbol, which becomes the dynamite that explodes the universe eventually into Mallarmé's constellations of unmasterable chance. Precisely these disintegrative implications of the unrestricted identification of all with language have manifested themselves persistently in the course and direction of symbolist poetry in its development ever since Baudelaire.[21]

Baudelaire was a believer in the identificatory power of the symbol, and he remained the undisputed master of this creative faculty for the symbolist poets that followed him. Yet he did not believe in the all-embracing, benevolent Nature in which symbols were supposed to be embedded and into which they beckoned invitingly, binding all things, including whoever could interpret them, together into one whole. For Baudelaire, this Romantic dream had become a nightmare, and, consequently, the symbol, in significant ways, became sinister. He was haunted by the symbol and its solicitations to communion with a Nature that he loathed. In "Obsession," Baudelaire recoils from nature, from its great forests that frighten him as do cathedrals with their windy organs ("Grands bois, vous m'effrayez comme des cathédrales; / Vous hurlez comme l'orgue . . ."). He would like the night to be without stars, for their light speaks to him, and it is a known language, whereas he is in

---

21. For sometimes contrasting views on this descent, see Charles Altieri, "From Symbolist Thought to Immanence: The Ground of Postmodern American Poetics," *boundary 2* (Spring 1973): 605–39.

search rather of the empty, the black or blank and naked, what is divested of signs and therefore devoid of significance:

> Comme tu me plairais, ô Nuit! sans ces étoiles
> Dont la lumière parle un langage connu!
> Car je cherche le vide, et le noir, et le nu!

> How you would please me, O Night, without these stars
> whose light speaks a known language!
> For I seek the empty, the black, and the naked!

This constitutes an anguished palinode that effectively retracts the soul's enchantment with the sweet native language of things in "L'invitation au voyage." Here Baudelaire is horrified by nature and its language, indeed by nature *as* language, and not because it is strange but because it is all too familiar. The familiar regards ("regards familiers") of "Correspondances" reappear, but now they have become terrifying. The forest is experienced as a cathedral whose significance is frightfully overdetermined rather than as the mysteriously alluring temple of "Correspondances." Nature is now already fully codified: the cries of the woods that reply to one another out of their depths ("Répondent les échos de vos *De profundis*") are already articulated as a church liturgy (*De profundis* is the *incipit* of Psalm 130). They are natural rites in a manner reminiscent of the temple of nature ("La nature est un temple") in "Correspondances," but here in "Obsession" precisely their symbolic force makes them a negative, indeed a nightmarish, experience.

Baudelaire is repelled not so directly by nature as by the significance of nature, which is a form of human culture, indeed a language. The ocean's waves, with their heaving and tumult, are execrable because they are already found by the mind within itself—"I hate you, Ocean! Your surgings and tumult, / are found again by my spirit in itself" ("Je te hais, Océan! tes bonds et tes tumultes, / Mon esprit les retrouve en lui")—just as the defeated man's bitter laugh full of sobs and insults is found in the enormous laugh of the sea. Even night fails to be other, and darkness—"les ténèbres"—consists in canvases ("des toiles") painted on, or destined to be painted on, by human signs. Nature offers no escape from the human, and the human has become just as abhorrent as the natural. The symbolic-linguistic mechanism that reduces everything to language is at the bottom of this viciously circular mirroring, since everything that can be reached through language is reduced to identity. All that is known is known through the identity of signs circulating in the linguistic system: it is all too familiar and too wretched, in effect, a prison-house without exit.

Of course, what Baudelaire loathes at bottom is himself because that is all that he can see at the bottom of Nature. He begins the desperate struggle to escape from himself by crying out after the name of "the other" that is still the watchword of so much French, left-bank culture today. What he is trying to escape is the viciously narcissistic self-reflexivity of the symbolist quest that is palpable in a poem like "La Chevelure" ("Head of Hair"), in which the poet imagines plunging his amorous and inebriated head into the black ocean in which "the other" is enclosed:

Je plongerai ma tête amoureuse d'ivresse
Dans ce noir océan où l'autre est enfermé . . .

I will plunge my amorous and inebriated head
Into this black ocean where the other is contained . . .

The "other" is sought in desperation in order to escape from the self, but this other is itself already "enclosed" ("enfermé"). Its darkness risks being confounded with the blackness of the self's own spleen. In the universe of total identity, there is really no escaping from the self. The seeker necessarily voyages endlessly in quest of the new and unknown, "le nouveau" and "l'inconnu." But the absolute identity of everything is the truth of the symbol that Baudelaire found himself imprisoned by and that he chafes to evade. All this he bequeathed, furthermore, to his poetic posterity.

Baudelaire adopts the symbol as a basic strategy but denaturalizes and also denatures it in the process. The universal identification of each with all, which is characteristic of symbolic vision and the basis for the correspondences of things, takes a peculiar turn when the identification of all things in the symbol is taken to be an identity of all with language. This, in effect, is what the symbolists explicitly do, rendering manifest the revolution in poetic language brought about *in nuce* by Baudelaire. It means that the identities of the symbolist vision, rather than being natural, indeed the deep structure or essence of nature, turn out to be purely artificial, indeed nothing but language. There is still an all-pervading logic of identity, but it takes on a very different significance, which is in important ways just the opposite of the significance it had in Romanticism. The natural order of things is no longer reassuring and restorative, healing human breaches and diseases. The order of things is only linguistic and therefore only a reflection of the human world of cultural artifacts and is, in fact, already infected with the endemic sickness of the self.

Baudelaire pursues to its furthest limits the logic of identity inhering in the symbol. He identifies everything with everything else. But the result he obtains is not oneness with the mystery of nature and the universe, even though he leaves behind him some traces of a deeply suffered longing for an encounter with the Other or the Unknown. What he actually achieves is rather an expansion of language so that, in effect, it encompasses everything—well beyond simply serving as the instrument of establishing the symbolic identity of all being. What remains is only for this linguistic mechanism to expose itself as such: it is then apt to collapse for lack of external support and, in so doing, to produce the brilliant artificial paradises and the scintillating chance constellations of symbolism. This sets up the program that symbolist poets, eminently Rimbaud and Mallarmé, were to follow in his wake. The linguistic turning and totalizing of the symbol that is achieved incipiently by Baudelaire constitutes the premise for the shattering even of language itself (once it is no longer held intact by anything beyond itself) that was to be pursued to its furthest extremes by later poets writing in this symbolist vein.

The identification of everything with language has remained an absolutely central preoccupation of French poetry and poetics in the twentieth century. It is at issue, for example, in Francis Ponge's *Le parti pris des choses* (1942), which hovers between treating words as natural things and then again ruthlessly unmasking this fiction and fighting against language in the name of the thing itself, "la chose même," which escapes it. Yet, the double aspect of the symbolism inaugurated by Baudelaire's poetry entails equally the breaking down of language, which collapses from within. This breakdown belongs together with the absorption by language of the world of things and with language's becoming itself a thing and acquiring thereby also the thing's vulnerability to amorcelation, dismemberment, and dissolution. Even this sort of resistance to the idealizations inherent in language suggests in indirect ways how later poets continue to remain Baudelaire's heirs. For although Baudelaire exquisitely expresses the ideal of a mysterious and profound unity in the symbol, in which "All is but order and beauty / Luxury, calm and voluptuousness" ("Tout n'est qu'ordre et beauté / Luxe, calme et volupté"), it is nevertheless possible to see how this complete freedom from discord and from external constraint contains the seeds of its own destruction and harbors the shattering of language as a total system into infinite disunity and limitless dis-semination. This is the decisive creative innovation that makes

Baudelaire's poetry so seminal for modern symbolist poetry in its widest ramifications.

II. The Linguistic Epistemology of French Symbolist Poetry

The disintegrative implications of the linguistic totalization of the symbol manifest themselves dramatically in the course of symbolist poetry as it flows from Baudelaire. This tendency, of course, appears mixed together with vestiges of the Romantic symbol as a harmonious whole. But whether in Baudelaire's immediate successors in France or in the descendants of symbolist poetry everywhere still today, the drive toward symbolic identification, by turning into identification of reality with language, eventually becomes a dismantling of language, its breaking up into the realities or irrealities of which it is compounded. The symbolic identification of all with language, so far from being a reduction to a known quantity, rather opens language up from within as itself inhabited by all the mysteries and *aporiae* of any possible or impossible universe. Language itself, rather than being the best known tool and the most human medium, becomes the *terra incognita* that it was formerly supposed to domesticate.

In the classical Coleridgean-Goethean definition and theory of the symbol in contradistinction to allegory, the symbol is preferred as the "living momentary revelation of the Inscrutable" ("lebendig-augenblickliche Offenbarung des Unerforschlichen").[22] Or again, the symbol is praised as organic, living form because it requires no logical operations but constitutes only the "unmediated vision of the imagination." As Coleridge writes, "The advantage of symbolic writing over allegory is that it presumes no disjunction of faculties, but simple dominance."[23] The immediacy of vision and presence so highly prized by Romantic theorists of the symbol led in the symbolist poets to efforts to concentrate on the word's value as immediate presentation, together with an evasion or relativizing of the representational function of language, which was strongly encour-

---

22. Johann Wolfgang von *Goethe, Gedenkausgabe der Werke, Briefe und Gespräche,* ed. Ernst Beutler (Zürich and Stuttgart: Artemis Verlag, 1949), 9:532.

23. Samuel Taylor Coleridge, *Miscellaneous Criticism,* ed. T. M. Raysor (London: Constable, 1936), 30. See, further, Geoffrey Hartmann, *The Unmediated Vision: An Interpretation of Wordsworth, Hopkins, Rilke, and Valéry* (New Haven: Yale University Press, 1954).

aged by the totally linguistic experience created by Baudelaire's poems. This was often done by taking the concretely present, physical qualities of the word, whenever it is enunciated or read, as its meaningful, symbolically significant, features. Not what words refer to in a conventional system of signification but what they palpably are as sounds and forms was explored as intrinsically meaningful. Traditionally, the phonetic and graphemic composition of a word had been considered purely aleatory and instrumental with regard to the word's meaning. But once the word is considered from the point of view of its sensuous presence rather than of its reference, the specific material qualities of a particular occurrence of the word become essential to the word's meaning or, we might rather say, "effect." Symbolist poets—and the French symbolists in an especially conscious, programmatic way—endeavored to educe the word's most essential meaning precisely from this, its sensory matter, whether visual or audible, rather than from its semantic content or what is confusingly called its "symbolic value" by linguistic science.

Crucial to the symbol still in its symbolist transmogrification is that it signifies by virtue of what it *is* rather than just by virtue of an arbitrary intention to use it as a substitute for something else. That the symbol be intrinsically or "naturally" significant, promising "the Orphic explanation of the universe" (Mallarmé), to this extent remains a criterion even when this nature reduces purely to chance and to the contingent connections and sedimentations that can be tracked by historical etymology. An image, word, or object signifies symbolically because of the connections it bears to other images, words, or objects in an order of relations that is not dependent on any users' conscious intentions but precedes and underlies them and is in this sense "natural." By this means, in the symbol, form is transformed into sense. The phonemic or graphemic form as verbal icon is meaningful in a way that exceeds its conscious employment as a sign in a linguistic system, and this "symbolist" meaning belongs to a materially—or phenomenally—real thing, not just to a representational construct. By means of analogy, this intrinsically meaningful thing, the symbol, can provide a hint of the sense of other things and of things in general.

After all, the physical, auditory properties of phonemes, as well as the concrete visual qualities of the written character, as material (or phenomenal) entities bear infinite affinities with all other material beings in the universe: all are conditioned by space and time and have unlimited degrees and specificities of attributes that are always more or less comparable along an unlimited variety of spectrums such as intensity, brightness, and homogeneity, not to mention their effects upon the whole range of a perceiving subject's receptivities. Any particular sense-object gives a kind of knowledge by analogy of all other particulars in the universe. Through the sensible constituents of language, it becomes possible again, as for the Romantics, "To see the world in a grain of sand / And a heaven in a wild flower . . ." (Blake, "Auguries of Innocence"). The extraordinary potential of the material and perceptual content of the signifier to become signifi-cant in and of itself, with at least some degree of independence from—or of excess with respect to—its semantic value, comes to be understood by poets in terms of a universal analogy of being.

Any particular sensuous content, symbolically considered, is part of a whole, indeed of *the* Whole. Language used symbolically as a poetic gnosis becomes the key to knowing all things as one. The symbol enables a knowledge of the whole of which it is a part, yet this knowledge by a concrete part gives only an indefinite *sense* of the whole without circum-scribing it by any determinate *concept*. The things or sensations on which symbolic knowledge is based have what Baudelaire calls in "Correspon-dances" the expansion of infinite things:

> Ayant l'expansion des choses infinies,
> Comme l'ambre, le musc, le benjoin et l'encens,
> Qui chantent les transports de l'esprit et des sens.

> Having the expansion of infinite things,
> Like ambre, musk, benjoin, and incense,
> Which sing the transports of the spirit and the senses.

This expansiveness of things in symbolic perception makes it possible to apprehend an infinity of beings in "a tenebrous and profound unity"; for anything apprehended under the aspect of the universal analogy of All has the expansion of something infinite, be it merely a perfume, a shade, or any kind of concrete sensation. It is potentially identical with everything else, synaesthetically fusing different sense modalities and even merging sense and intellect ("l'esprit et des sens").

Only as expansion or excess of meaning relative to a circumscribed, conventional sense can the symbolic character of the material signifier manifest itself. Matter is not in and of itself symbolic—it is abhorred generally by Symbolists (and Romantics) as devoid of all meaning, as the dead god of the crass materialism they shunned through their symbolic gnosis. Still, sensations, as the inescapable condition of the sign, can turn words into forms having the expansion of infinite things, in Baudelaire's phrase. In this event, the meanings assigned words by convention are not simply erased or made irrelevant; they are rather displaced by this explosion from within the materiality of the signifier, becoming themselves forms interacting with the forms that signify them: hence the oscillation and interaction between sense and sonority described by Mallarmé in "Crise de vers," where he attributes to the "essential," poetic words of a verse "the artifice of their alternating submergence in sense and in sonority" ("l'artifice de leur retrempe alternée dans le sens et la sonorité").[24]

The idea that linguistic forms should have intrinsic significances and natural affinities with the things they signify has as a rule been rejected in philosophy and linguistic theory ever since Hermogenes's conversation with Cratylus (in Plato's *Cratylus*)—and more recently on the basis of the Saussurian principle of the arbitrary character of the linguistic sign. But it is taken up again and explored intensively in the reflections on poetry of the symbolist poets, as well as being a constitutive principle of their poetry. This linguistic gnosis constitutes a way of transcending the subject-object dichotomy by finding the subject's own structures of meaning already inherent in the world as it is presented in and through language. To this end, language itself becomes the object of a superior, prophetic knowledge, with the implication that in language all objects of knowledge are virtually present or contained.

In the symbol, the meaning of things themselves, not just of semiological cyphers, is expressed: materially real things such as sounds and graphic marks are placed in intimate, intricate relation with ideal notions or abstract meanings. The interaction between the two, and the fusions created in comprehension, makes these concrete materials constitutive of, rather than merely instrumental to, linguistic significance. Conversely, signification, rather than consisting in arbitrary assignments of conventional meaning, becomes material and concrete. Thus, in the symbol, sense becomes sensuous, to echo Roman Jakobson's pithy definition of the poetic function of language.[25] It is not that sound simply supplants sense but rather that sound is divulged as intrinsically meaningful, while sense or meaning is made to become sensible and registers sensible qualities in its linguistic incarnation in the poetic word.

---

24. Stéphane Mallarmé, *Oeuvres complètes*, eds. Henri Mondor and G. Jean-Abbey (Paris: Pléiade, 1945), 368.

25. Roman Jakobson, "Closing Statement: Linguistics and Poetics," in *Style in Language*, ed. T. Sebeok (Cambridge: MIT Press, 1960).

This transformation of phonic and graphic form into sense and vice versa, to the end of attaining to the sense of things themselves, has been taken by Roland Barthes as the overarching project of modern poetry. According to Barthes, poetry endeavors to "re-transform the sign into sense: its ideal, tendentially, would be to attain not to the sense of words but to the sense of things themselves" ("re-transformer le signe en sens: son idéal—tendentiel—serait d'atteindre non au sens des mots, mais au sense des choses mêmes").[26] Putting this in precise linguistic terms, Barthes writes of "infra-signification" and of a "pre-semiological" state of language, which corresponds to the sort of "natural" signification that is traditionally imputed to the symbol. In this, it contrasts with the totalizing, appropriating constructions typical of myth: "Contemporary poetry is *a regressive semiological system.* While myth aims at an ultra-signification, an amplification of a primary system, poetry by contrast attempts to recuperate an infra-signification, a pre-semiological state of language" ("La poésie contemporaine est *un système sémiologique regressif.* Alors que le mythe vise à une ultra-signification, à l'amplification d'un système premier, la poésie au contraire tente de retrouver une infra-signification, un état pré-sémiologique du langage," 241). In a similar vein, Kristeva develops her theory of meaning in poetic language as operating below the level of semantic and syntactic convention and as manifesting psychic "pulsions" by deformations of the regular forms and structures of language.[27]

In this way, the reification of language, its becoming a real, concrete thing, as already in Romantic poetry, turns into an alphabetization and phonemic anatomization of all, that is, of all supposedly natural beings. To the symbolists, the transformation of all that is into language came to mean not just its apotheosis as total system, the Book of Creation, but just as importantly its amorcellation and disintegration. The symbolists turned the identity between thing and word around, insisting not so much on language as a natural being as on being and nature as language and therefore as themselves perfect artifice. The epistemological virtue of the poetic word as symbol is made to depend not so much on its capacity to synthesize totalities as on its opening a view into the sub-semantic and pre-semiological levels of language: poetry exposes language as consisting in sound or graphics—the phoneme and the letter. At these levels, real-

---

26. Roland Barthes, "Le mythe, aujourd'hui," *Mythologies* (Paris: Seuil, 1957), 239, 241.

27. Kristeva, *La révolution du langage poétique.*

ity is constituted and deconstituted not necessarily as a total order but as burgeoning or emergent in the moment of creation through the total expansion of the letter ("expansion totale de la lettre"; Mallarmé, "Le Livre, instrument spirituel").

One provocative, emblematic expression of the reification of language bound together with the linguistic reduction and shattering of the real in symbolist poetics is Rimbaud's "Voyelles": "A noir, E blanc, I rouge, U vert, O bleu. . . ." This sonnet treats language as a thing, as a perceptual object for the senses. The colors purportedly inherent in each of the vowels are drawn out of their "latent births" ("naissances latentes") and are connected directly with a plethora of concrete colored objects and sense impressions of color evidently suggested by analogies between the vowels' timbres and the objects' color-tones: velvety buzzing black bees for A, white glaciers and icicle lances for E, divinely vibrating green seas for U, laughing bloody red lips for I, stridently silent blue skies for O.

In *Une saison en enfer*, Rimbaud, reflecting on how he invented the color of vowels, comments: "I flattered myself that I was inventing a poetic verb accessible to all the senses" ("je me flatai d'inventer un verbe poétique accessible à tous les sens," "Alchimie du Verbe").[28] This is to treat the poetic word as itself an object of perception—and not only of one sense, as is generally the case with physical qualities, but of all. The sonnet's vision, moreover, finds all things, or at least an abundant sampling of them, present in language, in its most elementary constituents. The vowels are disclosed as constituent principles of creation, divine vibrations ("vibrements divins"), the first light of creation as the violet ray of His Eyes, for example, latent within the clarion O of omega ("O l'Oméga, rayon violet de Ses Yeux!"). Everything that is seems to lie latent, waiting for poetic evocation, in the letters that stand at the verbal artist's beck and call.[29]

Taking the signifier as *per se* significant engenders an atomization of language to its alphabetical components in the search for intrinsic meanings. Speculations on the intrinsic significatory values of letters and phonemes were carried out by Mallarmé in his prose writings, signally in his

28. Rimbaud is quoted from Arthur Rimbaud, *Complete Works, Selected Letters*, ed. Wallace Fowlie (Chicago: University of Chicago Press, 1966). However, as throughout the essay, unless otherwise indicated, translations are my own.

29. Rimbaud's sonnet bequeathed a founding charter to the "Symbolistes" of the 1880s, the original symbolists in the strict literary-historical sense of the term. See *La poésie symboliste*, ed. Bernard Delvaille (Paris: Seghers, 1971), and compare, for example, Jean Moréas's "Voyelles."

study of English words, *Les mots anglais,* as well as consistently in his poetic practice. In both genres, he relentlessly stresses the meaning inherent within words as acoustic image (sound) and as graphic icon (letter), that is, as form, apart from or in interaction with conventional sense. For example, letters like V and W in Mallarmé's poems visibly and mimetically embody their meanings rather than only signifying them through a system of conventions. Mallarmé saw images of the female shape and anatomy in these letters, which were thus naturally apt, in words like Venus, *v*ierge ("*v*irgin"), and *w*oman.[30]

The immediately sensed meaning of form, short-circuiting the indirection of signification, results in an uncontrolled proliferation, indeed an explosion, of meaning. Language becomes an immediate event of sense bypassing the conventional, rule-governed circuits of signification. Thus the symbol in French symbolist poetry was destined to become a matter not so much of participation in the larger whole that it represents as of the symbol's displacing and supplanting this reality by the supervening of language. Yet without any transcendent reference exterior to it, language itself enters into a phase of disintegration. And by virtue of their very identity with language, things themselves in the symbolic vision fall into disunity once language is exposed as consisting in atomic parts artificially synthesized and combined together.

In these ways, ironically, it turns out that symbolism in art and poetry, despite the accent on presence and participation in both the poetry and the theory, is, after all, haunted by absence and emptiness, severance and castration: such are the connotations with which the "term" *symbol* is laden in linguistic theory. In attempting to distance this counter-aesthetic, rigorously linguistic theory of the symbol from the symbolist project and yet circling back round to it, this essay has inadvertently confirmed the underlying unity of these seeming contraries. A quintessentially "symbolist" movement of assimilation at the level of language has been accomplished in the (merely rhetorical) failure of symbolist theory in this very essay to establish an identity, distinct from non-symbolist, non-poetic uses, for the term *symbol.* What seemed like a purely secularist reduction of all reality merely to language in modern symbolist poetry turns out to be a bursting open of language to the real as something unknown and unfathomable that inhabits the very material elements of which language is composed. It seems, then, that language proves itself to grant

---

30. See Robert Greer Cohn, *Toward the Poems of Mallarmé* (Berkeley: University of California Press, 1965), for numerous examples of this type of exegesis.

access to reality, or to be a kind of revelation, after all. Even in the very act of failing to be able to draw a map of reality, and in spite of (or even because of) being unable to objectively represent it, language makes the real elusively present in its very process of disintegration. Much is to be learned from Baudelaire about reading the meaning of language from its failures to comprehensively mean. Such total meaning is the dream of every symbol, and this dream comes true uncannily in Baudelaire—by being shattered. This is a breakthrough for and of modernity: it inaugurates a modality of broken expression that was to be pursued to some of its most provocative audacities by Emily Dickinson.

"the missing all"

emily dickinson's
apophatic poetics

I. The Apophatic Paradigm

Emily Dickinson has long been regarded as a peculiarly enigmatic figure for her puzzling and oftentimes paradoxical poems, as well as for her idiosyncratic religious faith. I will make no attempt to pry into that faith, except as it is expressed in the poetry.[1] However, if we focus on the faith together with the poetry as having the character of a negative theology, much that is enigmatic, without ceasing to be so, begins also to make a clear kind of sense. I contend that Dickinson's poetry is best understood as a form of negative theology or, more broadly, as what I will call "apophatic" discourse. My guiding idea is that Dickinson's exploration of modes of negation in poetic language enabled her to discover and express what are, in effect, negatively theological forms of belief. I will use *apophasis*, the Greek word for "negation," to designate the sort of radical negation of language per se—of any language whatsoever rather than only of specific formulations and of certain types of linguistic content—that

---

1. For more direct examination of Dickinson's faith, see Richard E. Brantley, *Experience and Faith: The Late-Romantic Imagination of Emily Dickinson* (New York: Palgrave, 2004).

characterizes this outlook, or rather sensibility, which suspects and subverts all its own verbal expressions.[2]

This term *apophasis* and its adjectival form *apophatic* evoke in the first place the ancient Neoplatonic tradition of speculation concerning the ineffable One as supreme principle of reality. Likewise commonly designated as apophatic are certain traditions of medieval mysticism, including Kabbalah and Sufism, concerning an unutterably transcendent Deity. In such traditions, the encounter in incommunicable registers of experience with the Inexpressible is marked by a backing off from language (*apo*—"away from," *phasis*—"speech" or "assertion"). Of course, this backing off is itself nevertheless registered in language, language that in various ways unsays itself.[3] The resultant apophatic modes of discourse, in their very wide diffusion throughout Western culture, especially in the domains of philosophy, religion, and literature, can be seen to have had a decisive bearing on Dickinson's writing. This can be inferred from the poetry itself, whether or not it is conscious and deliberate on her part. The apophatic tradition, I maintain, influences, whether directly or indirectly, Dickinson's reflections on the limits of her ability to express the reality she endeavors to approach and the experience she aims to convey in her poetry. Precisely the impediments to expression become her central message in telling ways, for they tell obliquely of something that is beyond language.

Apophasis is especially characteristic of advanced, highly self-reflective phases in the historical cycle of any given culture—for instance, the Neoplatonists in Hellenistic Rome, or late-medieval mystics, like Meister Eckhart and Marguerite Porete, after the collapse of Scholasticism. It emerges perhaps most conspicuously at similar crisis points reached in the Baroque and Romantic and postmodern ages. It is most often a form of secularized religious revelation, in which the experience of the divine returns, after having been subjected to severe rational critique on account of all of its naively positive expressions, which are exposed as

---

2. See my *On What Cannot Be Said: Apophatic Discourses in Philosophy, Religion, Literature, and the Arts*. Its brief introduction to Dickinson, vol. 2, 84–89, contains the core out of which the present chapter is elaborated.

3. A general orientation can be obtained from Michael A. Sells, *Mystical Languages of Unsaying* (Chicago: University of Chicago Press, 1994), and Sanford Budick and Wolfgang Iser, eds., *Languages of the Unsayable: The Play of Negativity in Literature and Literary Theory* (New York: Columbia University Press, 1989). The Neoplatonic background is presented in detail by Raoul Mortley, *From Word to Silence, I: The Rise and Fall of Logos* (Bonn: Hanstein, 1986), and *From Word to Silence, II: The Way of Negation, Christian and Greek* (Bonn: Hanstein, 1986).

merely myth. The essential experience of the "divine" (or of one does not know quite what) can be recuperated on the far side of such critique by acknowledging that in relation to such experience our discourse does not *know* what it is talking about and that precisely this unknowing is its peculiar force and warrant. All language is acknowledged to be merely worldly and so secular, yet the intrinsic incompleteness, inadequacy, and friability of language (such as was seen in the previous chapter to be a second aspect of Beatrice's legacy) is critically dwelt upon to the end of attempting to peer beyond its limits. Consequently, some kind of horizon of the infinite or incommensurable shows up in the very fissures that open up in the midst of the secular world. That world proves incapable of achieving its own closure and is left gaping open toward some other reality—or toward reality as other than itself. Dickinson represents one such moment in the late Romantic Age that also saw the rise of Transcendentalism as a sort of declericalized, secularized, pantheistic religion in America.[4]

Roger Lundin, in *Emily Dickinson and the Art of Belief,* treats Dickinson as "one of the major religious thinkers of her age." But Lundin seems finally to find atheism more than apophaticism at the bottom of Dickinson's art. He considers her one of the first "to trace the trajectory of God's decline."[5] In the end, my Dickinson is closer to Richard Brantley's: his emphasis on the "radical skepticism" underlying Dickinson's oscillation between her Calvinist and her Armenian heritages provides a historical analogue to the present philosophical argument for Dickinson's art as an instinctive, if not a conscious and deliberate, contribution to apophatic poetics.[6] As such, apophasis brings the secular activity of the imaginative writer face to face with its own inherent impasse and breaks the secular frame open to what it cannot fathom or comprehend in purely secular terms.

II. Dickinson Criticism and the Apophatic Paradigm

Dickinson's highly original writing makes her a maddeningly difficult poet, one whom eminent critics confess baffles them. Yet her poems

---

4. A rich array of sources and resources relating to this background is found in Perry Miller, *The Transcendentalists: An Anthology* (Cambridge: Harvard University Press, 1960).

5. Roger Lundin, *Emily Dickinson and the Art of Belief* (Grand Rapids: Wm. B. Eerdmans, 2004 [1998], 2nd ed.; citations 3 and 4.

6. Brantley, *Experience and Faith,* 154 and *passim.*

become startlingly intelligible when read according to their apophatic grammar and rhetoric: the words and phrases fall into place—the place they make for what they necessarily leave unsaid but let show up distinctly silhouetted in their hollows and shadows. The poems selected to illustrate Dickinson's apophatic poetics in this chapter generally thematize a negative method of thought and perception, but they are only the most explicit representatives of a poetic corpus that is, throughout, profoundly apophatic in nature and inspiration and that rewards being read as such, while it stiffly resists readings that ignore this orientation.

Although the poems often proved impossible for her contemporaries to penetrate, they have won immense appreciation in more recent critical appraisals, particularly in those at least implicitly or unconsciously attuned to apophasis and the poetics of the unsayable. Even if rarely with explicit acknowledgment of the apophatic tradition as a primary context, this framework has already been extensively operative in scholarship aiming to illuminate Dickinson's poems. Readings of Dickinson pointing in this direction have insisted on compression and abbreviation as features that distinguish her style, marking it out especially against the stylistic canons of her own time. Cristanne Miller's analysis of Dickinson's versification shows ellipsis—the omission and deletion of logical and syntactical links—to be its governing principle.[7] Carla Pomarè finds in this elliptical technique the means of producing the silence that paradoxically gives Dickinson her distinctive voice. Margaret Freeman, who analyzes Dickinson's poetry in terms of cognitive principles of discourse, similarly stresses omissions and absences as the signifying elements that grant the poetry its power, a power "through silence to capture the true essence of intimacy."[8]

Beyond such attention to linguistic gaps and lapses, the apophatic logic informing Dickinson's poetics has been discerned in a more conscious and comprehensive way by Shira Wolosky, particularly in her essays interpreting Dickinson's poems in light of their translation into

---

7. Cristanne Miller, *Emily Dickinson: A Poet's Grammar* (Cambridge: Harvard University Press, 1987). More recently, see Paul Crumbley, *Inflections of the Pen: Dash and Voice in Emily Dickinson* (Lexington: University Press of Kentucky, 1997), and the essays, including Miller's "Dickinson's Experiments in Language," in *The Emily Dickinson Handbook*, eds. Gudrun Grabher, Roland Habenbüchle, and Cristanne Miller (Amherst: University of Massachusetts Press, 1998).

8. Carla Pomarè, "A 'Silver Reticence': Emily Dickinson's Rhetoric of Silence," 211–22, and Margaret H. Freeman, "Emily Dickinson and the Discourse of Intimacy," 191–201, both in *Semantics of Silence in Linguistics and Literature*, eds. Gudren M. Grabher and Ulrike Jessner (Heidelberg: Universitätsverlag C. Winter, 1996).

German by the post-Holocaust poet Paul Celan. Reading through this lens, Wolosky stresses the valence of silence not as affirming a metaphysical reality, a transcendent ultimacy beyond telling, but as indicating a cataclysm of history, an irruption of time into the presumably metaphysical order. This irruption is likewise beyond telling, though for a different reason: "silence represents the collapse of meaning within historical processes." This view of silence builds a certain modernist bias into Wolosky's readings. It foregrounds affinities with later writers more than with the ancient apophatic traditions from which these modes of expression hail. According to Wolosky, the realm beyond language has become contested and is agonized over by Dickinson and Celan alike: "What Dickinson's and Celan's poetry repeatedly traces is a rupture between earthly experience and transcendent reference."[9]

Wolosky does situate Dickinson within a tradition of "theo-linguistic" thought deriving ultimately from "Hermetic and Platonic traditions" crystallized in classics such as Thomas à Kempis's *The Imitation of Christ*, John Bunyan's *Pilgrim's Progress*, and Sir Thomas Browne's *Religio Medici*. She notes how such traditions were reflected in the preaching of Jonathan Edwards and in Horace Bushnell's *Dissertation on the Nature of Language as Related to Thought and Spirit* in Dickinson's immediate cultural milieu. Yet Wolosky emphasizes particularly how this type of metaphysical framework is thrown into crisis and collapses in Emily Dickinson's poems.[10] However, just this sort of critical negation of concepts is in fact traditionally how apophatic or negative theology frees faith and spiritual experience from rigid metaphysical and theological dogma: it does not arise first with the crisis of modernity. This could still be said for even much later modern poets such as T. S. Eliot ("Burnt Norton" II and III) and Geoffrey Hill (for example, in *Tenebrae*, 1978): they continue and affirm this negative theological vein more than they abandon or overcome it.

The apophatic discursive paradigm that operates in Dickinson's poetics, then, has perhaps still not been fully realized and reflectively thought through.[11] And yet this paradigm can furnish a necessary key to inter-

9. Shira Wolosky, "Apophatics and Poetics: Paul Celan Translating Emily Dickinson," in *Language and Negativity: Apophaticism in Theology and Literature*, ed. Henny Fiska Hägg (Oslo: Novus Press, 2000), 63–83; citations 82 and 68.

10. Shira Wolosky, "The Metaphysics of Language in Emily Dickinson and Paul Celan," *Trajectories of Mysticism in Theory and Literature*, ed. Philip Leonard (New York: St. Martin's Press, 2000), 5–45.

11. A notable exception is Anthony Hecht, "The Riddle of Emily Dickinson," in *Emily Dickinson: A Collection of Critical Essays*, ed. Judith Farr (Upper Saddle River, NJ:

pretation of at least a central axis of Dickinson's poetic modus operandi. My wager is that it will prove profitable to read Emily Dickinson in relation to a spiritual as well as an aesthetic tradition of apophasis. There are numerous spiritual poets who have privileged the theme of silence, and certain of them have linked this theme with the spiritual traditions of apophatic mysticism. John of the Cross represents the confluence of the two, the poetics of silence and a theology of negation, a theology such as is expounded also, for instance, in *The Cloud of Unknowing*. John is re-echoed again by Silesius Angelus, who works Meister Eckhart's mystic philosophy (transmitted via John Tauler) into high-strung spiritual (*"Geist-reiche"*) verse. In such poetry, I believe, can be found some of the strongest affinities to crucial aspects of Dickinson's work. Her poetry, accordingly, is in some sense to be understood as a spiritual exercise, a use of poetry as a means of approach to an unknowable "divinity" or at least as an instrument for registering an impossible, inarticulable absoluteness in her experience of the ultimate reality.

The diffuse presence of apophatic ideas and conceits in Western cultural tradition, in many of its poets and philosophers and divines, as well as in writers and artists of various stripe, would have sufficed to enable Dickinson to pick up the requisite hints for developing her own perceptions and reflections along apophatic lines. Surely, if the links were explicit and direct, they would already have been made the object of intense scholarly study. The fact that apophasis has not been such a focus in Dickinson studies suggests rather that Dickinson develops these ideas largely by her own lights and on the basis of her own experience of language and its "beyond." So perhaps it is not really that she belongs *within* this *tradition,* as one who integrally receives and "hands down" a certain sensibility or teaching or technique, so much as that she is an original discoverer of the aporetic condition and predicament of language, and conjointly of a faith in a beyond of language. This alone could make for abundant parallels between her and poets like John of the Cross, the poet of the dark night ("la noche oscura"), or Silesius Angelus, for whom the rose is without why ("die Ros' ist ohn warumb").[12] Of course, in

Prentice Hall, 1996), 149–62 (reprinted from *Obbligati* [New York: Atheneum, 1986]). Hecht detects in Dickinson's resort to riddles "a religious seriousness, however unorthodox, and a profound sense that neither life itself nor the holy text by which we interpret it is altogether intelligible, and both require a riddling mind or interpretive skill" (162). He discovers in Dickinson an "ignorant knowledge" like that of the Book of Revelation, which reveals only a mystery—how "perfect understanding of love (which is ignorance) makes love inexpressible, an ineffable mystery, a riddle" (161).

12. On these and other parallels, see my *On What Cannot Be Said*, vols. 1 and 2.

less concentrated form, apophatic topoi and techniques can be found in Romantic poets from Wordsworth to Shelley and Keats or Whitman. But none enacts this mode as intensely, incisively, and pervasively as Dickinson does: her poetics can hardly be understood at all without some reference to this paradigm.

Harold Bloom employs, perhaps unwittingly, apophatic terms to describe Dickinson's poetry when he comments that her "unique transport, her Sublime, is founded upon her unnaming of all our certitudes into so many blanks; it gives her, and her authentic readers, another way to see, almost, in the dark."[13] And Marjorie Perloff acutely observes a number of the key characteristics of apophatic discourse in Emily Dickinson, yet without actually viewing her in the context of, or even as associated with, this tradition. Perloff does place Dickinson in the "other tradition," other with respect to Romanticism and Modernism and their Symbolist aesthetic—another tradition that has long captivated Perloff's interest.[14] Tellingly Perloff writes, "She did not believe that words were in themselves irreplaceable." Dickinson's poetics, Perloff points out, are contrary to the Symbolist doctrine of the *mot juste,* according to which "the chosen word is the *only* word that can convey a desired set of meanings."[15] Perhaps no word can be exactly right for Dickinson, and perhaps the words used do not ultimately matter, if her poems are concerned above all with what is beyond words, with what cannot be said.

Perloff characterizes Dickinson's poetry as "process poetry," and she salutes the approaches to Dickinson's "variorum poetics" by Martha Nell Smith, Susan Howe, Sharon Cameron, and especially Marta Werner.[16] These critics can be grouped as ones attentive to aspects of Dickin-

13. Harold Bloom, *The Western Canon* (New York: Harcourt Brace, 1994), 308–9.

14. Marjorie Perloff, *The Poetics of Indeterminacy: Rimbaud to Cage* (Princeton: Princeton University Press, 1981), vii.

15. From Perloff's essay "Emily Dickinson and the Theory Canon," available online at http://wings.buffalo.edu/epc/authors/perloff/articles/dickinson.html.

16. The works working along these lines cited by Perloff include Martha Nell Smith, *Rowing in Eden* (Austin: University of Texas Press, 1992); Sharon Cameron, *Choosing Not Choosing: Dickinson's Fascicles* (Chicago: University of Chicago Press, 1992); Marta L. Werner, *Emily Dickinson's Open Folios* (Ann Arbor: University of Michigan Press, 1995); and Susan Howe, "These Flames and Generosities of the Heart: Emily Dickinson and the Illogic of Sumptuary Values," in *The Birth-mark: Unsettling the Wilderness in American Literary History* (Hanover: Wesleyan University Press, 1993). There is more on the manuscripts and fascicles, including essays by Smith and Cameron, in *The Emily Dickinson Handbook,* eds. Gudren Grabher, Roland Hagenbüchle, and Cristanne Miller. For a recent "commonsense" study of Dickinson's "variorum poetics" see Domhnall Mitchell, *Measures of Possibility: Emily Dickinson's Manuscripts* (Amherst: University of Massachusetts Press, 2005).

son's writing practice in which language is never definitive but is projected always beyond itself. One important thing the material they work with reveals is how tentative and changeable, rather than final, Dickinson's verbal formulations are.

There has, accordingly, been a great deal of stir about the editing of Dickinson's works, particularly in the wake of the newer facsimile and variorum editions of her poems and letters. This has led to new and acute attention paid to her manuscripts, autographs, and folios. Werner writes:

> Driven on by the desire to establish a definitive, or 'fixed,' text—an end requiring among other things the identification and banishment of textual 'impostors,' errors and stray marks—a scholar-editor ends up domesticating a poet. How do we apprehend an author's passage through a forever unfinished draft? . . . Today editing Emily Dickinson's late writings paradoxically involves unediting them, constellating these works not as still points of meaning or as incorruptible texts but, rather, as *events* and phenomena of freedom. (5)

This is all implicitly apophatic in tenor in that it retreats from words as definitive, negating them as always inadequate, yet Werner, like Perloff and virtually all other critics, overlooks the traditional spiritual paradigm of apophasis, and their doing so is liable to give rise to certain distortions and confusions. For example, Perloff's idea that Dickinson distrusts beauty and musicality and is seeking only truth in her poetry results from the effort to categorize Dickinson's poetics by clear conceptual contrasts to other styles of poetics, particularly the Romantic and aesthetic. Yet Dickinson herself not infrequently praises beauty and music, albeit of a more sublime sort than the ordinary:

> The words the happy say
> Are paltry melody
> But those the silent feel
> Are beautiful—
>   (F 1767; J 1750)[17]

---

17. *The Poems of Emily Dickinson*, Variorum Edition, ed. R. W. Franklin (Cambridge: The Belknap Press of Harvard University Press, 1998). Citations of the poems follow the text of the Franklin edition (abbreviated F), but I also give the numbering of the poems in the Johnson edition (abbreviated J): *The Poems of Emily Dickinson*, ed. Thomas H. Johnson (Cambridge: The Belknap Press of Harvard University, 1955 [1951]).

Indeed melody and beauty both—like truth—are placed by Dickinson, in true apophatic fashion, beyond definition in a heaven that is indistinguishable from the unnamable divinity Himself:

> The Definition of Beauty, is
> That Definition is none—
> Of Heaven, easing Analysis,
> Since Heaven and He
> Are One—
>   (F 797; J 988)

Dickinson writes the same thing verbatim in exactly parallel fashion about melody in another variation of this verse:

> The Definition of Melody—is—
> That Definition is none—
>   (F 797; J 988)

Dickinson does not mistrust beauty and music more than other forms of representation; she simply sees the Unrepresentable as hiding behind them all. Leaving this crucial distinction out of account, Perloff tends to overdraw the contrast with modernist and symbolist poetics. It is true that Dickinson's poetics have an essential component that goes well beyond aesthetic symbolism, but so did the poetics of many others among the canonical Romantics and modernists. And like them, Dickinson sometimes evinces a rather powerful desire for totalizing and even for apocalyptic vision, although she is well aware that it can be expressed only fragmentarily and fictively.[18] On another front, whereas Perloff strives to differentiate categorically Dickinson's view of language from that of the deconstructive critics, and so claims that Dickinson does not cancel or take back meaning, this *does* happen repeatedly, not to say systematically, in Dickinson's poems.[19] The aim is not the deconstruction of

---

18. This is demonstrated, for example, by Beth Maclay Doriani, *Emily Dickinson: Daughter of Prophecy* (Amherst: University of Massachusetts Press, 1996), and Gary Lee Stonum, *The Dickinson Sublime* (Madison: University of Wisconsin Press, 1990).

19. Dickinson's poems' ways of unsaying what they say, their poetic of the "suspended syllable," is treated effectively by Virginia Jackson, *Dickinson's Misery: A Theory of Lyric Reading* (Princeton: Princeton University Press, 2005), 31ff, in relation to the verses:

> When what they sung for is undone
> Who cares about a Blue Bird's Tune—

metaphysics (and to this extent Perloff is right) so much as spiritual experience at the limits of language—apophasis vis-à-vis what defies linguistic formulation. There is, after all, a convergence between poststructuralist poetics of indeterminacy and Dickinson's poetics, but Perloff struggles not to see it in order to make her case that Dickinson is not comprehensible in a deconstructive theoretical optics like the poetry typically cited as exemplary by poststructuralist critics.

Perloff's own theoretical perspective is informed especially by Language (or L=A=N=G=U=A=G=E) Poetry, by writers like Charles Bernstein, David Bromige, and Ron Silliman, and by others like Rosemarie Waldrop and Lyn Hejinian working poetically with Wittgenstein's texts and philosophy of language.[20] Jerome McGann describes how this type of poetry grows out of the "literalism" of modernism.[21] Its thrust lies largely in eliminating symbolic reference to everything beyond the text, particularly to a world or a subject, and thereby riveting attention rather to the literal scene of writing itself. At least prima facie, apophatic poetics, with its orientation to a beyond of writing and language, is diametrically opposed to such a perspective. It seems that Wittgenstein's inspiration can be taken in both of these apparently antithetical directions: it has galvanized the writing of Language Poetry, but it can also turn us away from language toward the beyond of language. The latter is the dimension that the type of poetry I am calling apophatic explores. It is distinguished by its recalcitrance to any definitive linguistic formulation whatsoever of what it seeks to express. There is currently considerable excitement over discovering in Dickinson some of our own recently acquired obsessions and enthusiasms for the materialities of language, for the text's literal surfaces and for the self-reflexive scene of writing: current critics are keen to perceive the letter liberated from the spirit, from subjectivity and intentionality and such-like metaphysical ghosts. However, in the midst of this ferment, it is important not to lose sight of Dickinson's continuity with the apophatic tradition as a specifically spiritual tradition endowed with a powerfully poetic dimension.

Why, Resurrection had to wait
Till they had moved a stone
(F 1353)

20. Marjorie Perloff, *Wittgenstein's Ladder: Poetic Language and the Strangeness of the Ordinary* (Chicago: University of Chicago Press, 1996).
21. Jerome McGann, *Black Riders* (Princeton: Princeton University Press, 1993), particularly the afterword.

Many poems become astonishingly lucid and perspicuous, and in any case understandable, once we see them as not about what they say but as about what they cannot say. They point to a remoter abyss or "Sea" which language can mark but not articulate. This recess of speech darkly backgrounds almost everything in human life, including everyday emotions like gratitude. It lies beyond the reach (or "Plumb") of speech and beyond the meanings (or "Answer") that language can fish for with its verbal threads and cues, its "Line and Lead":

> Gratitude—is not the mention
> Of a Tenderness,
> But it's still appreciation
> Out of Plumb of Speech.
>
> When the Sea return no Answer
> By the Line and Lead
> Proves it there's no Sea, or rather
> A remoter Bed?
>   (F 1120c; J 989)

The difficulty, then, is not so much in the poem itself as in what it points out beyond itself and allows to be sensed or fathomed, but not to be comprehended. The extremely dense, discriminating, hairsplitting hermeneutics required by typical modernist poems, aiming at always greater precision, is not always called for nor necessarily conducive to letting Dickinson's poems happen—and so have their clearest and most intense effect. The assumptions of a mastery of language by the artist and of the formal perfection of the artwork cannot be applied so rigorously to Dickinson's kind of writing. If, as Perloff persuasively argues, Dickinson has not been part of the canon of poets regularly referred to in discussions of poetic theory, this suggests that some important key to the theoretical significance of her poetry may have been missing from the tools of her interpreters. I wish now, by placing some poems into an apophatic framework, to illustrate the aptness of the apophatic paradigm to unlock their most general intellectual significance and open to view not only the language-theoretical but also the spiritual underpinnings on which these poems are based. Dickinson's poems will thus be made to show the deep ambivalence of poetic writing as a secular form of creative expression. Such writing challenges and exceeds the secular frame that is also its enabling condition.

III. The Poems' Saying and Unsaying of Silence

The characteristically apophatic technique of the poems can be approached most simply and directly on the poems' own terms by attending first to the topic of silence taken together with the thematics of the intrinsic limits and foundering of language. There are numerous very short poems that effectively announce the theme of silence and suggest its potency as infinitely greater than that of any possible utterance. For example:

> There is no Silence in the Earth—so silent
> As that endured
> Which uttered, would discourage Nature
> And haunt the World.
> (F 1004; J 1004)

Silence must simply be endured. Any attempt to master it and give it utterance would be an artifice forcing it to be what it is not, manufacturing an unnatural *un*reality that would haunt the natural world.

Other lines intimate the approach, venturing well beyond the natural world and all its appearances, to a faceless divinity, or an Infinity, that can accept and sanction only silence as its (denial of) expression:

> Silence is all we dread.
> There's Ransom in a Voice—But Silence is Infinity.
> Himself have not a face.
> (F 1300b; J 1251)

Silence, in its desolation and emptiness, is dreadful, and so naturally we prefer that it be "ransomed" or redeemed in human and natural terms by a Voice. "But," just as God "Himself" does not have a face, so Silence itself can have no proper finite form or voice: it is "Infinity." This indeterminacy of its object in terms of language and concepts is the predicament of apophasis, and it is perhaps finally to be preferred to the "Ransom in a Voice." In any case, this silence is nearer to the nature of God Himself. It leads to the silence of the mystic, as well as to the mystic poet's struggles and declarations of failure to find any adequate expression.

Alongside such acknowledgments of a dimension of silence that is closest to the sacred source of all that is and of all that is said, Dickinson frequently alludes to indescribable moments of epiphany that she experiences as religious revelations and miracles and that transcend ordinary verbal expression. They consist in "thoughts" that are unique and incomparable, thoughts that "come a single time" and that cannot be reduced to any common currency of words. They must rather be tasted, like the communion wine in the sacrament of the Eucharist. However many times the experience is repeated, it is always unique and incomparable:

> Your thoughts don't have words every day
> They come a single time
> Like signal esoteric sips
> Of the communion Wine
> Which while you taste so native seems
> So easy so to be
> You cannot comprehend its price
> Nor its infrequency
> > (F 1476; J 1452)

Such thoughts that defy comprehension and articulation seem to be "native," familiar, as if *déjà vu,* and yet, at the same time, they seem to escape, never to return: they are assignable to no time and as such are timeless and ineffable:

> A Thought went up my mind today—
> That I have had before—
> But did not finish—some way back—
> I could not fix the Year—
>
> Nor Where it went—nor why it came
> The second time to me—
> Nor definitely, what it was—
> Have I the Art to say—
>
> But somewhere—in my soul—I know—
> I've met the Thing before—
> It just reminded me—'twas all—
> And came my way no more—
> > (F 731; J 701)

Dickinson's poetry is pregnant with the sense that unsayability itself can signify and that the poem's very failure to say what it strives to say may harbor its most powerful significance. She says as much in a poem like the following:

> If I could tell how glad I was
> I should not be so glad—But when I cannot make the Force,
> Nor mould it into word
> I know it is a sign
> That new Dilemma be
> From mathematics further off
> Than from Eternity
>   (F 1725; J 1668)

This incapacity of speech, or apophasis, is a sign of how far removed from "mathematics," that is, from any rationally calculable, articulable knowledge, is the intimation of the Eternity that Dickinson dwells on but cannot express. Still, her "hindered Words"—a good expression for apophatic rhetoric—are the key to telling of this Nothing (nothing that can be said, which is nevertheless everything), and thereby to renovating the world:

> By homely gifts and hindered words
> The human heart is told
> Of nothing—"Nothing" is the force
> That renovates the World—
>   (F 1611; J 1563)

As so often, something that is indicated as Nothing makes the poem and clinches its significance.

IV. Dickinson's Negative Poetics as Negative Theology (or as a Spiritual Practice and Aesthetic)

Primed by glancing through examples like these, we are now in a position to appreciate how Dickinson's poetry continually approaches and even coincides with characteristic themes of negative theology taken as a paradigm of spiritual understanding and experience. Negative theology is the kind of apophasis pertaining specifically to God, about whom we can only know (and therefore can only say) what "he" is *not*. God is Nothing (that can be said), even though he is the source and ground of all beings.

Still, he has no finite content, no attribute whatsoever by which he could be anything that can be articulated in language. In various ways, Dickinson articulates the principle that this Nothing is the All, the Absolute (1071). Even more acutely, she says that this is so because the All *is not*: it is "The Missing All."

> The Missing All, prevented Me
> From missing minor Things.
> If nothing larger than a World's
> Departure from a Hinge
> Or Sun's Extinction, be observed
> 'Twas not so large that I
> Could lift my Forehead from my work
> For Curiosity.
> (F 995b; J 985)

This is exactly the status of the Neoplatonic One, which is no thing but which everything that is anything emanates from and deeply depends on and indeed *is* in the abyss of its being. Whatever is *something* is incomparably less than this missing All, and therefore even the destruction of the entire finite universe would be insufficient to distract the speaker's attention from the contemplation of this infinite All that she knows is infinitely greater than anything finite whatsoever.

The mystic philosophy devolving from Plotinus (AD 205–270) known as Neoplatonism, as distinct from the Middle Platonism that evolved *between* Plato and Plotinus, inspired revivals far beyond the Hellenistic world of its origin, all through the Middle Ages and Renaissance, as well as in the seventeenth century among the Cambridge Platonists and their successors even in the Romantic age. Thomas Taylor (1758–1835) in particular was influential in disseminating Neoplatonic thinking among Romantic poets from Shelley to Emerson.[22]

According to this philosophical outlook, which accentuates the theological inspiration of Plato's thinking as oriented toward a transcendent, unifying principle of the universe as a whole, the One is All, the Absolute. But this also makes it Nothing, no *thing* that is determinate or finite, nothing that can be defined or said, for then it would not be absolute and

---

22. See, for example, Thomas Taylor, *Essays and Fragments of Proclus the Platonic Successor* (Somerset, UK: Prometheus Trust, 1999), and *Thomas Taylor the Platonist: Selected Writings*, eds. Kathleen Raine and George Mills Harper (Princeton: Princeton University Press, 1969).

unconditioned. As Dickinson writes: "The Object Absolute—is nought" (1071). While this Nothing in itself may be All or Absolute, whatever part or aspect of it is definable or even perceptible is *not* absolute. Something may be gained by perception for the appropriating subject, but only at the cost of losing the Absolute *as* absolute, as the perfect and divine, a "Perfectness," which thereafter we typically blame or "upbraid" for being so far removed from us:

> Perception of an object costs
> Precise the Object's loss—
> Perception in itself a Gain
> Replying to its Price—
> The Object Absolute—is nought—
> Perception sets it fair
> And then upbraids a Perfectness
> That situates so far—
>   (F 1103a; J 1071)

Dickinson here intuits that the presence of the Absolute as the absolute being of any object whatever is lost in being perceived and thereby reduced to the status of an object. The Object Absolute is the deeper reality of any object, but it is no object at all itself, and it is made to be naught by being objectified through perception.

Dickinson postulates an indistinct kind of knowledge of aura or "glory" that does not circumscribe any object of knowledge, since an object could only be finite and consequently *not* be this Absolute. She figures such objectless knowing rather as an intuitive, mystic *seeing* that transpired in immediacy and defies explanation:

> You'll know it—as you know 'tis Noon—
> By Glory—
> As you do the Sun—
> By Glory—
> As you will in Heaven—
> Know God the Father—and the Son.
>
> By intuition, Mightiest Things
> Assert themselves—and not by terms—
> "I'm Midnight"—need the Midnight say—
> "I'm Sunrise"—Need the Majesty?

Omnipotence—had not a Tongue—
His lisp—is Lightning—and the Sun—
His Conversation—with the Sea—
"How shall you know"?
Consult your Eye!
    (F 429a; J 420)

Midnight and sunrise, as the zero degrees of night and day, are absolute and therefore not to be said but "seen."[23]

On the basis presumably of this sort of "intuition" and not of "terms" (420), Dickinson feels her way to the same kind of vocabulary as was used by the Neoplatonic negative theologians as referred to and as revolving around the ineffable One[24]:

I found the words to every thought
I ever had—but One—
And that—defies Me—
As a Hand did try to chalk the Sun

To Races nurtured in the Dark—
How would your Own—begin?
Can Blaze be shown in Cochineal—
Or Noon—in Mazarin?
    (F 436; J 581)

It is impossible to find the right word for the One, if it is thought of strictly as without any determination or multiplicity. In like fashion, the sun, symbolically the source of all, cannot itself be delineated or illuminated, since everything visible can be delineated or illuminated only by

---

23. The apophatic tradition is intertwined with a broader tradition of theological aesthetics (for which see Hans Urs von Balthasar, *Herrlichkeit: Eine theologische Aesthetik*, 4 vols. [Einsieldeln: Johannes, 1969], trans. in 7 vols. as *Glory: A Theological Aesthetic* [Edinburgh: T&T Clark, 1982–91]), just as negative or apophatic theology works necessarily in tandem with affirmative, kataphatic (*kata*—"according to" + *phasis*—"speech") theology right from the source texts in the *Corpus Dionysiacum* of Pseudo-Dionysius the Areopagite (fifth to sixth centuries AD), as is emphasized especially by Denys Turner, *The Darkness of God: Negativity in Christian Mysticism* (Cambridge: Cambridge University Press, 1995).

24. The most radical and culminating development of this tradition in the ancient world can be found in the Neoplatonic philosopher Damascius (c. 462—538?). See my "Damascius. Of the Ineffable: Aporetics of the Notion of an Absolute Principle," *Arion: A Journal of Humanities and the Classics* 12/1 (2004): 111-31.

its light. Absolute brightness cannot be perceived apart from the colors or dyes that alone make it visible by toning down its total intensity, so as to bring it within the range of finite perception. A similar idea was expressed by another celebrated Platonist poet in the familiar verses: "Life like a dome of many-colored glass / Stains the white radiance of eternity" ("Adonais"). But Shelley's flowing eloquence and rhetorical grandeur are far removed from Dickinson's laconic anti-rhetoric, with its hard-edged, rare-dye quality that safeguards the peculiarly apophatic effect of the mystery of the unsaid. Whereas Shelley's language becomes transparent like light, Dickinson's poetry, with its rare words and rhythmic arrests—marked especially by her idiosyncratic use of dashes for spacings within and between lines—tends toward verbal viscousness and opacity.

These poems offer some of the most poignant and exact expressions anywhere in literature of how linguistic negation, or the self-erasure of words that act to cancel themselves out or to proscribe verbal expression, becomes the positive source of all that is perceived and can be said. They often place this experience in an aesthetic dimension of beauty, enchantment, and rapture, exclaiming, for example:

> To tell the Beauty would decrease
> To state the spell demean—

However, this spell is itself but the sign of something yet more indefinite and inarticulable:

> There is a syllable-less Sea
> Of which it is the sign
> My will endeavors for its word
> And fails, but entertains
> A Rapture as of Legacies—
> Of introspective mines—
>   (F 1689; J 1700)

There is no adequate expression for this experience that issues rather in a "syllable-less Sea." Yet the rapture left as a result or "legacy" of such experience testifies to interior riches that cannot be put into words, and so be exteriorized or objectified, but remain lodged, nevertheless, in "introspective mines"—where "mine(s)" suggests perhaps something irreducibly private and personal, even though this very expression crystallizes the subjective sensation as a mineral-hard grammatical fact.

Even some of Dickinson's lighter poems can be illuminated by being placed in the context of this problematic of negative theology and its corresponding apophatic rhetoric and spiritual practice. It is fundamental to the poetic theo-logic through which she sees the world. The reference to the unsayable and indefinable as the necessary background for all that she does say and articulate in her poems underlies even such a playful expostulation as:

> I'm Nobody! Who are you?
> Are you—Nobody—too?
> Then there's a pair of us!
> Don't tell! they'd advertise—you know!
>
> How dreary—to be—Somebody!
> How public—like a Frog—
> To tell one's name—the livelong June—
> To an admiring Bog!
>   (F 260; J 288)

Anyone who is merely *some*one is boring by comparison with the infinite mystery of the person who recognizes herself as Nobody. Of course, this is what must not be told ("Don't tell!"), for translated into words, it would be immediately betrayed: it would then be degraded to the level of the public gossip or "advertising" that passes so facilely from mouth to mouth, unthinkingly, like the croaking of frogs in a bog. What is articulated in this way becomes sound without meaning—the opposite of a plenum or surplus of meaning for which there is no adequate articulation. In this latter perspective, that of the experience of and even immersion in the unsayable, we may finally be indistinct from the divine, to the extent that we remain nameless—like the unnamable God, the great Nobody (for us, that is, as finite and merely natural, ungraced, creatures), who is worshipped in mystic raptures of apophatic discourse across the ages. In her own ingenious accents, Emily Dickinson, too, is participating in this tradition. In poem after poem, she demonstrates a powerful belief in the infinite positivity of Nothing. Likewise in her life, by her fabled reclusiveness, she seems to have said nothing—the nothing that actually contains everything.

Some will undoubtedly say that it is futile to speculate about what the poems do *not* say and that it is even more absurd and presumptuous if this is what they *cannot* say. True, such reading and such writing are not a matter of positive proof so much as of projection beyond what can be stated. This is nothing if not a spiritual exercise. Poetry of this order is, after all, a matter of faith, even if faith in what proves impossible to say. Where all categories of determination lose their grip in reference to what exceeds all terms of description and expression, religion and literature tend to coalesce: both aim at what neither can express, and an apophatic discourse is engendered as the effect of this impasse in the face of what Dickinson has christened, teasingly and oxymoronically, "The Missing All." This realization of the nothingness of all positive expressions (not to mention dogmatic terms) for divinity belongs to the secularization of religious revelation through poetry, but at the same time it reopens this revelation, which can never be exhausted, to untold and untellable mystery such as has been pursued by the millenary soundings of the religious imagination.

the dialectical logic of william butler yeats's byzantium poems

I. The Logic

Yeats is unusual, if not unique, among poets for having formalized his subject matter into an extra-poetic system. Although certainly poetry always remained his final aim, its fluid movement, subtle ambiguity, and defiance of confinement (especially characteristic of symbolic poetry) promised to frustrate any attempt to conceive a unified vision of the whole in it alone. He had first to achieve his unity of vision in the abstract; then he could proceed to weave it, with control and precision, into the rich and complex tapestry of his verse. Testimony to the predominance and urgency of this quest for unity appears in his 1919 essay titled "If I Were Four-and-Twenty": "One day when I was twenty-three or twenty-four this sentence seemed to form in my head, without my willing it, much as sentences form when we are half-asleep: 'Hammer your thoughts into unity.' For days I could think of nothing else, and for years I tested all I did by that sentence."[1]

---

1. William Butler Yeats, "If I Were Four-and-Twenty," in *Explorations* (New York: Macmillan, 1956), 23.

Yeats sought to attain the unity he so desired through the symbol. Because the symbol is able to comprehend vastly more than what it literally denotes, it fills the imagination with an awareness of the underlying unity of a multiplicity: multifarious images, emotions, and ideas, each with its own radiating associations, are all united in the symbol. In "The Symbolism of Poetry," Yeats describes how meaning emanates in all directions from a symbolic poem: "A little lyric evokes an emotion, and this emotion gathers others about it and melts into their being in the making of some great epic; and at last, needing an always less delicate body, or symbol, as it grows more powerful, it flows out, with all it has gathered, among the blind instincts of daily life, where it moves a power within powers, as one sees ring within ring in the stem of an old tree"[2].

This concept of the symbol entails, to some degree, a form of what is known to philosophers as "the doctrine of internal relations." This doctrine asserts that all of a thing's relations to other things pertain to the essence of the thing or are constitutive of its intrinsic nature.[3] Likewise, the symbol, conceived as a center of widening rings, carries an unlimited number of associations, each of which is part of its essential, intrinsic meaning and is not merely incidental or external to it; for although these symbolic relations are not properties that could be deduced from the concept of the object that the symbol literally is, they still do represent part—the truly vital part—of the symbol's essential meaning and import. Their imaginative and emotional content, as much as the symbol's analytic content (the set of predicates logically deducible from the subject), determine the essential nature of the symbol as an aesthetic object, even if this dimension of the symbol's significance is too elusive to be specified in a proposition that is simply true or false.

For this reason, there is something to be learned about Yeats's symbolism from the doctrine of internal relations. The doctrine entails that in an exhaustive description of any given thing, all items are essential. Such a description would include the thing's relations to all other things. On the highest level of abstraction, these are relations of being different from each of these other things, that is, of *not being* any of them, or of being a negation of each of them (in a mild sense of negation implying only difference, not diametric opposition or contrariety). But according to the doctrine of internal relations, as we have just noted, all these relations

2. William Butler Yeats, "The Symbolism of Poetry," in *Essays and Introductions* (New York: Macmillan, 1961), 157–58.

3. A concise description and history can be found in Richard Rorty, "Relations, Internal and External," in *Encyclopedia of Philosophy*, ed. D. M. Borchert (Detroit: Thomson Gale, 2006), 2nd ed., vol. 8, 335–45.

of negation (as relations categorically) are included in the thing's essence. This means that the thing can be what it essentially is only by virtue of *not* being what it is not, that is, by standing in a negative relation to each of its negations, or by being *different* from what is other than it. Thus all things other than the thing we have selected, through being essentially related to it, are constitutive of its identity. The thing in this sense takes up and includes all other things within itself—it becomes a locus of relations in which the whole is embraced. Yeats expresses something of this sort in "Vacillation":

> And half is half and yet is all the scene;
> And half and half consume what they renew . . .[4]

This logic of poetic symbolism now resembles the dialectical logic of Hegel, and it is rife with the paradox that so fascinated both Hegel and Yeats. From a dialectical point of view nothing simply is what it is; the distinctions between things break down as all forms flow out beyond their boundaries (the half into the whole) and—because they are essentially interrelated—radically interpenetrate. Yeats thought of his own psychological phase, the Demoniac Man, in terms very much resembling this type of dialectical flux: "As contrasted with Phase 13 and Phase 14, where mental images were separated from one another that they might be subject to knowledge, all now flow, change, flutter, cry out, or mix into something else. . . ."[5]

We arrive at such dialectical thinking as a result of a disposition to view things in their wholeness. By widening our perspective without limit—and what limit would not be arbitrary?—we would come eventually to a consideration of the sum of relations any given thing has to all other things. If we then consider the sense in which all these relations are essential—the sense, that is, in which all things other than the chosen thing, in respect of their relations to it, are included in its identity as a singular individual—we see the thing as a particular incarnation of the whole, that is, as a "concrete universal": hence, "To see the world in a grain of sand," as Blake wrote. In this way opposites—a thing and its negation—cease to be mutually exclusive and become dependent on each other. They are conceived of as contained within each other rather than as separated poles.

---

4. William Butler Yeats, *Collected Poems*. Definitive edition (New York: Macmillan, 1956).

5. William Butler Yeats, *A Vision* (New York: Collier, 1956; rpt. 1966), 141.

Yeats's use of this sort of logic is most evident in what he termed the "fundamental symbol" of his system, the double cone or vortex. It consists of two antithetical gyres which, far from being obdurately held apart, interpenetrate from vertex to base. In the gyres, Yeats finds his symbol for the whole, since it can be used, he says, to represent and interpret "every possible movement of life and of thought" (*A Vision*, 78). This is a truly universal symbol, one in which all things come together into unity. But the unity thus achieved is only a formal unity, and the symbol in which it is achieved is merely an abstract symbol; all things have been united only through a common form which was found by abstracting from the content of each individual thing. The human mind is unable to apprehend the totality of relations of a particular thing, where those relations are sensuous and concrete rather than being conceptually colligated in an analytic formula. The mind is capable of experiencing in poetry the unity of only a limited number of images and impressions. And thus, for the subjects of his poems, Yeats required less abstractly universal symbols that would evoke certain particular imaginative associations more vividly than others. One of the most powerful and richly poetic of all Yeats's unifying and concretely universal symbols is the Sacred City of Byzantium.

For Yeats, ancient and medieval Byzantium was an emblem of unity as well as a unifying symbol. His fascination with the city resulted in large measure from his imagining it as having attained to an ideal of cultural unity. He writes, "I think that in early Byzantium, maybe never before or since in recorded history, religious, aesthetic, and practical life were one." And he illustrates this oneness in the portrait he sketches of "some philosophical worker in mosaic," to be found in "some little wine shop," "who could answer all my questions, the supernatural descending nearer to him than to Plotinus even. . . ." Here everything could be woven "into a vast design, the work of many that seemed the work of one, that made building, picture, pattern, metal-work or rail and lamp, seem but a simple image . . ." (*A Vision*, 279–80). But the Byzantium poems could be written only after Yeats had worked out his system in *A Vision*. They present a concrete poetic embodiment of unity but do nothing to explicate it. Yeats had first to grasp the unity they express in his formal system of correspondences: that is what gave him the abstract design for the exquisitely cut cameos of the poems.[6]

---

6. For further sifting of Yeats's system and its intellectual underpinnings, see especially Neil Mann, Matthew Gibson, and Claire Nally, eds., *W. B. Yeats's* A Vision: *Explications and Contexts* (Clemson, SC: Clemson University Digital Press, 2012), as well as Matthew Gibson, *Yeats, Coleridge and the Romantic Sage* (London: Macmillan, 2000).

Before descending upon the poems themselves, we must draw out one further consequence of our theory of the symbol and its dialectical logic. The mind (including conscious sensibilities in general) is what forges the connections between objects in a symbolic poem. We may look to Yeats's "Symbols" for illustration of this fairly obvious, though deceptively simple, point:

> A *storm-beaten* old watch tower,
> A blind hermit rings the hour.
>
> All destroying sword-blade still
> Carried by the wandering fool.
>
> Gold-sewn silk on the sword blade,
> Beauty and fool together laid.

The links between the hermit and blindness, between destruction and the fool, or between Beauty and the fool, are not physical relations of empirical objects. Physical relations are extremely important in determining how things will be related in our minds, and admittedly our understanding of the words depends on our empirical experience. But there is also much more that is added by the emotions, the imagination, and the intellect, and it is these connotations, intimations, and allusions that enable us to experience the blindness of the hermit as really meaning something, as more than just a dumb fact. Because in our symbolist credo symbolic relations, which exist only in the mind and are therefore ideal, are taken as in a very meaningful sense real, we must adopt something of an idealist metaphysic. Even if we accept empirical verification as the only definitive test of objective existence or realness, ideal symbolic reality can still be held to qualify. This is the claim of astrology and of many other of Yeats's occult interests: it is believed that physical phenomena can be predicted and influenced by symbolic relationships. Less controversially, we can affirm that symbols have an aesthetic reality. On this basis, the symbol is conceived of as creating a poetic universe that we can enter into and experience imaginatively. Without necessarily committing ourselves to the view that mind is the metaphysical source and foundation of all reality and meaning, we can simply declare that we experience some sort of reality or meaning, though perhaps it comes all from fiction, from inventions of ideas and imaginings in art.

On this basis, art can be elevated to the status of an incarnation of divine spirit in the material, secular world. It entails the affirmation of an ideal reality, and this lies at the root of Yeats's symbolist technique. But from this affirmation springs a conflict between the ideal and the physical, which becomes one of Yeats's most obsessive themes, notably in his Byzantium poems. Byzantium is a symbol of a divinely regulated civilization and an inspired spiritual life. Accordingly, Yeats's aesthetic treatment of this symbol stresses the tension of the secular toward the transcendent, which is wrought to its highest pitch of intensity in these poems.

II. The Poems

The Byzantium poems pivot upon the conflict of the spiritual with the material, the ideal with the physical, and their reconciliation in art by means of the synthetic unifying powers of the imagination. These concerns are general parameters of Yeats's thought, and they are crucial in his poetry right from his earliest works. The ideal world by itself is depicted as sorrowfully sterile in an early poem, "Fergus and the Druid," where Fergus, feeling the burden of a worldly crown upon his head, takes from the Druid a "little bag of dreams," but in the wisdom he acquires from the bag he finds cause only for unrelenting exasperation and declares:

> But now I have grown nothing, knowing all.
> Ah! Druid, Druid, how great webs of sorrow
> Lay hidden in the small slate-colored thing!

This text must be set next to lyrics such as "The White Birds" of the same volume (*The Rose*, 1893) expressing ecstatic exaltation in an ideal existence outside time:

> I would that we were, my beloved, white birds on
>   the foam of the sea!
> We tire of the flame of the meteor, before it can fade
>   and flee;
> And the flame of the blue star of twilight, hung low
>   on the rim of the sky,
> Has awaked in our hearts, my beloved, a sadness that
>   may not die.
> . . . .
> I am haunted by numberless islands, and many a
>   Danaan shore,

Where Time would surely forget us, and Sorrow
    come near us no more;
Soon far from the rose and lily and fret of the
    flames would we be,
Were we only white birds, my beloved, buoyed out
    on the foam of the sea!

Such juxtaposition gives an indication of the great difficulty, for Yeats, of choosing between this world, the temporal world of the body, and the other world, the eternal realm of the soul. He confronts this choice directly, with divided will, in "To the Rose upon the Rood of Time":

Come near, come near, come near—Ah, leave me still
A little space for the rose-breath to fill!
Lest I no more hear common things that crave;
The weak worm hiding down in its small cave,
The field-mouse running by me in the grass,
And heavy mortal hopes that toil and pass;
But seek alone to hear the strange things said
By God to the bright hearts of those long dead,
And learn to chaunt a tongue men do not know . . .

This ever-present theme of the conflict between the natural and the transcendent is paralleled throughout the poems by the theme of its resolution in art. Art begins its career as a unifying value, bringing together all that is worthy of human attainment, in the very first lyric of the *Collected Poems*, "The Song of the Happy Shepherd," with the lines:

For words alone are certain good:
Sing, then, for this is also sooth.

Continually reworked in every subsequent group of poems, this motif, along with the related matter-spirit dichotomy, reaches perhaps its sublimest expression in the Byzantium poems, first, in "Sailing to Byzantium":

That is no country for old men. The young
In one another's arms, birds in the trees
—Those dying generations—at their song,
The salmon-falls, the mackerel-crowded seas,
Fish, flesh, or fowl, commend all summer long

Whatever is begotten, born, and dies.
Caught in that sensual music all neglect
Monuments of unageing intellect.

An aged man is but a paltry thing,
A tattered coat upon a stick, unless
Soul clap its hands and sing, and louder sing
For every tatter in its mortal dress,
Nor is there singing school but studying
Monuments of its own magnificence;
And therefore I have sailed the seas and come
To the holy city of Byzantium.

O sages standing in God's holy fire
As in the gold mosaic of a wall,
Come from the holy fire, perne in a gyre,
And be the singing-masters of my soul.
Consume my heart away; sick with desire
And fastened to a dying animal
It knows not what it is; and gather me
Into the artifice of eternity.

Once out of nature I shall never take
My bodily form from any natural thing,
But such a form as Grecian goldsmiths make
Of hammered gold and gold enamelling
To keep a drowsy Emperor awake;
Or set upon a golden bough to sing
To lords and ladies of Byzantium
Of what is past, or passing, or to come.

The opening stanza of the poem sets the dialectic of the time-eternity, body-soul antinomy into motion. These first eight lines purport to announce a rejection of Ireland, the land of time and the body. It is "no country for old men," such as this elderly expatriate. But the words spoken ostensibly in condemnation of Ireland present such an attractive picture, on the whole, that we cannot help feeling some undercurrent of half-heartedness, an ambivalence in the speaker's attitude of rejection. The world of nature, including some blissful human inhabitants, is enticingly limned with "The young / In one another's arms" and "birds in the trees." Furthermore, the "salmon falls" are emblematic of strength and vigor. Yeats would remember, as A. Norman Jeffares observed, "In Celtic legendry the salmon is used as a symbol of strength; the hero Cuchulain is renowned for his 'salmon leap,' and his energy is compared to the flight of a bird."[7]

Similar in effect, the phrase "mackerel-crowded seas," filling the mouth with the abundance it denotes, portrays nature as teeming with life, as at its climax rather than in decline. The "sensual music" thus becomes seductive and emits vibrant overtones celebrating the land being renounced. This mingling of attraction and repulsion is captured in the paradox of "Those dying generations." While these words seem intended simply to designate recurrent death, they also suggest, by dint of an ambiguity, life and generation and, moreover, the cycle through which life renews itself, which we cannot but feel as a positive value. Finally, "Monuments of unageing intellect" is too insupportably mighty a phrase, especially as a metaphor for a drooping old man, not to tremble with ironic resonance. Thus, from the first stanza we can sense the dialectical tension between the movement away from Ireland, toward eternal, immovable monuments, and the countermovement toward Ireland, with its temporal flux and the flow of nature.

I do not mean to suggest that the speaker's departure is unjustified. He is indeed an "aged man" who is perhaps too infirm of body to move in step with the sensual music of youth and sprightly life any longer. But there is not here simply an unequivocal espousal of the intellectual: there is rather a vigorous dialectic of the intellectual with the sensuous. This antithesis is further developed in the second stanza, where the speaker becomes "A tattered coat upon a stick," that is, a scarecrow, shriveled and lifeless and by implication antagonistic toward the birds that populate the scenery of Ireland in the first stanza. But the most significant development in this stanza is the introduction of the motif of art as the vehicle of transcendence. Singing is looked to as the soul's deliverance from "Decrepit age" and specifically as the antidote to mortality:

. . . and louder sing
For every tatter in its mortal dress . . .

7. Norman A. Jeffares, "The Byzantium Poems of W. B. Yeats," *Review of English Studies* 22 (1946): 47.

This is how the repellent images of age are to be made palatable and how they can even be used to attract us to the new lease on life that is granted through the embrace of art.

In the third stanza, the speaker invokes the sages standing inert "in God's holy fire / As in the gold mosaic of a wall." He appeals to them to "Come from the holy fire," to give up temporarily the eternal stillness of "the condition of fire," in which "is all music and all rest,"[8] and to "perne in a gyre," so that they may be the "singing-masters" of a soul yet spiraling through time. Thus the meeting of the eternal with the temporal takes place through art, art betokened here, as earlier, by song. The lines that follow embody perhaps the strongest repulsion in the poem between the natural and the supernatural, as the speaker entreats the sages to "consume my heart away," presumably by means of the purgatorial fires. The speaker then traces his heart's consternation to a deficiency in knowledge—"It knows not what it is"—employing the knowledge-power cognate of the divine-earthly polarity. But the poles do not fly apart. They are held together in dialectical interpenetration by the words "sick with desire," which confess the persisting attachment of the speaker, a "dying animal," to nature, even as he prays to escape it, and by the stanza's conclusion on a note that rings of art, which is consistently the sign of reconciliation and unity, with the phrase "the *artifice* of eternity." The suggestion of artificiality in "artifice of eternity" secures the connection with the primal materials out of which artworks are labouringly made, while at the same time the phrase chimes with the magnificent, unaging "Monuments" of the preceding stanza. It thus intones a hymn to great art as the author of eternity, be it through architecture, song, or artifact.

The paradoxical dialectic between nature and transcendence, in which each becomes inseparable from the other, culminates in the poem's final stanza, which concentrates on the unifying focal point of that dialectic—the state of artistic rapture. Nature, transcendence, and art all fuse together beautifully in the symbol of the golden bird. The speaker says:

Once out of nature I shall never take
My bodily form from any natural thing . . .

But, paradoxically, he goes on to explain that he will take his shape from

. . . such a form as Grecian goldsmiths make
Of hammered gold and gold enamelling

8. Yeats, "Anima Mundi," in *Essays and Introductions,* 524.

To keep a drowsy Emperor awake;
Or set upon a golden bough to sing
To lords and ladies of Byzantium
Of what is past, or passing, or to come.

As one of Yeats's correspondents, T. Sturge Moore, whom Yeats took very seriously on this point, noticed, "A goldsmith's bird is as much nature as a man's body, especially if it only sings like Homer and Shakespeare of what is past or passing or to come to Lords and Ladies."[9] Surely Moore is right that the eternal ideal is described in terms not entirely purged of physicality. This bird singing to the sensual ear and wrought of "hammered gold"—the adjective "hammered" solidly grasping the bird's contact with brute forces of mutation—does not escape nature but rather transfigures it.

The bird informs the natural with the eternal—in art. This synthesis of the worldly and the divine, achieved mainly in the paradoxical golden bird, is reinforced by the bird's association with the Emperor, who, as Yeats explains in his description of Byzantium in *A Vision*, is both a man and a "God dependent upon a greater God." (277). Furthermore, the bird's song keeps the Emperor in a state between sleeping and waking that had special significance for Yeats as uniquely disposed to artistic inspiration: "The purpose of rhythm, it has always seemed to me, is to prolong the moment of contemplation, the moment when we are both asleep and awake, which is the one moment of creation, by hushing us with an alluring monotony, while it holds us waking by variety, to keep us in that state of perhaps real trance, in which the mind liberated from the pressure of the will is unfolded in symbols."[10]

Thus time-eternity-art—substituting whichever of the many correlates for time and eternity and art are preferred—forms the general thesis-antithesis-synthesis pattern of "Sailing to Byzantium." In "Byzantium," the dynamics of this pattern, which remains basically the same, become more violently dialectical.

The unpurged images of day recede;
The Emperor's drunken soldiery are abed;
Night resonance recedes, night walkers' song
After great cathedral gong;

9. Ursula Bridge, *Yeats and T. Sturge Moore: Their Correspondence* (New York: Oxford University Press, 1953), 162.

10. Yeats, "The Symbolism of Poetry," in *Essays and Introductions*, 159.

A starlit or a moonlit dome disdains
All that man is,
All mere complexities,
The fury and the mire of human veins.

Before me floats an image, man or shade,
Shade more than man, more image than a shade;
For Hades' bobbin bound in mummy-cloth
May unwind the winding path;
A mouth that has no moisture and no breath
Breathless mouths may summon;
I hail the superhuman;
I call it death-in-life and life-in-death.

Miracle, bird or golden handiwork,
More miracle than bird or handiwork,
Planted on the star-lit golden bough,
Can like the cocks of Hades crow,
Or, by the moon embittered, scorn aloud
In glory of changeless metal
Common bird or petal
And all complexities of mire or blood.

At midnight on the Emperor's pavement flit
Flames that no faggot feeds, nor steel has lit,
Nor storm disturbs, flames begotten of flame,
Where blood-begotten spirits come
And all complexities of fury leave,
Dying into a dance,
An agony of trance,
An agony of flame that cannot singe a sleeve.

Astraddle on the dolphin's mire and blood,
Spirit after Spirit! The smithies break the flood.
The golden smithies of the Emperor!
Marbles of the dancing floor
Break bitter furies of complexity,
Those images that yet
Fresh images beget,
That dolphin-torn, that gong-tormented sea.

The first stanza of "Byzantium" again defines the antithesis of the human and the divine. The "unpurged images of day" and "The Emperor's drunken soldiery" smack of the impurity of the flesh (in Yeats's system, day is generally aligned with objectivity and the body), while an aura of austere spirituality hovers, as a nimbus from heaven, about the disdainful moonlit or starlit cathedral dome. Yeats ingeniously compresses the antinomy into phrases such as "mere complexities": "mere" because belonging to the lower world, whereas in the eternal realm of pure being all is simplicity and unity (Plato); and "complex" like everything else having to do with man and the natural world—that is, with "The fury and the mire of human veins." However, even in this first stanza, the collapse of the disjunction between the human and the superhuman, foreordained by the dialectical logic of merging opposites, seems to be adumbrated. For the night-walkers' song is inextricably associated with the unpurged images and drunken soldiers, which together recede from the scene, and we have learned from the companion poem to recognize the potentially supernatural powers of song and its great affinity with the spirit.

Of course, an antinomy must first be drawn to tautness in order to forcefully collapse, and besides, even at the climactic release, the clarity of the poem depends upon the poles retaining some sharp contrast with respect to each other. Thus the poem's incisiveness continues to augment through the second section, where the "image" (or "man or shade") floats in its distinctly supernatural element. Bound "in mummy-cloth," it "May unwind the winding path" that was spun during its natural life, thus rising out of nature into pure contemplation, or "mind's pondering," as it is termed in "All Souls' Night":

> I need some mind that, if the cannon sound
> From every quarter of the world, can stay
> Wound in mind's pondering
> As mummies in the mummy-cloth are wound . . .

Yet, supernatural as this specter may appear, it is not so entirely remote as to be unable to summon the "Breathless mouths" of humans—breathless with human excitement or exhaustion, though also breathless like the superhuman mouth that has "no moisture and no breath." Building upon this paradox, the section concludes with the crowning paradox, "I call it death-in-life and life-in-death," joining together the contraries of life and death, since in Byzantium, this capital city of symbols, opposites are mutually entailing.

The third stanza recalls the natural yet eternal, because artistically consummate, golden bird of "Sailing to Byzantium." This bird is the perfect symbol for the synthesis of nature and transcendence in art. Although in its aesthetic transfiguration it is "More miracle than bird or golden handiwork," it is nevertheless wrought of the hard and heavy "metal" of the earth. Since the bird is at once spirit (or divinity), nature, and art, it is interchangeably "Miracle, bird, or golden handiwork." This directly parallels (though not in the same order) the "image, man or shade" of the preceding stanza and the "religious, aesthetic, and practical life" of Yeats's prose descriptions of Byzantium.

In this manner, the whole poem, and indeed the whole Byzantium myth, is sucked into a vortex that swirls around the single concrete-universal symbol of the golden bird. This is Yeats's unity achieved. Such a complete coalescence necessarily draws in elements from every quarter of Yeats's system. The crowing of "the cocks of Hades," which the golden bird simulates, signifies the moment of divine influx, when time and eternity meet, just as in "Solomon and the Witch" a cockerel "crowed out eternity." This occurs at Phase 15, when the moon is full, a phase of supernatural incarnation, like the phase that coincides with the eleventh century of Yeats's Byzantium, the midpoint of the two-thousand-yearlong Christian Era. That the bird is "by the moon embittered" may be ambiguously interpreted either as envy of the full moon "Beyond the visible world" ("The Phases of the Moon," lines 60–63), which humiliates the bird for its material composition, or as antipathy, borne in allegiance to the full moon, toward all things that are not, like those under her aegis, "changeless," that is, antipathy toward things such as

> Common bird or metal
> And all complexities of mire and blood.

At midnight, the dark core of the night, which is another, like the full moon, of the symbols Yeats generally placed in the group favorable to Unity of Being,

> . . . on the Emperor's pavement flit
> Flames that no faggot feeds, nor steel has lit,
> Nor storm disturbs, flames begotten of flame . . .

Although these lines completely expunge corporeality, and sure enough "all complexities of fury leave" or are eradicated in "the fire that makes all simple" ("Anima Mundi," 511), there are nevertheless "blood-begotten spirits" that are taken into the dance and that are also necessary to the final synthesis. This synthesis is again achieved in art, and art that is once again intrinsically paradoxical: "Dying into a dance. . . ." Just as this line couples death and animation, so the succeeding line—"An agony of trance"—fuses incompatibles in an act that is both still and writhing. (We may well be reminded at this point of Yeats's remarks, quoted earlier, regarding the one moment of creation when we are held "in that state of perhaps real trance.") But in addition to being a category of art, the dance also has tremendous vitality of its own as a symbol for the synthesis of opposites. The dance itself, which is the form of the display, and therefore ideal (in Plato's sense), is indistinguishable from the dancer, the laboring material body: "How can we know the dancer from the dance?" ("Among School Children," l.64). Both move in unison, soul and body together, mingled into the transforming beauty of art. The stanza concludes, appropriately, with another incongruous union: because "All power is from the terrestrial condition" ("Animus Mundi," 523–24), a purely pneumatic flame "cannot singe a sleeve," and yet it is a flame of "agony."

A dialectical reconciliation is always one that contains and even depends upon conflict, such as swells up from the storming sea of the fifth stanza. The spirits moving through the sea toward the purificatory flames must ride "Astraddle" upon "the dolphin's mire and blood." They come in a "flood" of sea, which the golden smithies of the Emperor "Break," suggesting the violence of waves upon rock. Similarly, the marbles of the dancing floor "Break bitter furies of complexity," as they break "Those images that yet / Fresh images beget," or souls that have not yet escaped from the cycle of death and rebirth in nature. However, even in these furious clashes, the smithies of the Emperor, who rebuff the torrents of natural chaos, are themselves "golden smithies," and similarly the dancing floor is of "Marbles." In these forms, art withstands chaos and the storm of the elements. The final collision is between the Marbles and "That dolphin-torn, that gong-tormented sea," which images physical turmoil in the stirring of the dolphin, already identified with "mire and blood," while at the same time alluding, through "great cathedral gong," to the cathedral of the first stanza that disdainfully shines in the clear starlight of eternity. Thus, both in the poem and on the sea, the dialectic explodes in a shattering concussion of time and eternity held together by an intense artistic energy.

III. Later Poems

Later poems, as well as other poems from the same period, show Yeats continuing to vacillate "Between extremities" of the physical and the spiritual. In "The Tower," the title poem of the 1928 volume that begins with "Sailing to Byzantium," he announces that he has prepared his peace with:

> All those things whereof
> Man makes a superhuman
> Mirror-resembling dream,

while declaring in "A Dialogue of Self and Soul":

> I am content to live it all again
> And yet again, if it be life to pitch
> Into the frog-spawn of a blind man's ditch,
> A blind man battering blind men . . .

Perhaps the dialogue of Soul and Heart in "Vacillation," suggesting the interdependence between art, the forge of eternity, and its earthly material, strikes a more stable balance:

> The Soul. Seek out reality, leave things that seem.
> The Heart. What, be a singer born and lack a theme?
> The Soul. Isaiah's coal, what more can man desire?
> The Heart. Struck dumb in the simplicity of fire!
> The Soul. Look on that fire, salvation walks within.
> The Heart. What theme had Homer but original sin?

But on the whole Yeats's voices in *Last Poems* (1938–39) have an increasing tendency to make choices following that of "The Wild Old Wicked Man":

> "That some stream of lightning
> From the old man in the skies
> Can burn out that suffering
> No right-taught man denies.
> But a coarse old man am I,
> I choose the second-best,

I forget it all awhile
Upon a woman's breast."

Yet even here there is still an opposite side to the coin, a side that appears facing up in "An Acre of Grass":

Grant me an old man's frenzy,
Myself I must remake
Till I am Timon and Lear
Or that William Blake
Who beat the wall
Till truth obeyed his call . . .

This poem turns on the exaltation of "An old man's eagle mind" that can soar to heights of inspiration touching the heavens. Of course, it is especially the *artist*'s mind that Yeats has in mind as exemplary here:

A mind Michael Angelo knew
That can pierce the clouds,
Or inspired by frenzy
Shake the dead in their shrouds . . .

If these "old themes" ever finally deserted Yeats, they did so only after producing the sublime beauty of the Byzantium poems. And we may now add, in conclusion, that it was a beauty born of dialectic: it "Grew in pure mind" working "In the foul rag-and-bone shop of the heart."

IV. Addendum on Yeats's Poetic Logic in Current Criticism

Yeats's poetry and thought continues in contemporary criticism to lend itself to reinterpretations of a logic that can be discovered only, or at least best, through poetic creativity. It has become increasingly clear that the dialectical logic of Yeats's Byzantium poems leads him ultimately to a logic that is no longer bipolar. The fundamental impetus of Yeats's poetic vision as aiming at unity is the focus of a recent study bringing to bear contemporary environmental concerns that likewise demand a holistic outlook and that point in an apophatic direction of what cannot be said or grasped in the differential medium of language. Such unity is apprehended only as kenotic and as infinitely open. Sabine Müller, following the prompts of ecocriticism, reads Yeats's work as reaching beyond the conceptual to renewed union with nature discovered through profanation (an ultra-secularization) in its ineluctable sacredness.[11]

Breaking out of oppositional logic in this manner, Yeats's poems also derail the linearity of chronological time. They suspend their symbolic action in a time between an already and a not-yet, a time constructed by enfolding together prefiguration and apocalypse. This time can be symbolized by the figure of "eternity," but all such representations prove to be necessarily ambiguous and enigmatic. Yeats's use of such traditional metaphysical imagery is traversed by secularizing currents that are in fact practically inherent to its poetic fabrication and employment.

Nels Pearson, taking some cues from Dwight Purdy, connects the imagery of Yeats's "Byzantium," in which revelation leads to ambiguity and proclamation issues in enigma, with the biblical prophetic tradition that flourishes in Dante.[12] This procedure is based on typology opening to an eternal and unrealizable future that can only be prophetically anticipated and thereby, inevitably, also postponed. Alluding to such an eternity entails the imagery's breaking open the circuits of signification in ways that lend themselves to description in secular terms of literary theory, particularly post-structural semiotic theory. Yeats, in this way, can be understood as participating in the secular transmogrification of a spiritual vision hailing from the prophetic-poetic tradition of Dante and Blake.

11. Sabine Müller, "Conceiving Unity of Being: The Environmental Modernism of R. M. Rilke and W. B. Yeats." National University of Ireland, Galway (NUIG) doctoral dissertation, 2014.

12. Nels Pearson, "Postponement and Prophecy: Northrop Frye and 'The Great Code' of Yeats's 'Byzantium,' *University of Toronto Quarterly* 84/1 (2015): 19-33. Dwight Purdy, *Biblical Echo and Allusion in the Poetry of W.B. Yeats: Poetics and the Art of God* (Lewisburg: Bucknell University Press, 1994).

the religious vocation of secular literature

dante and postmodern thought

I. Literature and Secularization

Literature can be thought of quite broadly as a secularized form of religious revelation. This is especially so if we take "religion" to be concerned with underlying myths and rites and other forms of cultural invention and relation that constitute communities, often unconsciously. We are encouraged to take it this way by the etymological sense of "religion" as a tying or binding (*ligare*) back (re-) to source and origin.[1] Such a perspective on literature as secularized revelation is epitomized by Dante and his *Divine Comedy* near the origins of modern European literary tradition in the vernacular. The *Divine Comedy* marks the culmination of ancient and medieval epic in which the sacred aura of divine revelation had not yet been completely lost from literary expression and artifacts. Subsequently, the purposes and practices of literature and religion grew apart, at least apparently, throughout the modern period of fervent assertion of secular human autonomy in every domain of politics, society, and culture. But there may still be an underlying coincidence or

---

1. For this etymology of *religion*, see Lactantius, *Institutionum Divinarum* IV.28.

co-inherence of the two (literature and religion) to be discerned, especially if we bring to focus around Dante the periods before and after his incomparable achievement. Such a reflection promises to illuminate some aspects of the remarkable re(dis)covery of the deeply religious import of literature in our postmodern and indeed postsecular era.[2]

Dante has long been recognized as a founding figure of the modern world. His affirmation of a secular order with a finality of its own—independent of the spiritual, otherworldly destiny of humanity—is certainly one of the mainstays on which this judgment is based.[3] At the same time, however, Dante has become increasingly recognized as our contemporary in the postmodern and more precisely postsecular era.[4] He is not limited by the strictly humanistic horizon typical of the modern world, with its exclusion of transcendence and of any radical otherness to the human. Such is the modernity that allows human beings to make themselves the uncontested masters of the world. But Dante already stands in decisive ways beyond (paradoxically because he is before) these premises and parameters of the modern age. In what follows, by considering Dante's central place in the history of secularization in Western culture and by surveying the periods both preceding and following his own historical moment, we will be able to look past the strictures of the modern secularist paradigm in which literature and religion seem to lose touch with each other. This will help us to refocus secularization so as to see it as a crucial mode of theological revelation and to recognize secularization specifically in literature as the realization of an eminently religious outlook and experience.

In premodern times, the Italian peninsula was very much on the forefront of European intellectual discovery and renewal, particularly in the

---

2. Graham Ward, "How Literature Resists Secularity," *Literature and Theology* 24/1 (2010): 73–88, offers timely reflections on this current rediscovery. The imposing presence of this "era" is perhaps best attested by the reactions it provokes and by the impatience of some to move beyond it: witness *After the Postsecular and the Postmodern: New Essays in Continental Philosophy of Religion*, eds. Anthony Paul Smith and Daniel Whistler (Newcastle-upon-Tyne: Cambridge Scholars Press, 2010).

3. Reudi Imbach, *Dante, la philosophie et les laïcs* (Fribourg: Éditions Universitaires Fribourg Suisse, 1996), effectively contextualizes this crucial pillar of Dante's thought, which is rigorously argued by Dante in *Monarchia* III, xv.

4. The acute philosophical challenges of the *Commedia* for us today—reaching beyond its evident historical and philological interest—are pursued by leading contemporary Italian philosophers (Adorno, Sini, Givone, Gargani, Bodei, Curi, Rella, Reale, Malaguti, Ghisalberti, Giorello, Rovatti, De Montecelli, Ferraris, and Severino) in Nadia Ancarani, ed., *Filosofi d'oggi per Dante, Letture classensi* 32/34 *(Filosofi d'oggi per Dante)* (Ravenna: Longo, 2005).

process of reinterpreting Europe's religious heritage as it derives from both Judeo-Christian and Greco-Roman civilizations. Essential to the dynamic of European thought, as characterized especially by recurrent episodes of rebirth or "renaissance" throughout its history, are hermeneutic practices reinterpreting religious myth and symbol. This entails reconceptualizing what had been previously understood as divine revelation in terms of the free and creative arts and inventions of human beings. This interpretive process is often treated under the rubric of "secularization." It can be found at the origins of European literature already in Homer, particularly in the transition from the *Iliad* to the *Odyssey.* In the latter of these two tradition-founding epics, the figure of the poet acquires a remarkable degree of independence from the divine Muses. This process of autonomization is patent in the person of the protagonist, Odysseus. He practically invents his own identity through the poetic confabulation of books IX through XII delivering to the Phaeacians on the island of Scheria the marvelous and revelatory account of his adventures all around the Mediterranean basin, including its mythological appendages and reaching even to the domain of the dead. He no longer even invokes the Muses, although he acknowledges that his own power is dependent on the support of the gods, particularly Athena. No longer just a yielding receptacle, he becomes a self-assertive inventor of his own story and therewith of his own life and even afterlife. The first self-made man, Odysseus stands out as a symbol of secular humanism at the sacred sources of classical culture, which are thereby reconfigured in a secular guise.[5]

The secularizing interpretation of myth, which is begun in the Homeric poems themselves, is carried much further by philosophical interpretations of these poems especially in Stoic and Neoplatonic circles. Such philosophical-allegorical exegesis of epic poetry, with its rationalization of religious-poetic revelation, became a genre in its own right and achieved a kind of classic status in the third century of the Christian Era with Porphyry's *De antro nympharum* (*The Cave of the Nymphs*). The genre was further extended from Greek to Latin tradition, and its focus shifted from Homer to Virgil, in commentators including Servius, Macro-

---

5. Odysseus is taken as an emblem of the Enlightenment, the secular movement par excellence, by Theodor Adorno and Max Horkheimer, *Dialektik der Aufklärung: Philosophische Fragmente* (Frankfurt am Main: Fischer, 1969 [1947]), trans. E. Jephcott as *Dialectic of Enlightenment: Philosophical Fragments* (Stanford: Stanford University Press, 2002). See especially Excursus I, "Odysseus oder Mythos und Aufklärung," 58–83. I treat this subject in greater detail in "Homer's Musings and the Divine Muse: Epic Song as Invention and as Revelation," *Religion and Literature* 43/1 (2011): 1–28.

bius, and Fulgentius, with their allegorical interpretations of the *Aeneid* from the fourth to the sixth centuries. It continued to bear exquisite fruits throughout the Middle Ages down to Bernard Sylvestris's *Commentum super sex libros Eneidos Virgilii* (c. 1136). A little later, the *Divine Comedy* itself became the object of such philosophical interpretation in a bourgeoning commentary tradition that flourished in the Renaissance, for instance, with Christopher Landino's *Comento sopra la Comedia* (1481), and well beyond.

The pattern in such philosophical appropriation of epic literature, starting even within this literature itself, is to reinterpret revelation in rational, secular terms, yet this is done generally in order to vindicate the religious message therein rather than to debunk or dismiss it as passé. The allegorizers are trying to prove that these ancient poetic texts are profoundly true and meaningful, even if, with the passage of time, they may have ceased to be readily understandable. The secularizing interpretations of literature are generally proposed with a view to retaining the inherent religious revelation that poetry harbors and to realizing it in a world in which its secret language of wisdom has been forgotten or has become virtually unintelligible.

Secularization, as a fundamental axis of European thought and culture, can be followed from this matrix in the philosophical interpretation of epic all the way forward to contemporary postmodern thinkers who are militantly secularist but nevertheless keenly intent upon re-interpreting religious traditions. We may think of Jacques Derrida, among many others. This description holds still for such luminaries on the contemporary scene of critical thinking as Alain Badiou and Slavoj Žižek. Both have found in Saint Paul an emblematic figure for radical intellectual and spiritual revolution of the most far-reaching significance.[6] Žižek stresses that Christianity holds certain keys to a radical cultural critique that have otherwise been lost from contemporary debate.[7] In important respects the outstanding living representative of the philosophical tradition of the Enlightenment, Jürgen Habermas, likewise emphasizes the Christian

---

6. Alain Badiou, *Saint Paul: La fondation de l'universalisme* (Paris: Presses Universitaires de France, 1997), trans. Ray Brassier as *Saint Paul: The Foundation of Universalism* (Stanford: Stanford University Press, 2003); Slavoj Žižek, *The Fragile Absolute—or, Why is the Christian Legacy Worth Fighting For?* (London: Verso, 2000), 1–2, and *The Ticklish Subject: The Absent Centre of Political Ontology* (London: Verso, 1999), chapter 3: "The Politics of Truth, or, Alain Badiou as a Reader of St. Paul," 127–70.

7. Slavoj Žižek, *The Puppet and the Dwarf: The Perverse Core of Christianity* (Cambridge: MIT Press, 2003).

theological bases for any intelligible language of communicative action and community today.[8]

However, it is most of all Italian thinkers, notably Gianni Vattimo and Giorgio Agamben, who in important respects should be counted as best qualified among the protagonists of contemporary thought for bringing out the religious presuppositions and underpinnings of this current and ongoing species of revolution in cultural history. Most of the other leading European intellectuals just mentioned might well be characterized as religiously "unmusical," to borrow Richard Rorty's term, which in turn is borrowed from Max Weber.[9] The Italian Catholic culture with which, by their birthright, Vattimo and Agamben are permeated, on the other hand, provides fertile ground for nurturing insight into the religious roots of even the most secularized forms of culture. They lucidly recognize the rootedness of their subversively secular ideas in religious traditions of revelation. My purpose here is to bring out the continuity of this intellectual posture in which religious revelation is realized through secular expression in literature over a period spanning virtually the whole of Italian vernacular culture. I do so by comparing the proposals of these postmodern protagonists with Dante's project understood as also one essentially of the secularization of religious revelation. Dante, I wish to stress, furthermore, is eminently suitable for making us aware of some of the limits of secularization. His incomparable theological passion forces us to look beyond the strictures against the spiritual and the transcendent that are typical of many modern forms of secularization. He enables us to critique secularism's closures and thereby to restore the inalienably religious significance of literature to its full potency.

II. Negative Theology, Ineffability, Kenosis, Nihilism

A key to tracing this genealogy of secularization is to understand religion through the optics of negative theology[10]—that is, in terms not of dogmas

---

8. Jürgen Habermas, *Glauben und Wissen: Friedenspreis des deutschen Buchhandels 2001* (Frankfurt am Main: Suhrkamp, 2001), and, with Josef Ratzinger, *Dialektik der Säkularisierung: Über Vernunft und Religion* (Freiburg: Herder, 2005).

9. Richard Rorty's description of himself, in *The Future of Religion*, with Gianni Vattimo, ed. Santiago Zabala (New York: Columbia University Press, 2005), 30.

10. Early stages of this tradition are traced by Raoul Mortley, *From Word to Silence* (Bonn: Hanstein, 1986). Contexts close to and including Dante can be found in my *On What Cannot Be Said: Apophatic Discourses in Philosophy, Religion, Literature, and the*

and systems or laws and rites but of what lies always beyond any and all such positive formulations and expressions of religious belief, in what irretrievably exceeds our means of expression. In this perspective of the *apophatic* dimension of religion, Dante is truly the precursor of postmodern thinkers like Agamben and Vattimo. In his final work, the *Paradiso*, Dante sings himself to silence in acknowledgment of the quintessential ineffability of the divine vision toward which his whole poetic itinerary inexorably soars.[11] At the deepest sources of culture, from which the poem draws, the sacred and the secular are not yet distinct. Premodern and postmodern perspectives meet in aiming to access this unspeakable origin beyond the reach of representation and of every human technique or technology.

Literary representation from Homer to Virgil to Augustine to Dante progressively intensifies critical consciousness of the irremediable inadequacy of all representations of divinity.[12] The theological meaning that such religious poetry aims at is precisely what it cannot represent. Dante says as much, at the very climax of his paradisiacal vision, in his references to its escaping his grasp like the snow "unsealed" by the sun ("come la neve al sol si disigilla") or like the oracles of Sibyl scattered on wind-blown leaves ("così al vento ne le foglie levi / si perdea la sentenza di Sibilla," XXXIII.64–66). He makes the same point again in his forgetting of the twenty-five centuries of cultural history that his poem has so prodigiously gathered into memory when, in its final moment, his vision of God goes blank like that of Neptune submerged beneath the sea and looking up at the passing *shadow* of Jason's ship, the *Argo* ("che fé Nettuno ammirar l'ombra d'*Argo,*" XXXIII.94–96). There is a growing critical awareness of this ultimate predicament of unknowing, which becomes acute with Dante's intense theoretical reflection on the epistemological presuppositions and pragmatic premises of his poem. This takes place within his general recognition of the principles of negative theology in the tradition of Dionysius the Areopagite, which has left such a profound imprint on the poem, particularly on its final phase, the *Paradiso.*[13]

Arts, vol. 1: Classical Formulations. Further representatives extending to the postmodern are pursued in vol. 2: Modern and Contemporary Transformations.

11. William Franke, "Language and Transcendence in Dante's *Paradiso*," *The Poetics of Transcendence,* eds. Elisa Heinämäki, P. M. Mehtonen and Antti Salminen (Amsterdam: Brill/Rodopi: 2015), Currents of Encounter series, vol. 38, 107–31.

12. I trace this development in articles on Homer, Virgil, and Dante and expound it more integrally in *The Revelation of Imagination: From the Bible and Homer through Virgil and Augustine to Dante* (Evanston, IL: Northwestern University Press, 2015).

13. Among recent works focusing attention on negative theology in the *Paradiso* are

Postmodern thinkers who have turned their attention to religion are only catching up with traditional negative-theological reflection on how the truths that have been discredited—and the gods that have died—are all only so many forms of representation: the truth that was aimed at, or the gods who were invoked, remain beyond the reach precisely of all those representations. The postmodern moment opens this dimension of the *unknown,* which theology in its more deeply reflective (negative) forms has always pointed to and acknowledged as being beyond its grasp. Philosophy, too, has once again opened up to the mystery beyond any possible ground that it can define for itself—to what lies beyond any *cogito* (the "I think" of the subject) or *óntos ón* (what truly is, the pure presence of presencing) or *eidos* of the Platonic Idea that was supposed to serve as its foundation. Secular forms of culture, beginning with poems, and not least with theological poems, have, in fact, been the way that the mysteries of religion have revealed themselves progressively throughout the course of development of modern civilization. Modernity, most persistently since Max Weber, has typically interpreted this progress as banishing religion, as replacing its myths with rational explanations.[14] However, the most comprehensive explanations even of science have likewise been exposed as themselves systems of symbols that can never deliver up the real itself, for the latter withdraws always into a mystery infinitely more complex (and simple) than any logic can comprehend. Accordingly, we can see the sciences as fundamentally poetic, and, conversely, we can see our civilization's founding poems as the best approximations that we have to knowledge of reality as a whole.[15]

Religion lives in and through such secularization, whereby it becomes worldly and incarnate. Such poems explore what divinity is and does

Marco Ariani, *Lux inaccessibilis: Metafore e teologia della luce nel Paradiso di Dante* (Rome: Aracne, 2010), Diego Sbacchi, *La presenza di Dionigi l'Areopagita nel 'Paradiso' di Dante* (Florence: Olschki, 2006), and Antonio Rossini, *Il Dante sapienziale: Dionigi e la bellezza di Beatrice* (Pisa: F. Serra, 2009). Earlier important broachings of the subject include Giuliana Carugati, *Dalla menzogna al silenzio: La scrittura mistica della "Commedia" di Dante* (Bologna: Il Mulino, 1991), and Manuela Colombo, *Dai mistici a Dante: Il linguaggio dell'ineffabilità* (Firenze: La Nuova Italia, 1987).

14. Charles Taylor, *A Secular Age* (Cambridge: The Belknap Press of Harvard University Press, 2007). Highly influential sociological approaches include David Martin, *On Secularization: Towards a Revised General Theory* (Hants, UK: Aldershot, 2006), Talal Asad, *Formations of the Secular: Christianity, Islam, Modernity* (Stanford: Stanford University Press, 2003), and José Casanova, *Public Religions in the Modern World* (Chicago: University of Chicago Press, 1994).

15. Rorty's and Vattimo's *The Future of Religion* turns on the collapse of science into just another historically relative discourse without superior epistemological authority.

in terms of our world and experience. This is our only way of apprehending it. But we require the critical consciousness that emerges clearly with Dante (for example, in *Paradiso* IV.37–39 and VIII.1ff) in order to avoid simply identifying divinity with our representations of it, since they are fundamentally of the order of poetic fictions. If taken for reality per se, they become "false and lying gods," ("dèi falsi e buggiardi," *Inferno* I.72). Recent critical awareness focused on the modern myth of reason that was generated by the Enlightenment has opened up what we may call (and cannot help calling) the *postmodern* (and *postsecular*) age: in this age, the type of negative-theological wisdom that we can glean from Dante—particularly in the apophatic movement of the *Paradiso* toward ineffability—is being cultivated in philosophy by thinkers like Agamben and Vattimo, who return to the religious sources of our apparently secular culture.

The postulates of modernity, which pivot on an autonomous subject, have become questionable again in our postmodern age, and this enables us to reach back to Dante, to a moment before a Cartesian foundation in subjective self-certainty had become self-evident, and so to conceive of our being as beholden to a Ground or un-ground that we do not possess, indeed one that we can only be possessed by. Our being is not self-grounding but is given from—or in any case is open toward—a "beyond" that we cannot master. This has again become a defensible belief with the crisis of modern culture and the shaking of its supposedly secure foundations in the self-grounding, self-reflective consciousness of the subject in Descartes's *cogito ergo sum*. Vattimo announces the end of modernity and the new religious, or more exactly *Christian*, horizon of a certain postmodernity. Early on in his career, he followed the crisis of modernity into nihilism and resolved not to resist it but to accept and complete and *accomplish* these tendencies radically by his own brand of postmodern thinking. What then emerged for him was a rediscovery of the Christian religion as a form of unknowing, of orienting human thought and discourse to what humans cannot grasp or master. He recognized Christianity as the essential agent in the weakening of metaphysical forms of thought into what he calls "weak thought" ("pensiero debole"), which does not definitively know any objective grounds but remains open to infinite interpretation.[16]

Likewise, negative theology is essentially self-emptying *kenosis*: it denies all its own formulations for divinity and empties its own discourse

16. A manifesto of weak thought appeared as Gianni Vattimo and Pier Aldo Rovatti, eds., *Il pensiero debole* (Milan: Feltrinelli, 1983).

into silence. More broadly, it evacuates the reality of substantial being, starting from the supreme reality of divinity. It "weakens" supposedly impassible, universal being into lived experience and situated interpretation on the part of historical, encultured individuals and societies. As is emphasized by some of its more recent transmogrifications, negative theology can also puncture and deflate the abstractness of being and break it down into bodies—apophatic bodies, like the battered body of Christ.[17] Applications of the resultant figures of the flesh in patristic and medieval negative theologies have been pursued by Emmanuel Falque, particularly in *Dieu, la chair et l'autre: d'Irénée à Duns Scot.* More generally, the theological turn in French phenomenology brought about by writers such as Michel Henry, Jean-Luc Marion, and Jean-Louis Chrétien has focused attention on the invisible that comes with and inhabits the visible and embodied.[18]

Vattimo does not embrace negative theology, yet the apophatic turns up in the guise of what he calls an "accomplished nihilism" ("compiuto nichilismo"), in which no discourse can make strong claims to truth but rather can serve only for dissolving such claims. Vattimo's nihilism itself must be understood as a form of "weak thought." It is primarily the lack of foundations rather than any more aggressively destructive force that is evoked by the term *nihilism* as Vattimo employs it. This is akin to what Dante designates as *ineffability.* When ineffability is not just an index pointing to a strong metaphysical conception of God but is rather the general framework of the whole poem, so that all its names and notions are dissolved into the experience of the ineffable, as happens in the *Paradiso,* then *ineffabilità* has become in effect a weak thinking that deconstructs metaphysics rather than being just a moment inscribed within it and bolstering it by covering over its gaps.[19] An openness to what absolutely cannot be objectively given or grasped is the upshot of this realization—and it can be designated equally as Nothing or as God, to the

---

17. Especially interesting in this connection is Chris Boesel and Catherine Keller, eds., *Apophatic Bodies: Negative Theology, Incarnation, and Relationality* (New York: Fordham University Press, 2009).

18. Dominique Janicaud et al., *Phenomenology and the 'Theological Turn': The French Debate* (New York: Fordham University Press, 2000). See, further, Dominique Janicaud, *Le tournant théologique de la phénoménologie française* (Combas: L'Éclat, 1991), and most recently Emmanuel Falque, *Le combat amoureux: Disputes phénoménologiques et théologiques* (Paris: Hermann, 2014). Maurice Merleau-Ponty's *Le visible et l'invisible* (1964) is also a key text here.

19. I propose such a reading of the *Paradiso* in *Dante and the Sense of Transgression: 'The Trespass of the Sign'* (London: Continuum [Bloomsbury Academic], 2013).

extent that neither designation can be adequate or retain any objective content. In this regard, Vattimo's philosophical message today clarifies crucial aspects of what makes Dante's poem so timely for us, too.

In Agamben's case, the apophatic is found exemplarily in his logic of exception, a negative logic that is the secret underlying and undermining every apparently positive, assertive form of power. Agamben works this logic of exception out in *Homo sacer* in a comprehensive theory of sovereignty as consisting essentially in the power to make an exception to the norm and suspend the law (*Homo sacer*, I). Agamben extends his analysis to the power of the Church in *Il regno e la gloria, Homo sacer II, 2* and in *La chiesa e il regno*. Significantly, Dante's *Divine Comedy* is likewise built upon exceptions, emblematic cases being Cato, the pagan suicide placed among the saved souls as guardian of Purgatory, and the heathen hero Rifeus found, to Dante's utter astonishment, twinkling among the other just spirits in the heaven of Jupiter. Such anomalies are conspicuous reminders of God's absolute sovereignty over every form of system and rule. They interrupt the seamless logic of the divine realms that Dante elaborates and project them into an incalculable dimension of exception and grace.[20]

Agamben treats the apophatic also directly and thematically in relation to the myth of Persephone and the Eleusinian mysteries, where not some arcane and secret teaching but rather life itself (we might say "bare life," so as to link this discussion with Agamben's *Homo sacer* project) is the mystery that can be seen or touched but not said. Like the simple truth of things having no composition, according to Aristotle's *Metaphysics* 1051b, 22–24, it can be named but not said; its name is the "unsayable girl" (*aretos kore* in numerous ancient sources):

> La 'ragazza indicibile' poteva essere *nominata*, ma non *detta*. Nel mistero non vi era, cioè, spazio per il *logos apophantikos* (*De interpr.*, 17 b, 8), ma soltanto per l'*onoma*. E, nel nome, aveva luogo qualcosa come un 'toccare' e un 'vedere.'[21]

---

20. Justin Steinberg, *Dante and the Limits of the Law* (Chicago: University of Chicago Press, 2013), explains this logic of exception from a legal point of view and in terms of Dante's medieval culture (2–3 and *passim*).

21. Agamben and Monica Ferrando, *La ragazza indicibile: Mito e mistero di Kore* (Milan: Mondadori Electa, 2010), 15. The connections with Agamben will not be pursued further in this brief prolusion, which focuses rather on Vattimo. I take them up in another essay: "Agamben's Logic of Exception: Its Apophatic Roots and Offshoots," *Concentric: Literary and Cultural Studies* (September 2015).

The 'unsayable girl' could be *named,* but not *said.* In the mysteries, that is, there was no space for the *logos apophantikos* [Aristotle, *De interpretatione,* 17 b, 8], but only for the *name.* And in the name something like a 'touching' and a 'seeing' took place.

In each case (Agamben's and Vattimo's), a religious register of belief is attained negatively by attending to the absence of the sacred in any positively assertable form.[22] There is for both of these eminently postmodern thinkers a rupture in the objective order of things and an opening to an uncanny, anarchic dimension that cannot be authoritatively known or governed. For Dante, this is a dimension of the divine that transcends knowledge and defies human control. It can be elucidated in theological or, more precisely, negative-theological terms by what I call Dante's hermeneutic outlook. Dante's theological and existential hermeneutics are relevant not only to traditional textual interpretation and exegesis of the classics and the Bible but also to philosophical and particularly postmodern hermeneutics.[23] His poem gives a speculative turn to the cultural matrices that he actively deploys and transmits all through European (but more specifically Italian) culture and critical consciousness. Moreover, Dante's hermeneutics can help us to understand in what sense this nonobjective dimension of the unsayable that registers in poetic literature may be inherently religious.

III. Two Dantes: Secular and Religious?

First, it must be acknowledged that the question of Dante and religion is complex and vexed. He is read as staunchly secular by a long and venerable tradition of criticism that numbers among its founders Hegel and the distinguished Renaissance historian Jacob Burckhart. Its classic statement is Erich Auerbach's *Dante: Poet of the Secular World.* Secular approaches to interpreting Dante have been especially tenacious in Italy, where they have often tended to *exclude* the poet's theological convictions

---

22. Michel Foucault's "Préface à la transgression," *Critique* 195–96 (1963): 751–69, is a pertinent precursor in this line of thought.

23. The relevance of philosophical hermeneutics to Dante's project is highlighted by Christine O'Connel Bauer, *Dante's Hermeneutics of Salvation: Passages to Freedom in the Divine Comedy* (Toronto: University of Toronto Press, 2007), and by my *Dante's Interpretive Journey* (Chicago: University of Chicago Press, 1996).

and religious commitments. Benedetto Croce found it necessary to separate Dante's poetry from his theology, *poesia* from *non-poesia*, holding Dante's epoch-making aesthetic achievement to have been rather vitiated and obfuscated by his theological passion. A prejudice that has had a certain currency in Italy ever since Croce is the idea that Dante's medieval theological framework is no longer relevant for us today and must be left behind as we salvage from it the sublime poetry that serves as Italy's unsurpassable, exemplary classic and makes Dante her strongest literary progenitor.

Numerous American (and not only American) critics, on the other hand, have emphasized Dante's theological outlook as the soul of his inspiration as a poet and as perfectly inextricable from the poetic vision he conveys.[24] There are deep-seated cultural differences in the background here having to do with the suspicion of religion as an all-too-present and oppressive political power in the proximity of the Vatican versus a Romantic, Emersonian longing to recover all the enchantment of the medieval mystical vision from a safe distance across the Atlantic on the American continent.[25] Crucial to negotiating this tension is to realize the absolutely key role of *secularization* in Dante's poetic and theological project.

It turns out not to be necessary or helpful to polarize the secular and the religious. Poetry can be understood as intrinsically a kind of secularization of theological revelation in the tradition that Dante before all others has done so much to foster. By making the contents of religious revelation over into the substance of personal experience, literature of the order of Dante's poem effects an appropriation that gives an entirely different sense to theological dogmas. They are not affirmed purely on authority from above but are verified and validated in the world of experience by autonomous individuals. Dante's personal experience of Beatrice turns coldly systematic theological knowledge into passionately personal witness, a type of knowing in and through loving desire. The world of experience of an individual becomes the terrain of truth, which is made in this sense worldly or secular. The *Divine Comedy*'s remarkable addresses to the reader constitute a clarion call pointing in this direction of incar-

---

24. Outstanding in this regard is the work of Giuseppe Mazzotta, who poses Dante's challenge to our own time specifically in terms of Dante's "theology of the future."

25. See addendum to chapter 1, this volume. Mazzotta's transfer early in professional life from Italy to North America can in this light be understood to inform his fervidly theological view of Dante's poetry.

nate realization of theological revelation in the worldly experience of an individual subject and personal protagonist.

In poetry and art generally, religious revelation can be construed as secularization in the sense of making worldly and sensory impressions—aesthetic experience—into intimations of or from some other, invisible reality. In medieval art broadly speaking there is an extremely sensitive threshold between the visible and the invisible that also divides the human from the divine.[26] As the Swiss expressionist painter Paul Klee famously phrased it in his 1920 *Creative Credo*: "Art does not render the visible but rather renders visible" ("Kunst gibt nicht das sichtbare wider, sondern macht sichtbar").[27] Such a formula can work surprisingly well also for Dante's medieval poetic endeavor to render an invisible theological mystery in the sensory and finally visionary medium of his poetry. Dante is a leader in translating religious vision (and even more importantly non-vision) into literature, theological faith into art, and this is one of the decisive directions that Western culture, with its secularizing impetus and momentum, has been moving ever since. Dante's project of transforming the substance of more objective, dogmatic forms of knowing into intimate personal experience and poetry becomes possible once theological knowing itself is recognized as being most profoundly a form of *un*knowing, and this is what occurs consciously and explicitly in negative theology.

Dante lived in a great age of accumulation of knowledge—just after the exhaustive *summas* of high Scholasticism. He felt the need to rediscover the *un*knowable in order to restore a certain pathos and passion to the life of the intellect, and in this respect his experience runs closely parallel to that of contemporary thinkers like Vattimo and Agamben. One of the principal sources of Vattimo's postmodernism, Nietzsche, suggested that knowing things reduces them to insignificance: "With the full knowledge of the origin augments the insignificance of the origin" (*Aurora*, cited by Vattimo, *Fine della modernità*, 177). And this turns out to be prophetic of the predicament of postmodernity. Knowledge of everything is everywhere on hand, and yet it all tends to become only insignificant information. Relation to the invisible and unknowable source of meaning is erased.

---

26. Olivier Boulnois, *Au-delà de l'image: Une archéologie du visuel au Moyen Âge (Ve–XVIe siècle)* (Paris: Seuil, 2008).

27. Paul Klee, *Kunst-Lehre* (Leipzig: Reclam, 1991), 60.

IV. Interpretive Revolution and Vattimo's Christianity

For Vattimo, everything depends on and is even produced by interpretation. Exposing the interpretive nature of all reality, furthermore, unmasks its fundamental *nothingness*: it rests on nothing that is given or absolute; there is no solid foundation. Hence there is indeed a kind of nihilism inherent in Vattimo's radically hermeneutic perspective.[28] Everything is *nothing . . .* , nothing but interpretation. There is nothing else, no bedrock that is *not* produced by interpretation, no prior reality existing uninterpreted in and of itself. This is practically the same insight as Richard Rorty has propounded in Anglo-Saxon philosophical milieus, and indeed Vattimo and Rorty have recognized their affinities in this respect and have drawn out some of the consequences in their jointly authored *The Future of Religion*.

The principle that ontology itself is determined from its grounds up by interpretation is pursued in its fundamental implications especially by hermeneutic thinkers like Martin Heidegger and Hans-Georg Gadamer, on whose shoulders Vattimo and Rorty stand. The medium of interpretation is language, and therefore hermeneutic ontology culminates in the thesis that being itself is actually constituted by language (and therefore by interpretation). Heidegger dwelt on this point from early on, for example, in paragraph 34 ("Dasein and Discourse") of *Sein und Zeit* (*Being and Time*), through to his late writings on poetry and language in *Unterwegs zur Sprache* (*On the Way to Language*). Gadamer developed a linguistic ontology in part III of *Wahrheit und Methode* (*Truth and Method*) and gave lapidary expression to this idea in the dictum "Being that can be understood is language" ("Sein, das verstanden werden kann, ist Sprache").

That the world is produced by concrete acts of human interpretation is demonstrated in other ways also by American pragmatists, particularly John Dewey, William James, and Charles Sanders Peirce. All these thinkers, too, are of the first importance for both Vattimo and Rorty. Vattimo adds to this pragmatist perspective, however, something that Rorty could never countenance. For Vattimo, hermeneutics has penetrated the Western world specifically in the form of Christianity. Vattimo learned from Wilhelm Dilthey, particularly from his history of metaphysics in the *Introduction to the Human Sciences* (*Einleitung in die Geisteswis-*

---

28. Gianni Vattimo, *Nichilismo ed emancipazione: Etica, politica, diritto* (Milan: Garzanti, 2003), trans. William McCuaig as *Nihilism and Emancipation: Ethics, Politics and Law*, ed. Santiago Zabala (New York: Columbia University Press, 2004).

senschaften, 1883), that Christianity's "principle of interiority" fundamentally challenged the presumption of objective reality and truth on which Greek and subsequent metaphysics were based. Vattimo thus sees the deconstruction of metaphysics in the Western world as being primarily the work of Christianity. "Christianity is a stimulus, it is a message of liberation from metaphysics" ("il cristianesimo è uno stimolo, è un messaggio di liberazione dalla metafisica"), even of liberation from "truth" ("Per un cristianesimo non religioso," 51–52). For the principle of objective truth itself is rendered vain and powerless by Christ's saying "I *am* the truth" ("and the way and the life," John 14:6) and, further, by the Christian imperative of love. Truth is not an objective fact outside of and above him but rather the very essence of his subjective being as expressed in the act of love.[29] There is no ultimate objective or theoretical justification for one's beliefs: they are to be judged, rather, pragmatically by a criterion of charitable action toward others. Vattimo writes, accordingly, of "the postmetaphysical philosophy made possible by Christ" (*Future of Religion*, 50). Truth is entirely dissolved into "love" and into interpersonal agreement.

The Hedeggerian model that serves as constant reference for Vattimo is that of Being itself, which is ontologically different from all beings and is experienced as Nothing. But the historical paradigm here, in spite of Vattimo's resistance, is that of the mystic negative theology that Heidegger found in Meister Eckhart and Silesius Angelus and that Dante follows to his vision of God in the *Paradiso*, emphasizing its inviolable ineffability at every step of the way. Every strong claim to knowledge dissolves rather into a personal and mystical experience, of which the condition is humility and a giving up of all claims to know anything whatever, except as a gift graciously granted from . . . we do not know exactly what or whom.

The seminal insight for all of Vattimo's thinking is that of the interpretive nature and basis of all that is. Employing Heidegger's philosophical jargon, Vattimo calls this *hermeneutic ontology*. Following Nietzsche, who had proclaimed that truth is nothing but interpretation all the way down, and Heidegger, who had developed a hermeneutic ontology in the form of an analytic of existence, bringing out interpretation and understanding as intrinsic to the most basic features of our being-in-the-world,

---

29. Michel Henry works out the revolutionary implications of Christ's utterance phenomenologically in *C'est moi la vérité: Pour une philosophie du christianisme* (Paris: Seuil, 1998), trans. Susan Emanuel as *I Am the Truth: Toward a Philosophy of Christianity* (Stanford: Stanford University Press, 2003).

Vattimo develops his philosophical vision from this crucial insight into the interpretive constitution of all that is. While he takes this insight most directly from Heidegger and Nietzsche, he finds it already on hand at certain crucial junctures in the cultural history of the West. He gives Christianity a decisive priority in developing such a culture of interpretation. At least in "our" history, that of the West, Christianity has fostered a culture in which purported objectivities are dethroned so that, as a consequence, truth evolves into a subjective and even a purely pragmatic phenomenon.

This means, among other things, that truth is always relative to particular historical situations and communities. Vattimo recognizes his own roots in Western liberal democratic and specifically Italian Catholic culture. What is universal (at least potentially) is the deconstruction of all pretended objectivities so as to allow love among people to be the only authority over them. Christians are no longer under any objective regime requiring the name of truth. In choosing Christ, they choose love over any ideology laying claim to objective validity. They renounce claims to *know* how to discriminate the true and good from the illusory and evil, where all such determinations inevitably favor certain individuals and parties over others. The only truth revealed by Scripture is that of love: it is not in competition with science or with any other kind of knowledge claiming to state how things really are. It rather undermines all such claims. Love is how things *should* be *made to be* by us; it is a subjective imperative rather than an objective proposition about the true nature of the world. The only constraints on interpretation that really count are ones imposed not by how things objectively are but rather by a community and a tradition that furnish a language and create a life-world of their own as an indispensable context.

Now it may seem that all of this is worlds away from Dante. Indeed Vattimo always stresses *nihilism* as a necessary form of thought and culture in postmodern times. His *Fine della modernità* begins with an "Apology for Nihilism," as the title of the opening chapter announces. The tone of this nihilism, however, is not negative or despairing. It entails rather a kind of liberation and is, in fact, in Vattimo's estimation "our only chance" today.[30] Fundamentally, Vattimo's nihilism aims to clear the field of "metaphysical" illusions in order to open up to a free dimension of existence, one unencumbered by the purported objectivities that we unwittingly impose on ourselves.

---

30. Gianni Vattimo, *La fine della modernità* (Milan: Garzanti, 1985), 27. See, further, Vattimo, *Nichilismo e emancipazione*.

V. Negative Theology as Limitless Critique—in Poetry

Although Vattimo has not wished to acknowledge it, his approach is deeply consonant with the strategies of negative theology.[31] When Vattimo turns philosophy into a critical art of deconstructing all positive, objectifying claims, he is following the age-old practice of Christian negative theology, that of denying any positive attribution to the Godhead— and thereby to everything else, too, since in this perspective the being of everything depends directly on God's Being. There are very strong links between deconstructive philosophies and the negative theologies that are their counterparts in past tradition and that abide in some form as intrinsic to their current agendas.[32] Vattimo cites Wittgenstein to the effect that philosophy can only free us from idols (*Future of Religion*, 50)—but that is exactly what negative theologies have always done.[33] Vattimo rejects any theology of a transcendent God and even the crypto-theology of the absolutely other—the *tout autre*—of Levinas and Derrida (*Dopo la cristianità*, 41). However, all these descriptions and designations are also in the end negated by negative theology, at least if we do not read its "theology" too literally. And certainly Vattimo should be in favor of that: he pleads fervently against literal readings of the Bible.

Indeed, the extraordinary achievement of Dante's poem begs to be described in precisely the terms that Vattimo employs. Dante's poem deconstructs truth by translating dogmatic principles into poetic interpretation and personal aesthetic experience joined with resolute engagement in an existential faith. It does so through embracing a comprehensive life-commitment (embodying conversion) within a certain community and tradition. To this extent, the *Divine Comedy* ought to be recognized as the paradigmatic realization of Vattimo's idea of an "Age of Interpretation." Experiential and poetic truth becomes, in effect, the criterion for verifying all traditional and even all revealed "knowledge." Dante makes this point trenchantly, for example, in a passage concerning the number of the seraphs' wings, where he says that John is "with him" ("Giovanni è meco,"

---

31. Vattimo's typical distancing of himself from negative theology (one knows this maneuver well from Derrida and his disciples) registers, for example, in *La fine della modernità*, 37.

32. Such links are skillfully drawn by Bruce Ellis Benson, *Graven Ideologies: Nietzsche, Derrida and Marion on Modern Idolatry* (Downers Grove, IL: InterVarsity Press, 2002).

33. See especially Moshe Halbertal and Avishai Margalit, *Idolatry*, trans. (from Hebrew) Naomi Goldblum (Cambridge: Harvard University Press, 1992).

Purgatorio XXIX.105), thereby correcting Ezekiel's divergent account by direct appeal to his own personal experience in Paradise.[34]

I have previously endeavored to demonstrate that Dante's *Comedy* offers a compelling illustration of the "origin of the work of art"—the artwork as the origin and opening up of a world—as conceived by Martin Heidegger. I suggested, moreover, that Dante's hermeneutic vision is capable not only of illustrating but also of critiquing Heidegger's thought, and here I wish to suggest that the same goes for Vattimo's philosophy. Indeed Dante's hermeneutic ontology, such as I develop it in *Dante's Interpretive Journey,* is in certain respects more complete and responsive to what Heidegger calls the call of Being than is any modern hermeneutic which remains closed to the dimension of theological transcendence that animates Dante's vision: at least this is so once such transcendence is interpreted in a negative theological or apophatic key.

In Dante's poem, the interpretive art of poetry becomes the vessel and the vehicle of a revelation of Christian truth: truth is transformed by poetic interpretation from theological dogma into aesthetic experience and existential engagement. This corresponds precisely to the hermeneutic revolution that Vattimo champions. For the earlier, pre-Christian (or more likely pre-confessional) Vattimo of *La fine della modernità,* it is first of all aesthetics, not religion or theology, that opens the space of liberation beyond metaphysics. Vattimo understands postmodernity as essentially aesthetic in nature. What pierces the metaphysical cast of Western culture is, first of all, an aesthetic revolution from which the scientific revolution is then leveraged. Paradigm shifts in science (as expounded particularly by Thomas Kuhn) are modeled for Vattimo on artistic revolutions, which substitute one aesthetic style for another (*La fine della modernità,* chapter VI).

Vattimo recognizes art as the crucial catalyst in the hermeneutic revolution. He resists Gadamer's critique of aesthetic consciousness as imposing a subjective frame that preempts the truth that art can disclose (*La fine della modernità,* chapter VII). He defends and insists on the world-transforming power of the aesthetic. The artistic avant-gardes of the twentieth century are instigators of the modern social revolution that Vattimo espouses as liberating and that he wants to trace ultimately to Christianity. Dante's art, too, represented the avant-garde of formal innovation in his day and, furthermore, enacted a social revolution through its new

34. See Peter S. Hawkins, "John Is with Me," in *Dante's Testaments: Essays in Scriptural Imagination* (Stanford: Stanford University Press, 1999), 54–71.

existential hermeneutic and prophetic vision. But Vattimo does not recognize or exploit Dante and the epoch-making archive of his writings and their reception, the history of their effect (*Wirkungsgeschichte*).[35]

Admittedly, Dante's authoritarian, imperialist, Ghibelline ideology would be repugnant to Vattimo as a democratic reformer in the European Parliament, and presumably turn him away. Dante's great poem may seem to be an apology not just for Christianity but also for "Christendom"— a sort of "kingdom" based on supposedly Christian mores and spirituality. Nevertheless, Dante is adamant that no ecclesiastical instance but only a secular ruler can be the sole legitimate governing authority of the kingdom of this world. We may grant that the poem is an incomparable thesaurus of Christian ideology, one celebrating Christianity's saints and championing its crusades, even to the point of reproaching the pope for negligence in not mounting a campaign for the conquest and defense of the Holy Land. At the same time, however, the ultimate effect of Dante's poem, especially of its finale in Paradise, is to dissolve doctrine into personal experience and to transubstantiate theology into poetry. In this sense, too, the effect achieved by the work is profoundly secularizing. Its content is inextricably theological, but its theology is, finally, a negative theology that suspends its own content in turning to a God beyond (or perhaps imperceptibly within) all finite human concepts and words. Going beyond discursivity is the direction in which Dante is headed from the outset of the *Paradiso,* with its topos of ineffability continuously repeated all the way to the end—and even *as* the end. Only a loving incarnation of desire is finally capable of witnessing to the divine Word that cannot be spoken.

VI. The Spirit of Christianity as Interpretive Community

Vattimo does call attention to the Middle Ages and to Joachim of Flores as developing an acute and comprehensive sense of hermeneutics through the interpretation of Scripture, which in that day and age was viewed as the source and template of all possible experience of the real (*Dopo la cristianità,* chapter 2). Significantly, Joachim, the twelfth-century Cistercian abbot of the monastery of Fiori in the remote mountain fastnesses

---

35. Even Vattimo's contribution ("Heidegger: Il linguaggio come evento dell'essere") to a volume of studies on Dante, *Psicoanalisi e strutturalismo di fronte a Dante* (Florence: Olschki, 1972), vol. 1, 311–24, has no analysis and barely any specific mention of Dante or his texts.

of the Sila in Calabria, is recognized also by Dante as a crucial forebear. Dante's prophetic project is indeed internally linked with that of Joachim, who appears as a key figure at an especially climactic moment of the *Paradiso*. Dante places him in the Heaven of the Sun among the sapient souls and celebrates him as endowed with a prophetic spirit in a resounding reference to

> il calavrese abate Giovacchino
> di spirito profetico dotato.[36]
> > (XII.141–42)

> the Calabrian abbot Joachim
> endowed with a prophetic spirit.

Joachim elaborately developed the "spiritual" interpretation of Scripture. As he understands it, the true meaning of Scripture is not dictated by dogmatic authority but is informed instead by its worldly application in the experience of individual believers. All believers, moreover, are inspired directly by the Holy Ghost in the age of the Spirit. This age follows that of the Father, in which the Jews were under the authority of the Law (Old Testament times), and that of the Son (the New Testament era), which kept Christians under the tutelage of the Church and its magisterium. A new dispensation begins with the spiritualizing of revelation, with its becoming available to all through the direct visitation by the Spirit upon individual souls. This Age is for Joachim already incipient with the advent of Christian monasticism and its peculiar brand of spiritual perfection modeled especially by St. Benedict.

Dante's *Paradiso* exultantly sings the "true sparkling of the Holy Spirit" ("Oh vero sfavillar del Santo Spiro!" XIV.76) that has been imagined by Joachim as a pouring out of grace and truth and of the gift of prophecy upon all of God's people. Hierarchy within human society would then be obsolete, since all would be directly inspired and guided by God. This vision is for Vattimo a model of the breakdown of metaphysics and of all authority in a generalized interpretive free-for-all (or, more accurately, freedom-for-all). The Franciscan vision of a fraternal society in its radical Joachimite form based on a universally open activity of interpretation in the spirit replacing all institutionalized forms of author-

---

36. I quote and translate from *La Divina Commedia secondo l'antica vulgata*, ed. Giorgio Petrocchi, 4 vols. (Milan: Mondadori, 1966–67).

ity adumbrates the ideal of a Christian love-inspired, secular, democratic society that Vattimo longingly envisages. Dante receives the light of this vision into his *Paradiso* through its glorification of Joachim among the spirits of the blessed in the Heaven of the Sun.

Like Vattimo, Dante advocates for a society permeated by Christian values and charitable action or, more precisely, by free exercise of all possible intellect ("totam potentiam intellectus possibilis"), which he considers to be the proper fulfillment of humankind (*De Monarchia* I.i.1). This model society is to be integrally Christian and yet rigorously secular— free from ecclesiastical authority in all worldly spheres of life. The main thrust of Dante's defense of the authority of the Emperor aims precisely to liberate the secular domain from all ecclesiastical meddling—from all interference on the part of whatever priestly powers. Vattimo, in his own polemics against the pope, especially during the papacy of Joseph Ratzinger, could hardly wish for a more passionate precursor or a more compelling precedent than Dante.

Contemporary thought, as embodied in Vattimo's philosophy, has followed the secular destiny of modernity to the end of its possibilities and has discovered there an opening or a gap that issues in a return of religion. Dante, too, followed the secular thinking of his time radically to the point of its reversal, or at least apotheosis, in theological vision. Emblematically, he embraces Siger of Brabant as radical Aristotelian together with his ostensible opponent and nemesis Thomas Aquinas, the banner-bearing knight of ecclesiastical orthodoxy, in the Heaven of the Sun (*Paradiso* X.136–38). Just as Aquinas's speech completes its circle with reference to Siger immediately to his left, so Bonaventure ends his discourse with mention of the luminous spirit immediately to *his* left in his own circle, namely, Joachim (XII.140–41). Even as Aquinas had engaged in heavy polemics with Siger, so Bonaventure had fiercely attacked Joachim's teaching, particularly as it was relayed by the spiritual Franciscans of his own day.

There is prima facie an opposition between the secular and the religious, but in their enduring significance they tend rather to solicit and call one another forth. In a Christian spiritual and specifically incarnational perspective, the fulfillment of the secular is in the religious and vice versa. This becomes startlingly evident at certain historical moments. Among the most striking of them are Dante's moment at the end of the Middle Ages and the dawn of the modern age and, again, our own historical moment at the end of modernity, with its metamorphosis into what we can hardly escape calling "*postmodernity.*"

Dante's poem, and more generally his life's oeuvre, embody a hermeneutic revolution very much of the sort that Vattimo, as a philosophical prophet of postmodernism, proclaims. Dante's premodern outlook,
moreover, already critiques the postulates of modernity *avant la lettre*.
This is, in effect, the argument of my book *Dante's Interpretive Journey*,
which shows that a sort of demonstration of the interpretive ontology of
human existence, a phenomenological revealment of this existence not
unworthy of comparison with Heidegger's, is already well underway in
Dante's poem as leveraged particularly from its addresses to the reader.
Our existence is constituted by the call to which we respond. This is what
Vattimo is saying in the wake of Heidegger and at "the end of modernity." Dante, at the threshold of modernity, was able to have a similar
outlook, yet without its being circumscribed and confined by the postulate of the self-grounding subject and its correlative objective truths. For
Dante, too, all truth was interpretation, and it suspended his being in a
relatedness that opened beyond any fixed or knowable framework into
the mystery of the co-inherence of all things in what he called "God."
This is essentially the insight that Vattimo, too, is advocating in the
milieu of postmodern philosophy and religion today. Its being found in
Dante roots it in Vattimo's own historicity as an Italian, as well as in the
hermeneutic culture of the Middle Ages, which Dante develops to some
of its most provocative possibilities and most far-reaching conclusions.[37]

Vattimo does expressly recognize Dante as a classic without which
Italian literature would not be intelligible, just as Western culture is not
intelligible without the Bible, and he recognizes furthermore that the Bible
is necessary in order to understand Dante ("Per un cristianesimo non
religioso," 51). I have tried to suggest some avenues for developing this
important intuition in a more complete manner than Vattimo has done
or perhaps even thought to be possible. Yet such an adoption of Dante's
legacy is in my view indispensable to Vattimo's and to postmodernism's
own project and predicament. Vattimo finds himself sometimes accused
of Christian Eurocentric chauvinism, and the answer to this must be that
such ideology, which inheres in his historicity, and so is best openly admitted, nevertheless self-deconstructs—just as Dante's express, confessional
ideology and dogmatism dissolve in his more far-reaching and all-encompassing negative theology.

Allowing for their different historical contexts, the fundamental strategies of Dante and Vattimo as advocates for Christianity are, in the end,

---

37. Again, showing this is precisely the burden of *Dante's Interpretive Journey*.

strikingly alike. Both secularize religion into a form of interpretive tradition producing communal identity through collective symbols and consciousness-forming narratives ingeniously designed to engender passions such as solidarity and love. The claim to objective truth of this construction is strongly denied by Vattimo, but such strong denials run a risk, as Vattimo himself makes us aware, of taking on an air of objectivity themselves and so of converting into inverted assertions of truth in their own right. Dante's strength lies rather in the "weakness" of his poetic idiom, which does not as such assert but rather interprets.

Even the powerfully assertive and affirmative character of Dante's ideology, by being directed, in the end, toward the ineffable, works not dogmatically but rather poetically. It opens a horizon of meaning for free exploration rather than fixing final and determinate meaning in static formulas. Religion thus becomes literature for Dante, at least as author of the *Commedia,* just as religious belief is all a matter of interpretation for Vattimo. Indeed literature and religion are deeply one as interpretive practices conveying truth that cannot be adequately stated objectively. Such is the "weak," kenotic truth that prevails finally in the multi-millenary cultural heritage of Christianity that Dante and Vattimo together aspire to transmit. This is weak truth that, in the name of theological revelation, may yet prove the weakness of God (I Corinthians 1:25) to be stronger than all the mighty manifestations of human power that have so dominated the modern era.

Theological poetics in the wake of Dante have been concerned with negotiating the revelatory power of the movement of secularization throughout this modern period. The seeming reduction of poetry and revelation to worldly manifestations surprisingly releases another kind of power, one that exceeds human calculation and control in the direction of worldly and incarnate realization of the infinite potentialities of the poetic word. Entering into the flesh and becoming secular entail a crucifixion of the word and of religious truth narrowly conceived, but precisely this martyrization of the word has been an exceptionally fecund source of revelation throughout the modern era—and even beyond. The postmodern and premodern projects of Vattimo and Dante respectively rediscover, in mutually illuminating ways, the extraordinary potential of secularized interpretive understanding for releasing and fomenting the revolutionary ferment gestating in theological revelation in and for and beyond the modern age.

Adorno, Theodor and Max Horkheimer. *Dialektik der Aufklärung: Philosophische Fragmente*. Frankfurt am Main: Fischer, 1969 [1947]. Trans. as *Dialectic of Enlightenment: Philosophical Fragments*, ed. G. S. Noerr, trans. E. Jephcott. Stanford: Stanford University Press, 2002.

Agamben, Giorgio. *La chiesa e il regno*. Rome: Nottetempo, 2010.

Agamben, Giorgio. *Homo Sacer I: Il potere soverano e la vita nuda*. Turin: Einaudi, 1995.

Agamben, Giorgio. *Il regno e la gloria. Per una genealogia teologica dell'economia e del governo. Homo sacer*, II, 2. Vicenza: Neri Pozza, 2007. Trans. Lorenzo Chiesa (with Matteo Mandarini) as *The Kingdom and the Glory: For a Theological Genealogy of Economy and Government*. Stanford: Stanford University Press, 2011.

Agamben, Giorgio and Monica Ferrando. *La ragazza indicibile: Mito e mistero di Kore*. Milan: Mondadori Electa, 2010.

Altieri, Charles. "From Symbolist Thought to Immanence: The Ground of Postmodern American Poetics." *boundary 2* (1973): 605–39.

Altizer, Thomas J. J. *History as Apocalypse*. Albany: State University of New York Press, 1985.

Ancarani, Nadia. Ed. *Letture classensi 32/34 (Filosofi d'oggi per Dante)*. Ravenna: Longo, 2005.

Ariani, Marco. *Lux inaccessibilis: Metafore e teologia della luce nel Paradiso di Dante*. Rome: Aracne, 2010.

Ariani, Marco. Ed. *La metafora in Dante*. Florence: Olschki, 2009.

Asad, Talal. *Formations of the Secular: Christianity, Islam, Modernity*. Stanford: Stanford University Press, 2003.

Auerbach, Erich. *Dante als Dichter der irdischen Welt*. Berlin: Walter de Gruyter, 1929. 2nd ed. Afterword Kurt Flasch, 2001. Trans. Ralph Manheim as *Dante: Poet of the Secular World*. Chicago: University of Chicago Press, 1961.

Auerbach, Erich. "Figura." In *Scenes from the Drama of European Literature: Six Essays*. Gloucester, MA: Meridian, 1969. 12–67.

Austin, Lloyd. *L'univers poétique de Baudelaire: symbolisme et symbolique*. Paris: Mercure de France, 1956.

Badiou, Alain. *L'être et l'évévement*. Paris: Seuil, 1988.

Badiou, Alain. *Saint Paul: La fondation de l'universalisme*. Paris: Presses Universitaires de France, 1997. Trans. Ray Brassier as *Saint Paul: The Foundation of Universalism*. Stanford: Stanford University Press, 2003.

Baldwin, C. S. *Medieval Rhetoric and Poetic to 1400*. Gloucester, MA: Macmillan, 1928.

Balthasar, Hans Urs von. *Die Herrlichkeit des Herrn: Eine theologische Ästhetik*. 4 vols. Einsiedeln: Johannes, 1969. Trans. Erasmo Leiva-Merikakis as *The Glory of the Lord: A Theological Aesthetics*. San Francisco: Ignatius Press, 1989.

Barthes, Roland. "Le mythe, aujourd'hui." *Mythologies*. Paris: Seuil, 1957.

Baudelaire, Charles. *Oeuvres complètes*. Ed. Claude Pichois. Paris: Gallimard, 1975–76.

Bauer, Christine O'Connel. *Dante's Hermeneutics of Salvation: Passages to Freedom in the Divine Comedy*. Toronto: University of Toronto Press, 2007.

Bays, Gwendolyn. *The Orphic Vision: Seer Poets from Novalis to Rimbaud*. Lincoln: University of Nebraska Press, 1964.

Benjamin, Walter. "Die Aufgabe des Übersetzers." In *Illuminationen: Ausgewählte Schriften 1* (Frankfurt am Main: Suhrhamp, 1977. 50–62. Trans. as "The Task of the Translator: An Introduction to the Translation of Baudelaire's *Tableaux Parisiens*." In *Illuminations*. Ed. Hannah Arendt. New York: Schocken, 1969.

Benjamin, Walter. "Über einige Motive bei Baudelaire." In *Illuminationen. Ausgewählte Schriften 1*. Frankfurt am Main: Suhrkamp, 1977.

Benson, Bruce Ellis. *Graven Ideologies: Nietzsche, Derrida and Marion on Modern Idolatry*. Downers Grove, IL: InterVarsity Press, 2002.

Bible, The Holy. Containing the Old and New Testaments. Authorized King James Version. 1611. New York: American Bible Society.

Biral, Bruno. *La posizione storica di Giacomo Leopardi*. Turin: Einaudi, 1974.

Blake, William. *The Complete Poetry and Prose of William Blake*. Ed. David W. Erdman. Berkeley: University of California Press, 1982.

Blasucci, Luigi. "La Posizione Ideologica delle *Operette morali*." In *Critica e storia letteraria, studi offerti a Mario Fubini*. Padova: Liviana, 1970.

Bloom, Harold. *The Western Canon*. New York: Harcourt Brace, 1994.

Blumenberg, Hans. *Die Legitimität der Neuzeit*. Frankfurt am Main: Suhrkamp, 1966. Reissued revised as *Säkularisierung und Selbstbehauptung*. Frankfurt am Main: Suhrkamp, 1974. Trans. Robert M. Wallace as *Legitimacy of the Modern Age*. Cambridge: MIT Press, 1985.

Boesel, Chris and Catherine Keller. Eds. *Apophatic Bodies: Negative Theology, Incarnation, and Relationality*. New York: Fordham University Press, 2009.

Boitani, Piero et al. *Dante poeta cristiano*. Florence: Società Dante Alighieri, 2001.

Boitani, Piero. *Il vangelo secondo Shakespeare*. Bologna: Mulino, 2009.

Boucher, Holly Wallace. "Nominalism: The Difference for Chaucer and Boccaccio." *The Chaucer Review* 20 (1986): 213–20.

Boulnois, Olivier. *Au-delà de l'image: Une archéologie du visuel au Moyen Âge (Ve–XVIe siècle)*. Paris: Seuil, 2008.

Brantley, Richard E. *Experience and Faith: The Late-Romantic Imagination of Emily Dickinson*. New York: Palgrave, 2004.

Breton, Stanislas. *La philosophie du rien*. Kampen, Netherlands: Kok Pharos, 1992.

Bridge, Ursula. *Yeats and T. Sturge Moore: Their Correspondence*. New York: Oxford University Press, 1953.

Brix, Michel. "Modern Beauty versus Platonist Beauty." In *Baudelaire and the Poetics of Modernity*. Ed. Patricia Ward. Nashville: Vanderbilt University Press, 2000.

Budick, Sanford and Wolfgang Iser. Eds. *Languages of the Unsayable: The Play of Negativity in Literature and Literary Theory*. New York: Columbia University Press, 1989.

Burckhardt, Jacob. *Die Kultur der Renaissance in Italien* (1860). Trans. S. G. C. Middlemore as *The Civilization of the Italian Renaissance*, 2 vols. New York: Harper Torchbooks, 1958.

Burlin, Robert. *Chaucerian Fiction*. Princeton: Princeton University Press, 1977.

Calhoun, Craig, Mark Juergesnmeyer, and Jonathan VanAntwerpen. Eds. *Rethinking Secularism*. Oxford: Oxford University Press, 2011.

Cambon, Glauco. "Dante's Presence in American Literature." *Dante Studies* 118 (2000): 217–42.

Cameron, Sharon. *Choosing Not Choosing: Dickinson's Fascicles*. Chicago: University of Chicago Press, 1992.

Camilletti, Fabio. *Leopardi's Nymphs: Grace, Melancholy, and the Uncanny*. Oxford: Legenda, 2013.

Cantor, Georg. *Grundlagen einer allgemeinen Mannigfaltigkeitslehre (Foundation of a General Theory of Aggregates, 1883)*.

Cantor, Georg. "On the Theory of the Transfinite: Correspondence of Georg Cantor and J. B. Cardinal Frenzelin (1885–86). Afterword by Lyndon H. LaRouche, Jr." *Fidelio* 3/3 (Fall 1994): 97–110.

Caputo, John D. *The Prayers and Tears of Jacques Derrida*. Bloomington: Indiana University Press, 1997.

Caputo, John D. and Michael J. Scanlon. Eds. *Transcendence and Beyond: A Postmodern Inquiry*. Bloomington: Indiana University Press, 2007.

Caputo, John D., and Michael J. Scanlon. Eds. *God, the Gift, and Postmodernism*. Bloomington: Indiana University Press, 1999.

Carugati, Giuliana. *Dalla menzogna al silenzio: La scrittura mistica della "Commedia" di Dante*. Bologna: Il Mulino, 1991.

Casanova, José. *Public Religions in the Modern World*. Chicago: University of Chicago Press, 1994.

Cavell, Stanley. *Disowning Knowledge: In Seven Plays of Shakespeare*. Cambridge: Cambridge University Press, 2001. Updated ed.

Chaucer, Geoffrey. *The Riverside Chaucer*. Gen. ed. Larry D. Benson. New York: Houghton Mifflin, 1987. 3rd ed.

Chenu, M. D. *La théologie au douzième siècle*. Paris: J. Vrin, 1957.

Chiarenza, Marguerite Mills. "The Imageless Vision and Dante's *Paradiso*." *Dante Studies* 90 (1972): 109–24.

Cohn, Robert Greer. "Symbolism." *The Journal of Aesthetics and Art Criticism* 33 (Winter 1974): 181–92.

Cohn, Robert Greer. *Toward the Poems of Mallarmé*. Berkeley: University of California Press, 1965.

Coleridge, Samuel Taylor. *Miscellaneous Criticism*. Ed. T. M Raysor. London: Constable, 1936.

Coleridge, Samuel Taylor. *Biographia Literaria*. www.gutenberg.org.

Colish, Marcia. *The Mirror of Language: A Study in the Medieval Theory of Knowledge*. Lincoln: University of Nebraska Press, 1983. Rev. ed.

Colombo, Manuela. *Dai mistici a Dante: Il linguaggio dell'ineffabilità*. Firenze: La Nuova Italia, 1987.

Cox, John D. *Seeing Knowledge: Shakespeare and Skeptical Faith*. Waco, TX: Baylor University Press, 2007.

Crafton, John Michael. "Emptying the Vessel: Chaucer's Humanistic Critique of Nominalism." In *Literary Nominalism and the Theory of Rereading Late Medieval Texts: A New Research Paradigm*. Ed. Richard J. Utz. Lewiston: Edwin Mellen Press, 1995.

Croce, Benedetto. *Poesia e non poesia. Note sulla letteratura europea del secolo decimonono*. Bari: Laterza, 1964. 7th ed.

Crumbley, Paul. *Inflections of the Pen: Dash and Voice in Emily Dickinson*. Lexington: University Press of Kentucky, 1997.

Cusanus, Nicholas. *De visione Dei*. In *Nicolai de Cusa Opera Omnia*. Leipzig: Meiner, 1932–2006. Trans. Evelyn Underhill as *The Vision of God*. New York: Frederick Ungar, 1928.

Delvaille, Bernard. Ed. *La poésie symboliste*. Paris: Seghers, 1971.

Dante. *Convivio. Opere minori*, vol. 5, tome I, pt. II. Ed. C. Vasoli. Milan: Ricciardi, 1988.

Dante. *La Divina Commedia secondo l'antica vulgata*. Ed. G. Petrocchi, 4 vols. Milan: Mondadori, 1966–67.

Dante. *Monarchia*. Ed. Federico Sanguinetti. Milan: Garzanti, 1985.

Dante. *De vulgari eloquentia. Epistole. Opere minori*, vol. 5, tome II. Eds. Pier Vincenzo Mengaldo et al. Milan: Ricciardi, 1973.

Davis, Charles T. *Dante and the Idea of Rome*. Oxford: Clarendon, 1957.

De Benedictis, Raffaele. *Worldly Wise: The Semiotics of Discourse in Dante's 'Commedia.'* New York: Peter Lang, 2012.

de Certeau, Michel. "Penser le Christianisme." In *La faiblesse de croire*. Paris: Seuil, 1987.

Delany, Sheila. *Chaucer's House of Fame: The Poetics of Skeptical Fideism*. Chicago: University of Chicago Press, 1972.

Delasanta, Rodney. "Nominalism and the *Clerk's Tale* Revisited." *The Chaucer Review* 31 (1997): 209–31.

de Lubac, Henri. *Corpus mysticum: L'eucharistie et l'église au moyen âge*. Paris: Aubier, 1944. Trans. Gemma Simmonds, *Corpus Mysticum: The Eucharist and the Church in the Middle Ages*. South Bend: University of Notre Dame Press, 2007.

De Man, Paul. "The Double Aspect of Symbolism." *Yale French Studies* 74 (1988): 3–16.

De Man, Paul. "Lyric and Modernity." In *Blindness and Insight: Essays in the Rhetoric of Contemporary Criticism*. Minneapolis: University of Minnesota Press, 1971.

Derrida, Jacques and Antoine Spire. *Au-delà des apparences*. Latresne, Bordeaux: Le Bord de l'eau, 2002.

De Sanctis, Francesco. *Lezioni sulla Divina Commedia*. Bari: Laterza, 1955 [1854].

de Vries, Hent. Ed. *Religion: Beyond a Concept*. New York: Fordham University Press, 2008.

Dickinson, Emily. *The Poems of Emily Dickinson*. Variorum Edition. Ed. R. W. Franklin. Cambridge: The Belknap Press of Harvard University Press, 1998.

Dickinson, Emily. *The Poems of Emily Dickinson*. Ed. Thomas H. Johnson. Cambridge: The Belknap Press of Harvard University, 1955 [1951].

Donaldson, E. T. *Speaking of Chaucer*. London: Athlone Press, 1970.

Doriani, Beth Maclay. *Emily Dickinson: Daughter of Prophecy*. Amherst: University of Massachusetts Press, 1996.

Eagleton, Terry. *After Theory*. London: Allen Lane, 2003.

Eagleton, Terry. *Literary Theory: An Introduction*. Minneapolis: University of Minnesota Press, 1983.

Eldredge, Lawrence. "Boethian Epistemology and Chaucer's *Troilus* in the Light of Fourteenth Century Thought." *Mediaevalia* 2 (1976): 49–75.

Eliot, Charles W. Ed. *English Essays: Sidney to Macaulay; Shelley, A Defence of Poetry*. Cambridge: The Harvard Classics, 1909–14.

Eliot, T. S. "Milton I." In *On Poetry and Poets*. New York: Farrar, 1957.

Eliot, T. S. *The Waste Land and Other Poems*. New York: Harcourt, Brace & World, 1962.

Empson, William. *Milton's God*. London: Chattro, 1965.

Enders, Markus. *Zum Begriff der Unendlichkeit im abendländischen Denken: Unendlichkeit Gottes und Unendlichkeit der Welt*. Hamburg: Boethiana, 2006.

Falque, Emmanuel. *Le combat amoureux. Disputes phénoménologiques et théologiques*. Paris: Hermann, 2014.

Falque, Emmanuel. *Dieu, la chair et l'autre: d'Irénée à Duns Scot*. Paris: Presses Universitaires de France, 2008. Trans. William Christian Hackett as God, the Flesh, and the Other: From Irenaeus to Duns Scotus. Evanston, IL: Northwestern University Press, 2014.

Ferguson, Margaret W. "Saint Augustine's Region of Unlikeness: The Crossing of Exile and Language." *The Georgia Review* 29 (1975): 842–64.

Fink, Werner. "*Poeta vates*. Versionen eines mythischen Modells in der Lyrik der Moderne," *Formaler Mythos. Beiträge zu einer Theorie der ästhetischen Formen*. Ed. Matias Martinez. Munich: Schöningh, 1996. 124–62.

Finkelde, Dominik. *Politische Eschatologie nach Paulus: Badiou-Agamben-Zizek-Santner*. Vienna: Verlag Turia + Kant, 2007.

Fish, Stanley. "Discovery as Form in *Paradise Lost*." In *New Essays on 'Paradise Lost.'* Ed. Thomas Kranidas. Berkeley: University of California Press, 1971. 1–15.

Fish, Stanley. *Self-Consuming Artifacts: The Experience of Seventeenth Century Literature*. Berkeley: University of California Press, 1972.

Fish, Stanley. *Surprised by Sin*. New York: Macmillan, 1967.

Fletcher Angus. *Allegory: The Theory of a Symbolic Mode*. Ithaca: Cornell University Press, 1964.

Foucault, Michel. "Préface à la transgression." *Critique* 195–96 (1963): 751–69.

Franke, William. "Agamben's Logic of Exception: Its Apophatic Roots and Offshoots." *Concentric: Literary and Cultural Studies* (September 2015).

Franke, William. "Damascius. Of the Ineffable: Aporetics of the Notion of an Absolute Principle." *Arion: A Journal of Humanities and the Classics* 12/1 (2004): 111–31.

Franke, William. *Dante and the Sense of Transgression: 'The Trespass of the Sign.'* London: Continuum [Bloomsbury Academic], 2013.

Franke, William. *Dante's Interpretive Journey.* Chicago: University of Chicago Press, 1996.

Franke, William. "Homer's Musings and the Divine Muse: Epic Song as Invention and as Revelation." *Religion and Literature* 43/1 (2011): 1–28.

Franke, William. "Language and Transcendence in Dante's *Paradiso.*" In *Poetics of Transcendence.* Eds. Elisa Heinämäki, P. M. Mehtonen, and Antti Salminen. Amsterdam: Rodopi: 2014. 107–31.

Franke, William. "On the Poetic Truth That Is Higher than History: Porphyry and the Philosophical Interpretation of Literature." *International Philosophical Quarterly* 50/4 (2010): 415–30.

Franke, William. Ed. *On What Cannot Be Said: Apophatic Discourses in Philosophy, Religion, Literature, and the Arts,* 2 vols. Notre Dame: University of Notre Dame Press, 2007.

Franke, William. *A Philosophy of the Unsayable.* Notre Dame: University of Notre Dame Press, 2014.

Franke, William. *Poetry and Apocalypse: Theological Disclosures of Poetic Language.* Stanford: Stanford University Press: 2009.

Franke, William. "Poetry and Prophecy." *Oxford Research Encyclopedia of Religion.* Ed. John Barton. New York: Oxford University Press, 2015.

Franke, William. *The Revelation of Imagination: From the Bible and Homer through Virgil and Augustine to Dante.* Evanston, IL: Northwestern University Press, 2015.

Franke, William. "Symbol and Allegory." In *The Routledge Companion to Philosophical Hermeneutics.* Eds. Jeff Malpas and Hans-Helmuth Gander. New York: Routledge, 2015. 367–77 (chapter 29).

Freccero, John. *Dante: The Poetics of Conversion.* Ed. Rachel Jacoff. Cambridge: Harvard University Press, 1986.

Frey, Hans-Jost. *Studien über das Reden der Dichter.* München: Wilhelm Fink, 1986.

Friedrich, Hugo. *Die Struktur der modernen Lyrik.* Hamburg: Rowohlt, 1956.

Frye, Northrop. Ed. *"Paradise Lost" and Selected Poetry and Prose.* New York: Holt, 1951.

Frye, Northrop. *A Study of English Romanticism.* Chicago: University of Chicago Press, 1968.

Gadamer, Hans-Georg. *Die Aktualität des Schönen.* Stuttgart: Reclam, 1977. Trans. Nicholas Walker as *The Relevance of the Beautiful.* London: Cambridge University Press, 1986.

Gadamer, Hans-Georg. *Wahrheit und Methode.* Tübingen: J. C. B. Mohr, 1960. Trans. Joel Weinsheimer and Donald Marshall as *Truth and Method.* New York: Crossroad, 1989. 2nd ed. rev.

Gauchet, Marcel. *Le désenchantement du monde: Une histoire politique de la religion.* Paris: Gallimard, 1985.

Gibson, Matthew. *Yeats, Coleridge and the Romantic Sage*. Great Britain: Macmillan, 2000.

Goethe, Johann Wolfgang von. *Faust Eine Tragödie*. Stuttgart: Reclam. 1971.

Goethe, Johann Wolfgang von. *Gedenkausgabe der Werke, Briefe und Gespräche*. Ed. Ernst Beutler. Zürich and Stuttgart: Artemis Verlag, 1949.

Grabher, Gudren M., Roland Hagenbüchle, and Cristanne Miller. Eds. *The Emily Dickinson Handbook*. Amherst: University of Massachusetts Press, 1998.

Grabher, Gudren M. and Ulrike Jessner. Eds. *Semantics of Silence in Linguistics and Literature*. Heidelberg: Universitätsverlag C. Winter, 1996.

Greenblatt, Stephen. *Hamlet in Purgatory*. Princeton: Princeton University Press, 2001.

Habermas, Jürgen. *Glauben und Wissen: Friedenspreis des deutschen Buchhandels 2001*. Frankfurt am Main: Suhrkamp, 2001. Trans. H. Beister as "Faith and Knowledge" in *The Future of Human Nature*. Cambridge: Polity Press, 2003. 101–15.

Habermas, Jürgen and Josef Ratzinger. *Dialektik der Säkularisierung: Über Vernunft und Religion*. Freiburg: Herder, 2005. Trans. as *Dialectics of Secularization: On Reason and Religion*. San Francisco: Ignatius Press, 2005.

Halbertal, Moshe and Avishai Margalit. *Idolatry*. Trans. (from Hebrew) Naomi Goldblum. Cambridge: Harvard University Press, 1992.

Hamburger, Michael, *The Truth of Poetry: Tensions in Modern Poetry from Baudelaire to the 1960s*. New York: Harcourt Brace Jovanovich, 1969.

Hartmann, Geoffrey. *The Unmediated Vision: An Interpretation of Wordsworth, Hopkins, Rilke, and Valéry*. New Haven: Yale University Press, 1954.

Hawkins, Peter S. *Dante's Testaments: Essays in Scriptural Imagination*. Stanford: Stanford University Press, 1999.

Hecht, Anthony. "The Riddle of Emily Dickinson." In *Emily Dickinson: A Collection of Critical Essays*. Ed. Judith Farr. Upper Saddle River, NJ: Prentice Hall, 1996. 149–62.

Heidegger, Martin. "Das Wesen der Sprache." In *Unterwegs zur Sprache*. Pfullingen: Verlag Günter Neske, 1959.

Henry, Michel. *C'est moi la vérité: Pour une philosophie du christianisme*. Paris: Seuil, 1998. Trans. Susan Emanuel as *I Am the Truth: Toward a Philosophy of Christianity* (Stanford: Stanford University Press, 2003).

Henry, Michel. *Incarnation: Une philosophie de la chair*. Paris: Seuil, 2000.

Howe, Susan. "These Flames and Generosities of the Heart: Emily Dickinson and the Illogic of Sumptuary Values." In *The Birth-mark: Unsettling the Wilderness in American Literary History*. Hanover: Wesleyan University Press, 1993.

Imbach, Ruedi. *Dante, la philosophie et les laïcs*. Fribourg: Éditions Universitaires Fribourg Suisse, 1996.

Jackson, Virginia. *Dickinson's Misery: A Theory of Lyric Reading*. Princeton: Princeton University Press, 2005.

Jakobson, Roman. "Linguistics and Poetics." *Style in Language*. Ed. T. Sebeok. Cambridge: MIT Press, 1960.

Jakobson, Roman and Claude Lévi-Strauss. "'Les chats' de Charles Baudelaire." *L'Homme* II (janvier–avril 1962): 5–21.

Jameson, Fredric. "Baudelaire as Modernist and Postmodernist: The Dissolution of the Referent and the Artificial 'Sublime.'" In *Lyric Poetry. Beyond New Criticism*. Ithaca: Cornell University Press, 1985.

Janicaud, Dominique. *La phénoménologie éclatée.* Paris: L'Éclat, 1998.

Janicaud, Dominique et al. *Phenomenology and the 'Theological Turn': The French Debate.* New York: Fordham University Press, 2000.

Janicaud, Dominique. *Le tournant théologique de la phénoménologie française.* Combas: L'Éclat, 1991.

Jeffares, Norman A. "The Byzantium Poems of W. B. Yeats." *Review of English Studies* 22 (1946).

Kantorowicz, Ernst H. *The King's Two Bodies: A Study in Mediaeval Political Theology.* Princeton: Princeton University Press, 1997 [1957].

Kates, Judith. *Tasso and Milton: The Problem of Christian Epic.* Cranbury, NJ: Associated University Presses, 1983.

Keats, John. *Keats's Poetry and Prose.* Ed. Jeffrey N. Cox. New York: Norton Critical Edition, 2008.

Kermode, Frank. Ed. *The Living Milton: Essays by Various Hands.* London: Routledge, 1960.

Klee, Paul. *Kunst-Lehre.* Leipzig: Reclam, 1991.

Kierkegaard, Søren. *Fear and Trembling.* Trans. Alastair Hannay. New York: Penguin, 1985.

Kompridis, Nikolas. Ed. *Philosophical Romanticism.* New York: Routledge, 2006.

Kristeva, Julia. *La révolution du langage poétique.* Paris: Seuil, 1974.

Ladame, Alexis. *Dante, Prophète d'un monde uni.* Paris: Grancher, 1996.

Leff, Gordon. *Medieval Thought from St. Augustine to Ockham.* Baltimore: Penguin Books, 1958.

Leopardi, Giacomo. *Canti.* Eds. G. Getto and E. Sanguinetti. Milan: Mursia, 1977–82.

Leopardi, Giacomo. *Canti: Select Poems.* Trans. John Heath-Stubbs. *Poems from Giacomo Leopardi.* London: John Lehman, 1946.

Leopardi, Giacomo. *Opere.* Ed. Giovanni Getto. Milano: Mursia, 1966.

Leopardi, Giacomo. *Operette morali.* Ed. Saverio Orlando. Milano: Rizzoli, 1976.

Leopardi, Giacomo. *Operette morali.* Trans. Giovanni Cecchetti. Berkeley: University of California Press, 1982.

Lévi-Strauss, Claude. "L'efficacité du symbolique." In *Anthropologie structurale.* Paris: Plon, 1958.

Livi, François. *Dante e la teologia. L'immaginazione poetica nella 'Divina Commedia' come interpretazione del dogma.* Rome: Casa Editrice Leonardo da Vinci, 2008.

Lockhart, Adrienne R. "Semantic, Moral, and Aesthetic Degeneration in *Troilus and Criseyde.*" *The Chaucer Review* 8 (1973): 100–117.

Lollini, Massimo. *Il vuoto della forma: Scrittura, testimonianza e verità.* Genova: Marietti, 2001.

Lovejoy, Arthur O. *The Great Chain of Being: A Study of the History of an Idea.* New York: Harper & Row, 1960. William James lecture at Harvard, 1936.

Löwith, Karl. *Weltgeschichte und Heilsgeschehen: Die theologischen Voraussetzungen der Geschichtsphilosophie.* Stuttgart: Kohlhammer, 1949. Trans. as *Meaning in History: The Theological Implications of the Philosophy of History.* Chicago: University of Chicago Press, 1949.

Lundin, Roger. *Emily Dickinson and the Art of Belief.* Grand Rapids, MI: Wm. B. Eerdmans, 2004 [1998]. 2nd ed.

Lupton, Julia Reinhard. *Citizen-Saints: Shakespeare and Political Theology.* Chicago: University of Chicago Press, 2005.

Lupton, Julia Reinhard. *Thinking with Shakespeare: Essays on Politics and Life.* Chicago: University of Chicago Press, 2011.

Luzzi, Joseph. *Romantic Europe and the Ghost of Italy.* New Haven: Yale University Press, 2008.

MacCaffrey, Isabel. *Paradise Lost as "Myth."* Cambridge: Harvard University Press, 1959.

MacCullum, Hugh Reid "Milton and Figurative Interpretation of the Bible." *University of Toronto Quarterly* 31.4 (1962): 396–415.

Madsen, John. *From Shadowy Types to Truth: Studies in Milton's Symbolism.* New Haven: Yale University Press, 1968.

Maimonides, Moses. *RAMBAM: Readings in the Philosophy of Moses Maimonides.* Ed. and trans. Lenn Evan Goodman. New York: Viking, 1976.

Malinowski, Bernadette. *"Das Heilige sei mein Wort": Paradigmen prophetischer Dichtung von Klopstock bis Whitman.* Würzburg: Königshausen und Neumann, 2002.

Mallarmé, Stéphane. *Oeuvres complètes.* Eds. Henri Mondor and G. Jean-Abbey. Paris: Pléiade, 1945.

Mann, Neil, Matthew Gibson, and Claire Nally. Eds. *W. B. Yeats's* A Vision: *Explications and Contexts.* Clemson, SC: Clemson University Digital Press, 2012.

Martin, David. *On Secularization: Towards a Revised General Theory.* Hants, UK: Aldershot, 2006.

Matalene, H. W. Ed. *Romanticism and Culture: A Tribute to Morse Peckham and a Bibliography of his Work.* Columbia, SC: Camden House, 1984.

Mazzale, Ettore. "Osservazioni sul *Discorso di un italiano.*" In *Leopardi e il Settecento: Atti del I Convegno internazionale di studi leopardiani.* Florence: Olschki, 1964.

Mazzotta, Giuseppe. *Dante's Vision and the Circle of Knowledge.* Princeton: Princeton University Press, 1993.

Mazzotta, Giuseppe. "Reflections on Dante Studies in America." *Dante Studies* 118 (2000): 323–30.

McFague, Sallie. "Intimations of Transcendence: Praise and Compassion." In *Transcendence and Beyond.* Ed. John D. Caputo and Michael J.Scanlon. Bloomington: Indiana University Press. 154–59.

McFague, Sallie. *Speaking in Parables: A Study in Metaphor and Theology.* Philadelphia: Fortress Press, 1975.

McFarland, Thomas. "Romantic Imagination, Nature, and the Pastoral Ideal." In *Coleridge's Imagination: Essays in Memory of Pete Laver.* Eds. R. Gravil, L. Newlyn, and N. Roe. London: Cambridge University Press, 1985.

McGann, Jerome. *Black Riders.* Princeton: Princeton University Press, 1993.

McGinn, Bernard. *Meister Eckhart and Beguine Mystics: Hadewich of Brabant, Mechthild of Magdeburg, and Marguerite Porete.* New York: Continuum, 1994.

Merleau-Ponty, Maurice. *Le visible et l'invisible.* Paris: Gallimard, 1964.

Michaud, Guy. *Message poétique du symbolisme.* Paris: Nizet, 1947.

Miller, Cristanne. *Emily Dickinson: A Poet's Grammar.* Cambridge: Harvard University Press, 1987.

Miller, Perry. *The Transcendentalists: An Anthology.* Cambridge: Harvard University Press, 1960.

Mitchell, Domhnall. *Measures of Possibility: Emily Dickinson's Manuscripts.* Amherst: University of Massachusetts Press, 2005.

Moltmann, Jürgen. *Gott im Projekt der modernen Welt: Beiträge zur öffentlichen Relevanz der Theologie.* Gütersloh: Chr. Kaiser, 1997. Trans. as *God for a Secular Society: The Public Relevance of Theology.* Minneapolis: Fortress Press, 1999.

Montemaggi, Vittorio and Matthew Treherne. Eds. *Dante's 'Commedia': Theology as Poetry.* Notre Dame: University of Notre Dame Press, 2010.

Moretti, Franco. *Signs Taken as Wonders: On the Sociology of Literary Forms.* London: Verso, 2005 [1983].

Mortley, Raoul. *From Word to Silence, I: The Rise and Fall of Logos,* and vol. II, *The Way of Negation, Christian and Greek.* Bonn: Hanstein, 1986.

Müller, Sabine. "Conceiving Unity of Being: The Environmental Modernism of R. M. Rilke and W. B. Yeats." National University of Ireland, Galway (NUIG) doctoral dissertation, 2014.

Muscatine, Charles. *Chaucer and the French Tradition.* Berkeley: University of California Press, 1957.

Nancy, Jean-Luc. *Déconstruction du christianisme,* vol. 1: *La Déclosion.* Paris: Galilée, 2005.

Nancy, Jean-Luc. *Déconstruction du christianisme,* vol. 2: *L'Adoration.* Paris: Galilée, 2010.

Nasti, Paola. *Favole d'amore e 'saver profondo': La tradizione salamonica in Dante.* Ravenna: Longo, 2007.

Neumann, Gerhard. "'L'inspiration qui se retire.' Musenanruf, Erinnern und Vergessen in der Poetologie der Moderne." *Memoria—Vergessen und Erinnern (= Poetik und Hermeneutik XV).* Ed. Anselm Haverkamp and Renate Lachmann. Munich: Fink, 1993. 433–55.

Neuse, Richard. Chaucer's Dante: Allegory and Epic Theater in The Canterbury Tales. Berkeley: University of California Press, 1991.

Newman, Barbara. *Medieval Crossovers: Reading the Secular against the Sacred.* Notre Dame: University of Notre Dame Press, 2013.

Nietzsche, Friedrich. *The Gay Science.* Trans. Walter Kaufman. New York: Random House, 1974.

Pannenberg, Wolfhart. *Christentum in einer säkularisierten Welt.* Freiberg im Breisgau: Herder Verlag, 1988. Trans. as *Christianity in a Secularized World.* New York: Crossroad, 1989.

Parris, Benjamin. "'The Body is with the King, but the King is not with the Body': Sovereign Sleep and *Hamlet* and *Macbeth*." *Shakespeare Studies* 40 (2012): 101–42.

Patrides, C. A., W. B. Hunter, and J. H. Adanson. *"Bright Essence": Studies in Milton's Theology.* Salt Lake City: University of Utah Press, 1973.

Pearl, Matthew. "'Colossal Cipher': Emerson as America's Lost Dantean." *Dante Studies* 117 (1999): 171–94.

Perloff, Marjorie. *The Poetics of Indeterminacy: Rimbaud to Cage.* Princeton: Princeton University Press, 1981

Perloff, Marjorie. "Emily Dickinson and the Theory Canon." http://wings.buffalo.edu/epc/authors/perloff/articles/dickinson.html.

Pelikan, Jaroslav. "The Otherworldly World of the Paradiso." In *Eternal Feminines: Three Theological Allegories in Dante's Paradiso.* New Brunswick: Rutgers University Press, 1990.

Penn, Stephen. "Literary Nominalism and Medieval Sign Theory: Problems and Perpsectives." In *Nominalism and Literary Discourse: New Perspectives.* Eds. Hugo Keiper, Christoph Bode, and Richard J. Utz. Amsterdam: Rodopi, 1997.

Perella, Nicholas. *Night and the Sublime in Giacomo Leopardi.* Berkeley: University of California Press, 1970.

Perloff, Marjorie. *The Poetics of Indeterminacy: Rimbaud to Cage.* Princeton: Princeton University Press, 1981.

Perloff, Marjorie. *Wittgenstein's Ladder: Poetic Language and the Strangeness of the Ordinary.* Chicago: University of Chicago Press, 1996.

Pertile, Lino. *La punta del disio: Semantica del desiderio nella Commedia.* Florence: Cadmo, 2005.

Pearson, Nels. "Postponement and Prophecy: Northrop Frye and 'The Great Code' of Yeats's 'Byzantium.'" *University of Toronto Quarterly* 84/1 (2015): 19-33.

Peyre, Henri. *Qu'est-ce que le symbolisme?* Paris: Presses Universitaires de France, 1974.

Poulet, Georges. *La poésie éclatée.* Paris: Presses Universitaires de France, 1980.

Purdy, Dwight. *Biblical Echo and Allusion in the Poetry of W. B. Yeats: Poetics and the Art of God.* Lewisburg: Bucknell University Press, 1994.

Quilligan, Maureen. "Milton's Spenser: The Inheritance of Ineffability." In *Ineffability.* Eds. P. Hawkins and Anne Schatter. New York: AMS Press, 1984.

Raffa, Guy P. *Divine Dialectic: Dante's Incarnational Poetry.* Toronto: University of Toronto Press, 2000.

Rapaport, Herman. *Milton and the Post-Modern.* Lincoln: University of Nebraska Press, 1983.

Reisner, Noam. *Milton and the Ineffable.* Oxford: Oxford University Press, 2009.

Rennie, Nicholas. *Speculating on the Moment: The Poetics of Time and Recurrence in Goethe, Leopardi, and Nietzsche.* Göttingen: Wallstein, 2005.

Rimbaud, Arthur. *Complete Works, Selected Letters.* Ed. Wallace Fowlie. Chicago: University of Chicago Press, 1966.

Robertson, Jr., D. W. "Chaucerian Tragedy." *English Literary History* 19 (1952): 1-37.

Rorty, Richard. "Relations, Internal and External." *Encyclopedia of Philosophy.* Ed. D. M. Borchert. Detroit: Thomson Gale, 2006. 2nd ed., vol. 8, 335-45.

Rorty, Richard and Gianni Vattimo. *The Future of Religion.* Ed. Santiago Zabala. New York: Columbia University Press, 2005.

Rossini, Antonio. *Il Dante sapienziale: Dionigi e la bellezza di Beatrice.* Pisa: F. Serra, 2009.

Rowe, Donald W. *O Love O Charite! Contraries Harmonized in Chaucer's "Troilus."* Carbondale: Southern Illinois University Press, 1976.

Samuel, Irene. *Milton and Dante: The "Commedia" and "Paradise Lost."* Ithaca: Cornell University Press, 1966.

Sbacchi, Diego. *La presenza di Dionigi l'Areopagita nel 'Paradiso' di Dante.* Florence: Olschki, 2006.

Schillebeeckx, Edward. "Silence and Speaking about God in a Secularized World." In *The Spirit and Power of Christian Secularity.* Ed. Albert Schlitzer. London: University of Notre Dame Press, 1967.

Smith, Martha Nell. *Rowing in Eden.* Austin: University of Texas Press, 1992.

Schmitt, Carl. *Hamlet oder Hekuba: Der Einbruch der Zeit in das Spiel.* Stuttgart: Klett-Cotta, 1985 [1956]. Trans. David Pan and Jennifer Rust as *Hamlet or Hecuba: The Intrusion of Time into the Play.* New York: Telos Press, 2009.

Schmitt, Carl. *Politische Theologie. Vier Kapitel zur Lehre von der Souveränität.* Berlin: Duncker & Humblott, 1922. Trans. as *Political Theology: Four Chapters on the Concept of Sovereignty,* trans. George Schwab. Cambridge: MIT Press, 1985.

Schwartz, Regina. *Sacramental Poetics at the Dawn of Secularism: When God Left the World.* Stanford: Stanford University Press, 2008.

Schwartz, Regina. Ed. *Transcendence: Philosophy, Literature, and Theology Approach the Beyond.* New York: Routledge, 2004.

Scofield, Martin. *The Ghosts of Hamlet.* Cambridge: Cambridge University Press, 1980.

Scott, John A. "The Unfinished *Convivio* as a Pathway to the *Commedia.*" *Dante Studies* 113 (1995): 31–56.

Segal, Charles. *Orpheus: The Myth of the Poet.* Baltimore: Johns Hopkins University Press, 1989.

Sells, Michael A. *Mystical Languages of Unsaying.* Chicago: University of Chicago Press, 1994.

Shakespeare, William. *Hamlet.* Norton Critical Edition. Ed. Cyrus Hoy. New York, 1963.

Shakespeare, William. *The Riverside Shakespeare.* Text ed. G. Blackmore Evans. Boston: Houghton Mifflin Co., 1974.

Shalkwyk, David. *Shakespeare, Love and Service.* Cambridge: University of Cambridge Press, 2008.

Shelley, Percy Bysshe. *Shelley's Poetry and Prose.* Eds. Donald Reiman and Neil Freistat. New York: Norton Critical Edition, 2002.

Shoaf, R. A. *Dante, Chaucer, and the Currency of the Word.* 2 parts. Norman, OK: Pilgrim Books, 1983.

Shook, Lawrence K. "The *House of Fame.*" In *Companion to Chaucer Studies.* Ed. Beryl Rowland. Oxford: Oxford University Press: 1979. Rev. ed.

Smith, Anthony Paul and Daniel Whistler. Eds. *After the Postsecular and the Postmodern: New Essays in Continental Philosophy of Religion.* Newcastle upon Tyne: Cambridge Scholars Press, 2010.

Spitzer, Leo. "L'Aspasia di Leopardi." *Cultura Neolatina* (fasc. 2–3, col. XXIII, 1963).

Steinberg, Justin. *Dante and the Limits of the Law.* Chicago: University of Chicago Press, 2013.

Starobinski, Jean. *La mélancolie au miroir: trois lectures de Baudelaire.* Paris: Julliard, 1989.

Stevens, Wallace. *The Collected Poems of Wallace Stevens.* New York: Knopf, 1923–90.

Stone, Gregory B. *Dante's Pluralism and the Islamic Philosophy of Religion.* New York: Palgrave Macmillan, 2006.

Stonum, Gary Lee. *The Dickinson Sublime.* Madison: University of Wisconsin Press, 1990.

Tatlock, John S. P. "The Epilog of Chaucer's Troilus." *Modern Philology* 18 (1920): 625–59.

Taylor, Charles. *A Secular Age.* Cambridge: The Belknap Press of Harvard University Press, 2007.

Taylor, Charles. *Sources of Self: The Making of the Modern Identity.* Cambridge: Cambridge University Press, 1987.

Taylor, Karla. *Chaucer Reads 'The Divine Comedy.'* Stanford: Stanford University Press, 1989.

Taylor, Mark. *Disfiguring: Art, Architecture, Religion.* Chicago: University of Chicago Press, 1992.

Taylor, Thomas. *Essays and Fragments of Proclus the Platonic Successor.* Somerset, UK: Prometheus Trust, 1999.

Taylor, Thomas. *Thomas Taylor the Platonist: Selected Writings.* Eds. Kathleen Raine and George Mills Harper. Princeton: Princeton University Press, 1969.

Terrell, Katherine H. "Reallocation of Hermeneutic Authority in Chaucer's *House of Fame.*" *The Chaucer Review* 31/3 (1997): 279–89.

Tillyard, E. M. W. *The Elizabethan World Picture.* New York: Macmillan, 1944.

Timpanaro, Sebastiano. "Alcune Osservazioni sul Pensiero del Leopardi." In *Classicismo e illuminismo nell'Ottocento.* Pisa: Nistri-Lischi, 1965.

Took, John. *Conversations with Kenelm: Essays on the Theology of the Commedia.* London: Ubiquity Press (University College London Arts and Humanities Publications), 2013.

Took, John. *Dante's Phenomenology of Being.* Glasgow: University of Glasgow Press, 2000.

Turner, Denys. *The Darkness of God: Negativity in Christian Mysticism.* Cambridge: Cambridge University Press, 1995.

Ungaretti, Giuseppe. "Secondo Discorso su Leopardi." *Paragone* 10. Firenze: Sansoni, 1950.

Vahanian, Gabriel. "Theology and the Secular." In *Secular Theology: American Radical Theological Thought.* Ed. Clayton Crockett. New York: Routledge, 2002. 1

Valéry, Paul. *Œuvres* II. Paris: Gallimard (Bibliothèque de la Pléiade), 1960 [1941].

Vance, Eugene. "Mervelous Signals: Poetics, Sign Theory, and Politics in Chaucer's *Troilus.*" *New Literary History* 10 (1979): 293–337.

Vattimo, Gianni. *Dopo la cristianità: Per un cristianesimo non religioso.* Milan: Garzanti, 2002. Trans. as *After Christianity.* New York: Columbia University Press, 2002.

Vattimo, Gianni. *La fine della modernità.* Milan: Garzanti, 1985.

Vattimo, Gianni. "Heidegger: Il linguaggio come evento dell'essere." In *Psicoanalisi e strutturalismo di fronte a Dante,* vol. 1, 311–24. Florence: Olschki, 1972.

Vattimo, Gianni. *Nichilismo e emancipazione: Etica, politica, diritto.* Milan: Garzanti, 2003. Trans. as *Nihilism and Emancipation: Ethics, Politics and Law,* ed. Santiago Zabala, trans. William McCuaig. New York: Columbia University Press, 2004.

Vattimo, Gianni. "Per un cristianesimo non religioso." In *Cos'è la religione oggi?* Eds. Giovanni Floramo, Emilio Gentili, and Gianni Vattimo. Milan: ETS, 2005.

Vattimo, Gianni and Aldo Rovatti. Eds. *Il pensiero debole*. Milan: Feltrinelli, 1983.

Vattimo, Gianni and John Caputo. *After the Death of God*. Ed. Jeffrey Robbins. Columbia University Press, 2007.

Vega, Amador. *Arte y santidad. Cuatro lecciones de estética apofática*. Pamplona: Universidad Pública de Navarra, 2005.

Vega, Amador. "Estética apofática y hermenéutica del misterio: elementos para una crítica de la visibilidad." *Diánoia* 54, no. 62 (2009): 1–25.

Venard, Olivier-Thomas. *Littérature et théologie: Une saison en enfer*. Geneva: Ad Solem, 2002.

Ward, Graham. "How Literature Resists Secularity." *Literature and Theology* 24/1 (2010): 73–88

Ward, Patricia. *Baudelaire and the Poetics of Modernity*. Nashville: Vanderbilt University Press, 2000.

Warner, Michael, Jonathan VanAntwerpen, and Craig Calhoun. Eds. *Varieties of Secularism in a Secular Age*. Cambridge: Harvard University Press, 2010.

Werner, Marta L. *Emily Dickinson's Open Folios*. Ann Arbor: University of Michigan Press, 1995.

Westphal, Merold. *Hegel, Freedom, and Modernity*. New York: SUNY Press, 1992.

Wetherbee, Winthrop. *Chaucer and the Poets*. Ithaca: Cornell University Press, 1984.

Wittgenstein, Ludwig. "Lecture on Ethics." In *Philosophical Occasions 1912–1951*. Eds. James C. Klagge and Alfred Nordmann. Indianapolis and Cambridge: Hackett, 1993. 37–44.

Wittgenstein, Ludwig. *Tractatus Logico-Philosophicus*. Trans. C. K. Ogden, with introduction by Bertrand Russell. London: Routledge, 1992 [1920].

Wolfson, Elliot R. *Language, Eros, Being: Kabbalistic Hermeneutics and Poetic Imagination*. New York: Fordham University Press, 2005.

Wolosky, Shira. "Apophatics and Poetics: Paul Celan Translating Emily Dickinson." In *Language and Negativity: Apophaticism in Theology and Literature*. Ed. Henny Fiska Hägg. Oslo: Novus Press, 2000.

Wolosky, Shira. "The Metaphysics of Language in Emily Dickinson and Paul Celan." *Trajectories of Mysticism in Theory and Literature*, Ed. Philip Leonard. New York: St. Martin's Press, 2000.

Wordsworth, William. Preface to 2nd ed. of *Lyrical Ballads*. www.gutenberg.org.

Yeats, William Butler. "Anima Mundi." In *Essays and Introductions*. New York: Macmillan, 1961.

Yeats, William Butler. *Collected Poems*. Definitive edition. New York: Macmillan, 1956.

Yeats, William Butler. "If I Were Four-and Twenty." In *Explorations*. New York: Macmillan, 1956.

Yeats, William Butler. "The Symbolism of Poetry." In *Essays and Introductions*. New York: Macmillan, 1961.

Yeats, William Butler. *A Vision*. New York: Collier, 1956; rpt. 1966.

Žižek, Slavoj. *The Fragile Absolute—or, Why is the Christian Legacy Worth Fighting For?* London: Verso, 2000.

Žižek, Slavoj. *The Puppet and the Dwarf: The Perverse Core of Christianity.* Cambridge: MIT Press, 2003.

Žižek, Slavoj. *The Ticklish Subject: The Absent Centre of Political Ontology.* London: Verso, 1999.

Made in the USA
Middletown, DE
14 February 2022

61188861R00161